Number Eight: Environmental History Series

MARTIN V. MELOSI, General Editor

U.S. FOREST SERVICE GRAZING AND RANGELANDS

U.S. FOREST SERVICE GRAZING AND RANGELANDS

A History

by

WILLIAM D. ROWLEY

Texas A&M University Press

COLLEGE STATION

Library of Congress Cataloging in Publication Data

Rowley, William D.
U.S. Forest Service grazing and rangelands.

(Environmental history series ; no. 8)
Bibliography: p.
Includes index.
1. Grazing—United States—History.   2. Forest
reserves—United States—History.   3. United States.
Forest Service—History.   4. Range policy—United States—
History.   5. Forest policy—United States—History.
I. Title.   II. Series.
SD427.G8R74   1985   333.74′0973   85-40048
ISBN 0-89096-218-9

Manufactured in the United States of America
FIRST EDITION

To Patricia

Contents

Illustrations

Sheep grazing on Rio Grande National Forest

Cattle grazing on crested wheatgrass

Tractor removing sagebrush from land to be reseeded

Cattle grazing on reseeded rangeland

Official Forest Service grazing permit, 1954

Forest Service ranger, range foreman, and sheep herder

Preface

THE story of regulated grazing control on lands managed by the U.S. Forest Service reveals many of the conflicts over resource policy on the public lands since the beginning of the century. In grazing regulation the Forest Service came first. It became a pioneer and a leader in the development of management techniques for all types of range stock. Its research efforts sought knowledge about the condition of the range, optimum grazing capacities, and the impact of grazing upon other forest resources. Some foresters found it difficult to reconcile grazing with the protection and growth of trees, but forest officials recognized the necessity of accommodating graziers in the forests if government forest reservations were to survive in the West. From that point on, the question of grazing in the forests becomes primarily a description of the relationship between the Forest Service and the livestock indusry. This relationship experienced both stormy and easy times, with the forage resources many times being the primary casualty in the conflicts between agency and stock operators.

The decade of the 1970s saw important changes in public land laws which can be no more than touched upon in a study of this breadth and length. It is too early for historians to detect the far-reaching effects that this most recent decade will have upon government regulatory policies. Good history is like good wine: it must go through an aging process.

To the History Section of the U.S. Forest Service, guided by the able leadership of Dennis Roth, must go thanks for funding and encouragement on the initial project. The author experienced complete freedom of inquiry and interpretation in addition to access to mountains of files and personal memos. I would also like to thank Frank Harmon of the Forest Service's History Section for his helpful work with the text. At the National Archives in Washington, D.C., Milton O. Gustafson offered valuable advice on how to navigate the intricate paths of historical research in the city, and Richard

Crawford and J. Douglas Helms spent much time in retrieving the documents from the depths of archival storage.

Closer to home, Paul F. Tueller of the University of Nevada, Reno, Range, Wildlife, and Forestry Division, deserves credit for encouraging me to undertake this study and offering helpful guidance in many of the technical aspects of range management and ecological terminology. Robert Nylen, who is now with the Nevada State Museum in Carson City as the official registrar, traveled with me to various archives to help in the massive job of compiling information vital to this study. W. R. Chapline, who was for many years involved in the Forest Service's range research programs, spent many hours reading and criticizing this manuscript. While at times I disagreed with him, I know that I and the manuscript profited from his keen criticism. Robert S. Rummell, now retired from the Forest Service's Grazing Office, read the early versions of the manuscript with a critical eye. Garwin Lorain of Reno also read the manuscript to check my description of technical range management problems, and Mary Lorain was the patient typist. These people and many others served to make this work an effective piece of scholarship, but I know that I am ultimately responsible for the final product, which I hope will give the reader a broad overview of many of the problems and challenges that face government management of public forest rangelands.

WILLIAM D. ROWLEY

Reno, Nevada
November, 1984

Abbreviations

AAA	Agricultural Adjustment Act
BLM	Bureau of Land Management
Dr.	Drawer
Fd.	Folder
FRC	Federal Records Center
FS, RM, WO	Forest Service, Range Management Division, Washington Office
FS, WO	Forest Service, Washington Office
NA, RG 95	National Archives and Records Service (Washington, D.C.), Record Group 95, Records of the Forest Service
NF	National Forest
RM	Range Management
Sec.	Section
WNRC Acc. No.	Washington National Records Center (Suitland, Md.), Accession Number
WPA	Works Progress Administration

U.S. FOREST SERVICE GRAZING AND RANGELANDS

1

The Open Land and the Herdsman Frontier

The "range" system of raising cattle and horses with its attendant
cruelties and losses, is gradually giving way to more humane and
thrifty methods.

> —Edgar T. Ensign, *Report*
> *on the Forest Conditions of the Rocky*
> *Mountains*, 1889

FROM its earliest days in the region, the livestock industry was inescapably
identified with the western United States. The cowboy, the cattle drives
northward from Texas, the struggle between sheepmen and cowmen, the
stockmen's battles with the encroaching "nesters" (homesteaders)—all
helped shape popular views of the western American herdsman frontier.
When, at the turn of the century, the federal government created the forest
reserves from portions of the public domain, administrators found themselves in the midst of the ongoing controversies over forest range use. The
young science of forestry was generally concerned with trees and watershed protection; not questions of range use. But federal foresters also faced
immediate basic decisions about regulating and even continuing the practice of domestic livestock grazing in the new government forests. By 1900
questions of grazing, not timber, were among their most urgent problems.

Forests in the United States contained not only timber stands, which
supplied construction materials and fuel, but also places to graze cattle,
sheep, horses, goats, and swine for the herdsmen and frontier homesteaders. Forestry education in schools of the eastern United States was
heavily influenced by European ideas; consequently it failed to prepare
early foresters for the westerners' demand that forest reserves accommodate and guarantee grazing use. To the new cadre of foresters these assertions at first seemed incompatible with the goals of progressive forestry,

but the singular needs of the West compelled Americans to integrate grazing into forest management. Admittedly, the inclusion of grazing within the
ranks of forestry brought to western graziers the irritations of complying
with new rules governing forest ranges, and the traditions of a free and
open range died hard. But many graziers preferred nominal regulation to
the chaos that had occurred by the turn of the century: the deadlines, the
violence, and the serious, widespread depletion and spoilage of ranges in
forests and high mountain meadows. Deadlines meant just that: animals
crossing the lines were shot.

Creation of the Forest Reserves and Utilization of the Range

In 1891, Congress passed the General Land Law Revision Act, which
included a provision, sometimes called the Creative Act, authorizing the
president to set aside forest reserves from the unreserved public domain.
During the period extending from March 30, 1891, to February 25, 1893,
Benjamin Harrison designated over thirteen million acres as forest reserves
in seven western states and Alaska. President Grover Cleveland set aside
twenty-six million more acres during his second term.

These forest reserves became protected lands, nominally closed both
to settlers and resource use—that is, timber cutting, mining, farming, and
grazing. The Creative Act was a major legislative breakthrough in the long
fight for federal forest protection and the first step in closing America's vast
nineteenth-century open land frontier. By assuming the role of perpetual
owner of these lands and their resources, the federal government began a
reversal of a three-century-long policy of land privatization on the frontier.
The land and its resources had appealed to fortune seekers and homebuilders alike. The forested lands now drew special interest not only because of their obvious richness in lumber, but because of a national concern over the disappearance of good timber stands to sustain an expanding
economy.[1]

Timber, however, was only one natural resource in the newly reserved
lands. Other resources were soil, water and ranges upon which domesti-
cated cattle, sheep, goats, horses, and sometimes hogs fattened in the late
spring, summer, and fall, along with native wild animals. These lands also

[1]Harold K. Steen, *The U.S. Forest Service: A History*, pp. 27–38; E. Louise Peffer,
The Closing of the Public Domain; Disposal and Reservation Policies, 1900–1950,
pp. 15–16.

contained mineral lodes, the mining of which received special encouragement from Congress. The organic resources of the forests, on the other hand, would pose very specific questions of utilization.

How much use could be made of the forests and vegetation cover without endangering their ability to renew themselves? Without the renewal, the important watershed function of the forests—protection against erosion and floods—could be threatened. Those who called for the protection of western water supplies for urban and irrigation needs often quoted the old adage, "If you want clean water, you've gotta get the hogs out of the creek," and a few demanded an almost absolute denial of grazing because of harmful results. Mining, however, was so entrenched that almost no voice was raised against its abuses on the reserves for a long time.

But how important were forage resources to a system of forest reserves whose primary purpose was to protect and foster timber production? For several years, the Department of the Interior avoided the question. In the early years, according to the conservation historian Samuel P. Hays, "Grazing . . . became the primary commercial use of the forests." When it did attempt to prohibit grazing, the department was confronted with "interests of considerable magnitude." Ever since the Civil War the ranges and resources of the trans-Missouri West drew stockmen in get-rich schemes to the free grass of the public domain. Although today's national forests comprise only a small percentage of the former public domain, their withdrawal constituted an important first step toward public management of the forests. Very shortly public agencies recognized that they also had to manage the range resources of the forest. It was on these forest reserves that the General Land Office instituted a stock permit grazing program in 1899.[2]

The public-land history of western stockraising from 1865 to the 1890s was marked by chaos, violence, and depletion of the ranges through overgrazing. The move toward regulated grazing in the forest reserves became part of an effort to achieve stability and permanency in an industry that had experienced destructive competition and the resultant devastation of range forage. The stockmen's invasion of the western ranges was one of the many forces pushing the nation westward during a time when industrial-urban centers flourished after the Civil War. The growing cities of the Midwest and the East demanded large quantities of beef, mutton, and wool. As

[2] Samuel P. Hays, *Conservation and the Gospel of Efficiency: The Progressive Conservation Movement, 1890–1920*, p. 49; U.S. Department of Agriculture, *Yearbook of Agriculture, 1901*, p. 336.

The Forest Service
United States Department of Agriculture

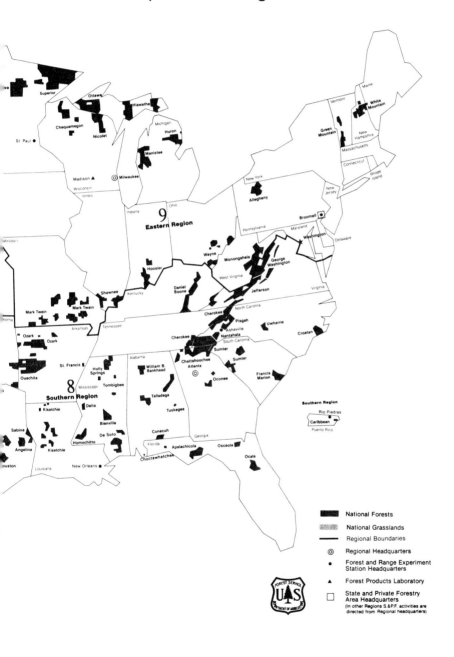

National Forests

National Grasslands

Regional Boundaries

◎ Regional Headquarters

• Forest and Range Experiment Station Headquarters

▲ Forest Products Laboratory

☐ State and Private Forestry Area Headquarters
(In other Regions S.&P.F. activities are directed from Regional headquarters)

railheads moved into the grasslands of the West after the war, these lands offered the bonanza of free grazing within easy distance of lucrative mid-western markets.

The great era of the cattlemen on the western ranges was short-lived, encompassing only the two decades from 1867 to 1887. These were the years of the long drive from Texas northward in which the American folk figure of the cowboy emerged. The transient and even violent nature of this business on the open range often pitted cattlemen against sheepmen and stockmen against settlers. The cowboy frequently took the brunt of these conflicts, adding a darker dimension to his romanticized role in the open-range cattle industry. From 1866 until the late 1880s, the great cattle drives from Texas moved north in widely varying numbers, depending on market conditions. Weather and markets conspired in some years to wreak havoc on the range cattle industry. In other years great fortunes were made as Texans moved their eight-dollar- and ten-dollar-per-head cattle for resale at Kansas and Nebraska railheads for twenty-five and thirty dollars. Despite threatening winters, years of low market prices, and prohibitions against Texas cattle, the northern Great Plains and Intermountain West ranges beckoned to stock entrepreneurs. Texans, among others, established them-selves along the narrow water sources in these arid lands, sheepmen came from New Mexico, and finally the homesteaders arrived to threaten the free grazing itself.[3] It is difficult to determine exactly how many cattle came up the trails from Texas to Kansas and other western railheads in the years after the Civil War. An 1885 official report to Congress summarizes the numbers in Table 1.

While prices continued to rise in the 1880s, drawing heavy invest-ments in the stock industry, organizations arose on the plains to impose regulations on the use of the open and free range. The chaotic individu-alism of the 1870s subsided as cattlemen combined into pools and associa-tions. Stock growers' associations formed to solve those difficulties that plagued the spectacular growth of the open range industry. They faced problems relating to the stealing of cattle by the everpresent rustlers, ap-

[3] Ray A. Billington, *Westward Expansion: A History of the American Frontier*, pp. 669–70; Samuel T. Dana and Sally K. Fairfax, *Forest and Range Policy: Its Development in the United States*, p. 49; John K. Rollinson, *Wyoming Cattle Trails*, pp. 19–30; Walter P. Webb, *The Great Plains*, pp. 216–23; Edward E. Dale, *The Range Cattle Industry: Ranching on the Great Plains from 1865 to 1925*, p. 14; Joseph G. McCoy, *Historic Sketches of the Cattle Trade of the West and Southwest*, pp. 104–108.

TABLE 1. Estimated Number of Cattle from Texas,
1866–85.

Year	Number	Year	Number
1866	260,000	1876	321,998
1867	35,000	1877	201,159
1868	75,000	1878	265,646
1869	350,000	1879	257,927
1870	300,000	1880	394,784
1871	600,000	1881	250,000
1872	350,000	1882	250,000
1873	405,000	1883	267,000
1874	166,000	1884	300,000
1875	151,618	1885	220,000
	Total	5,201,132 (estimated)	

SOURCE: U.S. Congress, House, *Letter from the Secretary of the Treasury Transmitting a Report from the Chief of the Bureau of Statistics [Ranch and Range Cattle Traffic;* report prepared by Joseph Nimmo, Jr.], 48th Cong., 2d sess., 1885, H. Exec. Doc. 267.

portioning water access, customary range rights, the conduct of general roundups, and registering brands. The stock organizations became strong forces in the territorial and state legislatures, obtaining sanctions in law for their regulations and the endorsement of range rights according to local usage customs. State commissioners recognized brands registered with the associations and refused to authorize shipment of cattle with illegitimate brands. Local organizations also resisted the continuation of the long drives from Texas, as local ranchmen claimed overstocking on the ranges and worried about the spread of disease by Texas cattle.

To restrict the flow of Texas cattle northward and reduce range competition, local governments seized upon the dangers of "Texas fever" (a highly contagious disease carried by ticks) in cattle from the South. A government study (the Nimmo report) said its dangers were exaggerated "and that the Texas cattle trail might safely be continued under proper sanitary conditions." Nevertheless, states north of Texas continued to pass and enforce quarantine legislation prohibiting or restricting the passage of Texas cattle infected with fever. The legislation appeared in the mid-eighties at a time when the end of the cattle bonanza was in sight. The plains became overstocked for the available markets and prices reduced, reflecting the growing danger. The Kansas Quarantine Act of 1885 prohibited the passage of Texas cattle between March 1 and December 1 of each year and made drovers liable for damages from the fever to local herds. In addition, Colorado, Nebraska, Wyoming, and New Mexico all passed similar quarantine laws in 1884 and 1885, later reinforced by federal quarantine regulations under the Division of Animal Husbandry (established in 1901). In response, defenders of Texas cattle accused the cattlemen on the northern ranges of opposing "the driving of Texas cattle to the northern ranges upon considerations of a purely commercial and economic nature."

To overcome the quarantine laws and bypass the westward extension of settlement, Texans advocated a national cattle trail. Congress was urged to create "a great free highway for the special purpose of a cattle trail" out of the public domain lands in Kansas, Nebraska, and Dakota. With passage of the Kansas quarantine law, the proposal shifted the trail outside of western Kansas and into Colorado. Texas representatives in Congress supported the proposal in the form of a bill, but state representatives from the northern Great Plains ardently opposed it. The bill called for a trail to begin at the southern border of Colorado, extending to Canada. The trail would be two hundred feet wide at river crossings and 6 miles wide in open country where sufficient land was required to provide feed along the trail. The total length of the trail would be 690 miles, for an area of 2,070 square miles or 1,324,800 acres. Supporters argued that the precedent existed for aid to a national cattle trail because of previous governmental land grants for railroad construction and wagon roads.

The opposition to the trail, however, proved too great. Established northern ranches, although largely stocked from Texas, wanted to exclude further competition. Additional cattle from Texas reduced local market prices at the railheads and exhausted the range grasses to which northern ranchers believed they now had a "prescriptive right." Also, the continued introduction of Texas herds onto the range disrupted attempts to "upbreed" stock quality by the importation of costly highgrade eastern bulls.[4] Finally, the more settled communities growing up on the plains opposed Texas cattle drives because they resented the periodic invasion of the cowboys, who assaulted community decorum.[5]

[4]U.S. Congress, House, *Letter from the Secretary of the Treasury Transmitting a Report from the Chief of the Bureau of Statistics* [*Ranch and Range Cattle Traffic*; hereafter cited and mentioned in text as *Nimmo Report*], 48th Cong., 2d sess., 1885, H. Doc. 267, pp. 38–39; John T. Schlebecker, *Cattle Raising on the Plains, 1900–1961*, p. 27.

[5]Robert R. Dykstra, *The Cattle Towns*, p. 239.

If the Texans were to have a national cattle trail, the northern ranchers wanted leasing rights to the public domain to reinforce their contentions of a "prescriptive right," or what more popular sources called "range rights." These were not rights of actual ownership, but rights to the range based upon "priority of occupation and continuous possession." Support for both of these programs offered opportunity for the two regions to join in a unified policy toward the use of the public domain by the cattle interests. As one delegate from Wyoming to the National Cattlemen's Convention in Saint Louis said in November, 1884: "You favor us in a measure which is very dear to us, and we will favor you with all earnestness and in good part, in favor of every pet scheme from the south." All that the northern ranchers desired, he said, was a fair control of the ranges occupied. On the other hand, without this guarantee, the northern men feared being overwhelmed by the immense herds of surplus cattle from Texas to the point where "we were in danger of obliteration and extinction." The newly established northern ranchmen, without title to their vast rangelands, sought a stability and guarantee in their use of these lands through a governmental leasing system.[6]

The public lands of Texas already had a leasing system. In 1883, Texas ranchmen began to accept the guarantees provided by leasing on state lands. The state of Texas came into the union in 1845 with the right of ownership to its own public domain and generally followed the liberal policy of selling huge tracts of land to stock interests. Leasing, however, encountered resistance when ranchmen refused to pay the nominal leasing fees and insisted that custom and personal agreements better guaranteed range rights. Although leases could be made for ten-year periods, many still refused to accept them. Some ranchers openly used the lands without paying anything, escaping penalties because local juries refused to convict. Later lease laws provided for competitive bidding, and subsequent Texas legislatures struggled to develop adequate leasing procedures for the remaining (and quickly disappearing) open range in the state.[7]

The appropriateness of a national leasing program applied to the open country of the central and northern Great Plains posed many problems for the developing frontier. Any offer by the federal government of long-term leases to the public grazing lands limited future access by newcomers. New stockmen, including sheepmen, looked askance at a system of quasi-land

[6] *Nimmo Report*, p. 38; Rudolf A. Clemen, *The American Livestock and Meat Industry*, p. 182.

[7] Dale, *Range Cattle Industry*, p. 112.

tenure that might limit their future in the region. Railroads, desirous of population growth along their routes, objected to a permanent labeling of the lands for grazing purposes only. They anticipated further development of a diverse trade to this interior region—a trade that might extend beyond the task of carrying cattle to the tasks of carrying crops out of, and manufactured goods back into, the region. These strong voices denounced any system of leasing on the public domain that constricted the future of the area and most of all limited new enterprises seeking opportunities. For too many years the free and open land frontier had served to widen the varied horizons of American enterprise. Proposals to declare the lands a permanent grazing area met with scorn.

In the mid-1880s, Joseph Nimmo's report on the range cattle industry denounced any proposal to lease large parcels of public lands for long periods as contrary to traditional American land-disposition policies. Past policies, the report said, benefited the commercial and industrial interests of the United States. More directly, the Nimmo report denounced the leasing proposal on the grounds of expanding settlement:

Evidently it will be much more in harmony with the sentiments and wishes of the people of this country if the National Government shall adhere to its present line of policy regarding the disposition of the public lands and provide additional safeguards and offer new inducements to settlers rather than place any possible barrier to the occupancy of the public lands by them or to their enjoyment of the privileges which they have already secured under existing laws. In a word, it will be much more promotive of the public interests if the lands now held by the Government shall be dedicated to the rearing of men rather than the rearing of cattle.[8]

Events on the ranges soon forced the questions of who should control the ranges and whether they should raise cattle or men to be resolved. The ranges became overstocked as eastern and foreign capital sought the great returns on investments afforded by the open-range stock industry. Further crowding of the Kansas, Colorado, and Panhandle ranges occurred in 1885 when President Cleveland ordered moved over two hundred thousand head of cattle that had been placed in the Cheyenne-Arapaho Indian Reservation under leasing agreements. This overgrazing was made worse by the summer drought of 1885, leaving the cattle in a weakened condition to face the harsh and cold winter of 1885–86, which proved one of the worst ever on the southern Great Plains. Cattlemen experienced losses of up to 85 per-

[8] *Nimmo Report*, p. 48.

cent. The disaster prompted fast sales of remaining cattle to raise cash. It further depressed beef prices, which had already turned downward in 1884 with the general overstocking of the western ranges.

The low prices worried northern ranch investors and operators, but the weather pattern in the North during the summer of 1886 continued to be of more concern. The pattern seemed to be following that of the southern Great Plains during the previous year. Drought and deterioration of the range during the summer spelled disaster if the coming winter was hard. By November, winter showed signs of imminent fierceness as many ranchers sought to ship their young cattle to midwestern farms. In Montana, some outfits drove herds northward to better ranges in Alberta and took out leases from the provincial government.

None of these measures could prevent the impending disaster. Many of the animals, already in poor condition from deteriorated summer ranges, could not survive the early winter. A warm chinook wind in early January offered some relief, but bitterly cold winds raced down from the north by the end of January and persisted well into March. The losses were catastrophic. The great winter of 1886–87 thus ended the era of the "beef bonanza" and the open-range livestock industry. Those who had invested the most by recently purchasing expensive eastern calves lost the most. Once-great fortunes were now lost in the carnage of the plains winter. Springtime brought the grief of estimating the losses that in many cases reached 90 percent. After the disaster it was understood that animals could never again be permitted to roam freely and fend for themselves on the open range during winter months. One observer from the U.S. Department of Agriculture's Division of Forestry wrote, "the 'range' system of raising cattle and horses, with its attendant cruelties and losses, is gradually giving way to more humane and thrifty methods." Henceforth, range and ranch started to become synonymous as the necessity of raising hay crops and winter feeding became apparent.[9]

Stockmen now saw the necessity of owning good base-ranch property with water supplies and irrigable haylands. The haylands provided the essential ingredient of the new range stock operation—winter feeding. The cowboy was no longer the romantic, dashing figure, always upon horseback. He had to climb down from his horse to join the ranks of western

[9] Ernest S. Osgood, *The Day of the Cattleman*, pp. 219–21; Edgar T. Ensign, *Report on the Forest Conditions of the Rocky Mountains*, Bulletin no. 2, U.S. Department of Agriculture, Division of Forestry, p. 64.

agricultural labor. He now had to operate agricultural machinery; plow fields; irrigate them; sow, cut, and stack alfalfa; and scatter feed to hungry stock during winter snows. The lives and work patterns of those who stayed in the plains cattle industry were forever changed by the twin disasters of overgrazing and the destructive winters of the mid-1880s.

As the cattle kingdom retreated, other contenders for the resources of the public domain moved confidently into the West. Settlers tried to bring crop agriculture to areas whose soil and climate resisted. They therefore profited far less than had been expected by the designers of the Homestead Act. This act, passed in 1862 by the U.S. Congress, provided for the transfer of 160 acres of unoccupied public land to each homesteader on payment of a $10.00 filing fee after five years of residence; land also could be acquired at $1.25 an acre after six months of residence. One hundred sixty acres were adequate in the humid areas east of the hundredth meridian, but many more acres were needed for successful crop and stock agriculture in the arid west. The homesteader also brought barbed wire that broke up the free and open range. Ranchers used the wire in defiance of government rulings against fencing public lands. Sheepmen also began crowding into the plains, deserts, and mountain ranges, challenging the prior claims of cattlemen to land, forage, and water. By 1900 the cattle industry was in major retreat and sheep outnumbered cattle in most western states.[10]

The older cattle interests, operating through their powerful stock associations, often did not accommodate smaller ranchers, farmers, and sheepmen. The 1892 Johnson County War in Wyoming exemplified the determination of established cattle interests to resist the influx of smaller competitors who sometimes established new herds by using rustled cattle— a common practice on the open range. The cattle associations and large ranchers employed detectives or "hired guns" to seek out offenders and administer extralegal justice. These same detectives warned and shot sheep herders who grazed flocks on ranges customarily used by cattle.[11]

Many Americans in the late nineteenth century still could not become alarmed about these conflicts. Such struggles were regarded as the natural outcome of the free productive forces in the economy. There was little that governmental policy could accomplish to prevent these confrontations,

[10]U.S. Bureau of the Census, *Twelfth Census of the United States, 1900*, vol. V, *Statistics for Agriculture*, pp. 704, 708.

[11]T. A. Larson, *History of Wyoming*, pp. 268–84; Asa S. Mercer, *The Banditti of the Plains, or the Cattlemen's Invasion of Wyoming in 1892*.

given the prevailing laissez-faire attitudes toward the public domain. The Nimmo report for instance, regarded with detachment the violent confrontations among herdsmen and conflicts with settlers, noting them "to be but the natural and unavoidable result of the interaction of productive forces in the development of the resources of the country." Out of such struggle came "the advancement of the commercial and industrial interests of a great people." [12]

The Free Range Causes Chaos and Destruction

The prevailing policies, discouraged large free acquisitions of the public domain and prohibited leasing options, created chaotic conditions in many western range areas by the late 1880s and 1890s. Little thought was given to the spoilage of range resources, but much to who could use the grass first and establish rights to it by the constant presence of stock. As early as 1878, John Wesley Powell took note of the forage resources already disappearing because of overgrazing in his landmark work *Report on the Lands of the Arid Region of the United States*. Clearly the West needed its land classified for determining its best advantage. Powell suggested viable ranch units should be 2,560 acres or four square miles. The West also needed fair and equitable systems for water distribution to be devised through community action, the building of irrigation works, and the protection of watershed. [13]

Others who lived in the West during this period were not so polite as Powell in their description of events on the open and free rangelands. They described range wars, bloodshed, and destruction of the range resources by uncontrolled, brutally competitive use. Albert F. Potter, who directed the Grazing Section of the early Forest Service, ranged cattle through the period in Arizona from 1880 to 1900 and became prominent among sheepmen. Looking back in 1912, he wrote: "In the absence of lawful regulation it was quite natural that the period from 1880 to 1900 should become one of spoilation." He noted that the pioneer ranchers, looking for quick profits, overstocked their ranges, an action which led to increasing speculation and incredible numbers of stock on the range. In reply, stock operators pro-

[12] *Nimmo Report*, p. 50.
[13] John W. Powell, *Report on the Lands of the Arid Region of the United States*, 45th Cong., 2d sess., 1878, H. Exec. Doc. 73, pp. 21–29.

tested that they were forced to keep large numbers on the ranges to prevent encroachments from newcomers.

Improved transportation brought more settlers trying to claim the best lands and competing with the earlier users of the free range. The use of the range, Potter said, became a struggle in which only the fittest survived, "and the permanent good of the industry was sacrificed to individual greed." The result on the western rangelands was not a happy picture by the end of the century, if the following generalizations of Potter are to be accepted:

The grazing lands were stocked far beyond their capacity; vegetation was cropped by hungry animals before it had opportunity to reproduce; valuable forage plants gave way to worthless weeds and the productive capacity of the lands rapidly diminished. Class was arrayed against class—the cowman against the sheepman, the big owner against the little one—and might ruled more often than right. Deadlines stretched their threatening lengths across the country, jealously guarded by armed men; battles were fought and lives sacrificed; untold thousands of animals were slaughtered in the fight for the range. Probably no class of men deplored this state of affairs more deeply than did the stockmen themselves, but they were victims of circumstance and governmental inaction with no course open to them other than the one they followed.[14]

Contributing to the crowding of western ranges were the increasing numbers of sheep. The process of sheep raising in many ways stood in sharp contrast to the conduct and values of the cattle community. The isolated, methodical work of a sheep herder on foot had little in common with the dashing work of the cowboy mounted on a horse moving thousands of cattle from Texas to the wild cow towns of the central and northern plains. Sheep could not be permitted to graze freely and had to be kept on the move toward better pasture at a relatively constant pace. Cattle, too, were much more able to take care of themselves on the open range than the helpless, wooly creatures that only drew contempt from cowmen. But a closely tended flock of sheep near the home ranch during the winter survived better than cattle on the open range in harsh winters. Cattlemen complained that sheep devastated available grass and browse much more than cattle did. The watering needs of sheep were minimal, an attribute crucial to survival in an arid country. All things considered, sheep were better competitors for scarce forage in arid lands than were cattle.

[14] Albert F. Potter, "The National Forests and the Livestock Industry," 1912, p. 8, Potter Papers, present location unknown, quoted in Paul H. Roberts, *Hoof Prints on Forest Ranges: The Early Years of National Forest Range Administration*, p. 46.

Sheepmen also utilized the public domain. The sheepman typically owned only 160 acres with water and good hayland; this was the home and winter ranch. During the summer the sheep grazed in more remote ranges, higher in the mountains. The home ranch might also be on leased railroad lands that offered convenient access to shipping. Sheep produced both wool and mutton for market, and flockmasters by the early 1890s considered both products in selecting breeds. Because of their ability to survive the winters under closer care and the two money crops they provided, sheep began to outnumber cattle in the western mountain states. Montana reflected this trend in 1890 when reports showed the number of sheep in Montana to be 1,555,116 and cattle, 649,757. By the year 1900 in most western states sheep far outnumbered cattle.[15] Some large outfits in New Mexico and California evolved out of the large land grants created when the southwest was under Spanish and later Mexican rule. More prevalent in New Mexico were small herdsmen of Hispanic heritage who pursued a subsistent, sedentary existence. Their sheep and goats grazed forest ranges, and the lives of the people were tied to local village economies. In many areas of the remaining mountain west an entirely differnt group of sheep graziers were numerous landless, itinerant herdsmen who drove sheep bands owned by absentee corporate owners.

By the 1890s many cattlemen who once abhorred the sheep industry, forcibly resisting the incursions of the wooly herds, turned to sheep as a safer investment. Americans had begun trailing sheep across the trans-Mississippi West with the first emigrant parties to California in 1841. Much earlier, in the seventeenth and eighteenth centuries, Spanish padres had introduced sheep and goats through the mission system on the northern frontier of New Spain. After the 1848 discovery of gold in California, twenty-five thousand sheep were herded from New Mexico to the San Joaquin Valley. In 1852 Richard ("Uncle Dick") Wootten drove sheep from New Mexico through Utah across the Great Basin to the gold country of California. California sheep were supplied to mining towns in Nevada, Idaho, and Montana by the mid-1860s. Nearly half a million sheep were brought from New Mexico to California in the decade of the 1850s as California supplied other places in the interior-mining West and Pacific Coast. Oregon, with its green mountain pastures, mild climate, and concentration on agriculture, became a favored center of a West Coast sheep industry.

[15] Ezra A. Carman, H. A. Heath, and John Minto, *Special Report of the History and Present Condition of the Sheep Industry of the United States*, p. 716.

New Mexico nonetheless remained the focus and source of the industry, sending thousands of head of sheep northward between 1870 and 1880 to stock ranges in Colorado, Kansas, Utah, Wyoming, and Nebraska. In 1892 a Bureau of Animal Industry report asserted: "It may be stated that New Mexico is the mother of the sheep industry of the Rocky Mountain region and the Great Plains." New Mexico's sheep even stocked the Texas ranges. Paralleling the growth of the cattle empire, the sheep industry expanded quickly in the 1880s. Propaganda about the attractiveness of western rangelands for sheep graziers also drew capital investments from the East and Europe. Not only were sheep, under supervision of herders and dogs, better able to survive winters, but mutton and wool prices remained more stable than cattle prices. Little wonder that sheep supplanted cattle as the most numerous class of livestock on western ranges by the end of the century.[16]

Within the ranks of the sheep industry, problems existed concerning access to and use of the public domain. Sheepmen who owned or even rented a home ranch and took their flocks regularly year after year to selected mountain ranges found the lands occupied by "tramp bands," which did not operate from base ranches. Those sheep were purchased, placed under a herder's care and sent onto the public domain. The shepherds, often newly arrived immigrants, spoke no English. Their employers were absentee owners who contracted for their labor and may have advanced money for their travel from the Spanish Pyrenees Basque country or Scotland. Such ventures offered quick profits wth no investment either in buildings or land. The tramp bands naturally drew protests from landed stockmen, who resented the competition for the ranges by men who had no community roots, paid no taxes on land, and who were not even citizens. In partial response to this situation, states initiated head taxes, collected by county assessors, on itinerant sheep bands. Nonetheless, tramp bands persisted and even increased.

Sheepmen, like cattlemen earlier, perceived that stability on the range required permanent guarantees to range rights. How were such guarantees to be achieved without their purchasing of the lands? Leasing based on traditional use rights appeared to be the answer. Congress, however, rejected the idea of leasing the public domain for grazing uses in the nineteenth cen-

[16] Ibid., p. 915; Edward N. Wentworth, *America's Sheep Trails: History, Personalities*, p. 135.

tury. Solving the public range problem in this manner was tantamount to imposing a status quo on the land, cutting out opportunity for newcomers, according to many in Congress. Yet the system of free access, as Potter indicated, produced violence and depleted range resources. In some areas stock associations, which had maintained some order, grew less effective and failed to enforce range regulations. They fell into disrepute under attacks from new settlers, who believed the associations represented large-landed local interests and monied eastern corporations. These charges appealed to many when Populist party doctrines became widespread during the economically depressed 1890s.[17]

Range conservation appeared to be an important need by the end of the 1880s. In part, weather conditions enforced conservation on the lagging cattle industry. To most stockmen, conservation meant a limiting in some manner of the numbers of stock allowed to use the ranges. Cattlemen often blamed sheepmen and benchland farmers for devastated ranges. Also, forage opportunities for their herds were a constant invitation to a parade of new cattle graziers as well. Those graziers who had arrived earlier attempted to establish prescriptive rights to the range by their customary occupancy and acceptance of those rights among themselves, their stock organizations, and roundup committees. Some western writers have compared these range rules to the customs of the mining districts in their attempt to regulate and distribute access to ore in rich stream beds or quartz lodes. As with mining-district rules, western legislatures sometimes reinforced the regulations of stock organizations by authorizing inspections of cattle shipments for legitimate brands and passing water laws that gave rights to the first users. It was in the area of water rights that early arrivals established their most effective power. Whoever controlled the water sources often controlled great areas of land. Without access to the limited water sources, newcomers could not survive even with open and free ranges.[18] These restrictions, however, would not totally discourage new homesteaders from trying their luck on the western rangelands.

Of particular interest to many stockmen in the arid West were the high mountain summer ranges where nutritious grasses provided a necessary complement to the lower ranges, which became exhausted from winter

[17] Bert Hasket, "The Sheep Industry in Arizona," *Arizona Historical Review* 7(1936): 24; Osgood, *Day of the Cattleman*, pp. 244–55.

[18] Charles H. Shinn, *Mining Camps: A Study in American Frontier Government*, pp. ix, 221–23; Rollinson, *Wyoming Cattle Trails*, p. 29.

grazing and were unusable in hot and dry summers. The intensive competition for these ranges demonstrated the need for a rational allocation method. Their distance from home ranches, and diverse water sources excluded the normal stock association procedures for laying forceful, if sometimes extralegal, claims to ranges.

The race to the mountains in the spring became an ecological disaster: "That which was free for all to use, came to be regarded as free for all to despoil." [19] Sheepmen often arrived too early, destroying the new forage crop before it could be safely grazed. Ultimately, the less palatable perennial species and the genetically aggressive annual species replaced the more nutritious hitherto dominant, native perennial grasses. This reduction in range-carrying capacity, not only led to poorly fed stock, but also watershed erosion as the stock damaged or eliminated the more sturdy perennial grass cover and also retarded the growth of seedling trees. This kind of grazing threatened city water supplies, jeopardized water storage for irrigation projects, and finally led to numerous uncontrolled periodic floods as the soils and their grass covering failed to retain the runoff water.

Despite the importance of conservation efforts, the American Association for the Advancement of Science and the various American forest congresses made little reference to forage resources. Studies often referred to watershed protection, but the trees were given the chief role as guardians of this resource. The leasing of public rangelands was the closest any proposal came to halting the ever-increasing use of the ranges by more numerous herdsmen. Leasing, of course, was not a conservation measure, but merely a proposal to bring stability to the industry, and orderliness and peace to the range by guaranteeing the preeminence of the already established grazier. The symbol and rallying point for the growing conservation movement focused on the trees of the land, not its depleted range grasses and forbs. But within the tree lands were also grazing lands. Grazing expert Potter recalled:

At the beginning the mountains and heavily timbered areas were used but little, but as the situation grew more acute in the more accessible regions the use of these areas became general and in course of time conditions within them were even more grave than elsewhere, for experience had demonstrated that they were the choicest ranges and they were in strong demand. The mountains were denuded of their vegetative cover, forest reproduction was damaged or destroyed, the slopes were seamed

[19] J. J. Thornber, *The Grazing Ranges of Arizona*, Arizona Agricultural Experiment Station Bulletin no. 65, 1910, p. 336.

with deep erosion gullies, and the water-conserving power of the drainage basins became seriously impaired. Flocks passed each other on the trails, one rushing in to secure what the other had just abandoned as worthless, feed was deliberately wasted to prevent its utilization by others, the ranges were occupied before the snow had left them. Transient sheepmen roamed the country robbing the resident stockmen of forage that was justly theirs.[20]

Even with the creation of the forest reserves in 1891 and their subsequent extensions, the resources of the forest range received only passing notice until graziers demanded use of the mountain rangelands. Admission to the limited range within the forests could not be denied without a bitter political struggle. The first steps toward a controlled grazing policy appeared on the horizon through effective forest administration. Much rangeland was included in national forests for the protection of watershed and the desire to bring stability to range use. Eventually a system of grazing control was initiated on these lands, dedicated to the peaceful allotment of range forage and the more distant goals of range renewal and conservation.

But the forest reserves were only a small part of the public domain. Outside of the forests remained vast public lands whose grazing resources would not come under government supervision until the passage of the 1934 Taylor Grazing Act. Since the forest reserves predated the arrival of large range-control programs for the public domain by over thirty years, early forestry officials became the pioneers of government-range regulation and resource use.

[20]Darrell H. Smith, *The Forest Service: Its History, Activities and Organization*, Brookings Institution Monograph no. 58, pp. 6–9.

2

Pioneers in Grazing Regulation

> He may make such rules and regulations and establish such service
> as will insure the object of such reservations, namely to regulate
> their occupancy and use and to preserve the forest thereon from
> destruction.
>
> —Amendment to Sundry Civil
> Appropriations Bill, 1897

Before 1894, seventeen forest reserves with a total estimated area of 17.5
million acres were under the Department of the Interior and its land agency,
the General Land Office. What the department was supposed to accomplish with the reserves other than protect the trees from depredation remained a mystery. The question of whether stock would be permitted on
the ranges was not even addressed until late in the 1890s.

Although the Department of the Interior took possession of the reserves, the General Land Office did not have the personnel to perform a
protective function. In 1892 the Secretary of the Interior, Hoke Smith,
called for the use of federal troops to bar trespassers from the reserves.
Troops already had been used in Yellowstone National Park, but there was a
fear that their presence in the forests might be judged unconstitutional.[1]
The lack of regulations for the administration of the reserves created uncertainty about their purpose and future. Trespasses became open and de-
fiant with too few officials in the local reserves to bar livestock grazing and
even timber cutting. The government, however, disclaimed charges that it
intended to lock up the resources of the reserves. It simply had no workable
plans for the use of the resources and therefore was forced to take the position that no use at all could occur. Officially, the lands were closed. Under
the 1891 law, no timber could be cut, no minerals mined, or roads built

---

[1] John Ise, *U.S. Forest Policy*, p. 121.

on the reserves. This state of affairs had to change, but Congress was slow to act, not even granting funds for the enforcement of trespass laws.

Grazing interests became understandably restless under pointless policies that threatened their future access to forest grazing areas. The wanton, illegal use of the forest by the tramp herders continued despite paper restrictions against roving through and grazing forest lands. Those who abided by the restrictions only opened more extensive pastures for those who did not. More specific and enforceable rules were demanded. The creation of the Cascade Reserve in 1893 marked a moratorium on the creation of more reserves until a method for their administration could be developed.[2]

Western stockmen were not the only group attentive to forest policy; recreationists, watershed protectionists, and timber harvesters were all concerned. Unfortunately, the goals of one group would often clash with those of another. The forests could not be turned into national parks and at the same time satisfy the powerful use-oriented interests of lumbermen and ranchers. Some recreationists, aesthetic utilitarians, and watershed advocates, mainly interested in western urban and irrigation supplies, cheered restrictions on use. But as Bernhard E. Fernow, chief of the Department of Agriculture's Division of Forestry, contended, the purposes of the reserves should be protection of government property and the production of revenue—that is, resource use. Such a policy promised much to the timber interests, but little to grazing.

By 1893, Congress finally moved to consider bills to authorize the utilization of forest reserves. Timber, of course, attracted the most attention, but other interests demanded a part in the formation of forest policy. Although many westerners welcomed the formation of the reserves, they became uneasy over the prospect of the forests becoming untouchable preserves. Such a fate might occur by administrative inaction or by congressional action to extend the principle of the national parks to the reserves. Beginning in 1892, bills appeared in Congress for protection and administration of the forests. In 1893 considerable debate took place on Arkansas Congressman Thomas R. McRae's bill, "To Protect Forest Reservations." The bill provided for sale of the timber to the highest bidders under compe-

---

[2] Paul W. Gates and Robert W. Swenson, *The History of Public Land Law Development*, p. 558; H. Duane Hampton, *How the U.S. Cavalry Saved Our National Parks*, pp. 81–94.

tent management plans. Western Congressman Binger Hermann from the sheep-grazing state of Oregon attacked the bill. He demanded that lands suitable for grazing, mining, and agriculture be excluded from forest reserves.[3]

Much talk and many proposals emerged in Congress. No legislation occurred until 1897. The first official statement of administrative policy on grazing matters was in a regulation dated April 14, 1894. On all forest reserves the "driving, feeding, grazing, pasturing, or herding of cattle, sheep, or other livestock" was prohibited.[4] This order made the search for an equitable system of forage use in the forests crucial to legitimate western livestock interests. Blatant violation of the order occurred by those who saw no reason to obey it if the department could not enforce it. In the congressional debates the views of western representatives were as diverse as the many forest resources. The defenders of grazing in the forests were only one group among many other claimants to resources. Conservationists and western urbanites believed the defenders' arguments lacked force and sophistication, especially when it was charged that grazing harmed both the growth of trees and water supplies. Western stockmen, the grazing interest, did not command broad based support outside their region. Rather, they spoke for a narrow, but highly organized user group whose activities inspired suspicion on the part of conservationists. The conservationists charged grazing consumed resources, threatened tree growth, increased the threat of fires, and degraded watershed for irrigation and urban water supplies. Despite these considerations, the political power of the grazing interests in the West compelled attention and finally obtained official admission of stock to the forest reserves.

The conservationists' concerns were shared by aesthetic and recreational groups. These latter groups were most prominently represented by John Muir and the publisher of *Century* magazine, Robert Underwood Johnson. In February of 1895, *Century* conducted a written symposium on the future of the reserves. Protection against all types of trespass was considered to be of foremost importance. Professor Charles S. Sargent of Harvard advocated the training of forest officers at the U.S. Military Academy at West Point, while others contended that the Civil Service Commission was the best qualified and most constitutionally acceptable agency to pro-

[3] *Congressional Record*, 53rd Cong., 1st sess. 1893, vol. 25, pt. 2, p. 2372.
[4] Frederick V. Coville, *Forest Growth and Sheep Grazing in the Cascade Mountains of Oregon*, U.S. Department of Agriculture, Division of Forestry Bulletin no. 15, p. 10.

vide personnel to protect the forests. Sargent also proposed a Forest Experiment Station near West Point and the enlistment of a forest guard unit to carry out the principles of applied forestry. Others responded that forestry training should fall to the state agricultural or land grant institutions to develop a proper civil service for the practice of government forestry. Perhaps the wisest comment was that found in the journal *Irrigation Age*: "The question as to whether the army or the civil service can do this work best is of very small importance when we reflect that absolutely nothing is being done now, and that either branch of the service would be able to introduce a greater and urgent reform." [5]

The symposium barely touched upon the question of grazing and then only to condemn the practice. John Muir, the lone speaker, said sheep flocks caused desolation, and endorsed a military guard for the forests: "One soldier in the woods, armed with authority and a gun, would be more effective in forest preservation than millions of forbidding notices." The early forester, Gifford Pinchot, admitted that, for a time, "I fell for it to some extent myself." But he said he soon understood that "out in the woods mere orders do not go." However, to him a civil service with the confidence of the public was more acceptable than a military order backed by guns. [6]

Cautious advocates of forest conservation feared to move too swiftly in the promulgation and enforcement of regulations for the reserves. The formation of the reserves had been a tremendous achievement. Their future existence should not be risked by the strict application of hastily developed policies. Fernow advised caution and "a common-sense treatment and more careful exploitation of our national forests." Others, like Pinchot, mindful of western interests, objected to the lack of forthright, purposeful policies, but admitted that a general and vague forest administration was preferable to overly restrictive rules that invited attacks on government involvement in forest conservation.

In 1894 Congressman McRae attempted to have passed a bill authorizing a general administrative law for the reserves. Although the bill finally died in 1896, Pinchot and other management advocates welcomed its introduction because the bill merely authorized the secretary of the interior to "establish such service as shall be required for the Forest reserves." The

[5] "Progress of Western America," *Irrigation Age* 8 (March, 1895): 72–73.
[6] Gifford Pinchot, *Breaking New Ground*, pp. 86–88; "A Plan to Save the Forests," *Century* 27 (February, 1895): 626–31.

McRae bill contained no specific restrictions on settlers, miners, water users, and others who might be required to apply for resource-use permits. Significantly, it avoided any reference to grazing because, as Pinchot put it, "grazing was the best organized interest of the West." Any mention of fees, permits, or licenses would have provoked immediate and effective protests. It advocated the practice of turning over forest resource administrative problems to the discretionary abilities of a government agency; that special interests in Congress could not seek to derail bills for each different aspect of forest administration.

With the failure of the McRae bill, pressure mounted for a general study of the forest problem. Promptings from the American Forestry Association and the continued failure of Congress to pass a forest administration bill moved Secretary of the Interior Smith to ask the National Academy of Sciences in 1896 to appoint a committee to investigate and make recommendations on the future of the reserves. Some, like Fernow, correctly feared that the so-called scientific investigation would be more of a "junket" that left little time for a seriously researched report. The young and enthusiastic Pinchot, on the other hand, supported the formation of the commission, as did the influential editor and conservation crusader, Robert Underwood Johnson.[7]

The Philadelphia-based National Academy of Sciences appointed seven men to the Forest Committee. They were Charles S. Sargent, director of the Harvard Botanic Garden and author of *Silva of North America*; Henry L. Abbot, expert on the physics and hydraulics of streams; Alexander Agassiz, curator of the Harvard Museum of Comparative Zoology; William H. Brewer, a natural scientist and professor at Yale; Wolcott Gibbs, head of the National Academy of Sciences; Arnold Hague, a geologist and geological explorer; and, as secretary, Gifford Pinchot, the youngest member and the only forester in the group.[8]

Gibbs, the chairman of the committee, declared that the task could not be completed before the end of the congressional session. Yet, with Pinchot and Sargent leading the way, the committee undertook its charge with enthusiasm and awe at the twenty million acres of forest it was sup-

[7]Lawrence W. Rakestraw, "History of Forest Conservation in the Pacific Northwest, 1891–1913" (Ph.D. diss., University of Washington, 1955), p. 60; U.S. Congress, *Senate Report of the Committee Appointed by the National Academy of Sciences upon the Inauguration of a Forest Policy for the Forested Lands of the United States*, 55th Cong., 1st sess., 1897, S. Doc. 105, vol. 5, p. 7 (hereafter cited as *NAS Report on Forest Policy*).

[8]Pinchot, *Breaking New Ground*, p. 92; Steen, *U.S. Forest Service*, p. 31.

posed to study. Committee members visited the western forests and some complained of the swiftness of their visits. Likewise Fernow still feared that the conclusions of a hasty investigation would offend powerful western interests. He and others always had sought a cautious forest policy to avoid offending the westerners, who might wreck the entire undertaking if they believed the report would recommend the exclusion of many resource users from the forests.[9]

Throughout the summer of 1896 the committee gathered information, and it submitted a preliminary report on February 6, 1897. This report to the president supported doubling the size of the reserves before more damage could be done and more land filed upon by settlers and lumbermen. Departing President Grover Cleveland added 21,378,840 acres to the forest-reserve system, announcing the addition on February 22 in a George Washington's Birthday proclamation. News of the reserves, which came simultaneously with the report's recommendations that grazing be eliminated from the forests, caused the predicted furor in the West. The extensive written comments contained in the report on grazing damage reflected the views of naturalist John Muir. Muir traveled with the committee in the western mountains and became well acquainted with Pinchot during the summer's investigations.

Muir's influence on the report is obvious throughout by its strong stand against grazing: "Fire and pasturage chiefly threaten the reserved forest lands of the public domain. In comparison with these, the damage which is inflicted on them by illegal timber cutting is insignificant." Especially singled out for condemnation was the nomadic sheep industry because of the damage caused by animals in the forests of California and western Oregon. The report used Muir's famous epithet for sheep—"hoofed locusts"—in its description of their impact on the forests. In addition, it charged, these animals were often owned by foreigners, "who are temporary residents of this country." These nomadic herders came into the high Sierra and Cascade range in the spring as soon as the snow permitted and "[carried] desolation with them." The destruction caused by these animals loosened the forest floor and produced conditions favorable to floods, making the sheep not only a threat to the forests, but to watershed protection.

The report played upon the concerns of the irrigation movement in the West and western urban centers, reemphasizing the destructive impact of sheep grazing on watersheds. It described the patterns of destruction: in

[9] Steen, *U.S. Forest Service*, p. 33.

summer, bands of sheep reached into the highest mountain valleys, then reteated in autumn. On their return the herders set fires to destroy the undergrowth and stimulate new herbage in the spring. These abuses increased water runoff, threatening the usefulness of streams for irrigation and the upstream storage of water needed by both cities and reclamation projects during hot summer months. Without a doubt, the report declared, "In every western state and territory the nomadic sheepmen are dreaded and despised." The present damage was glaring, but the effects on the future of mountain forests, the flow of streams, and the agricultural possibilities of their valleys would be far more profound.

The report downplayed the sheep industry's commercial importance, saying that it was "certainly insignificant relative to the injury it inflicts on the country." Lax governmental supervision of grazing restrictions in the forests caused hardship to others: "The Government in permitting free pasturage on the public domain to sheep owners in the public land states and territories, clearly commits an injustice to persons engaged in this industry in other parts of the country, who are obliged to own or hire their pastures." The report acknowledged that the sheep pasturage had been so long permitted that stockmen "have come to believe that they have acquired vested rights in the public forests"; it then contended that only vigorous action could check these attitudes, and cited examples of the use of soldiers in Yosemite and General Grant national parks in California.[10]

The attack on grazing, specifically sheep herding, affronted powerful western grazing interests. The doubling of the forest reserves and the hardline attitude toward grazing made the academy's report highly controversial. Many accused it of putting forth eastern solutions for western problems. These doubts in turn inspired a suspicion of the scientific experts enlisted by the committee. Western grazing interests keenly felt their exclusion when the report recommended use of reserves for mining and lumber resources, but the absolute prohibition of grazing. In retrospect the report was ill-considered, and caused more harm than good. It was, however, highly gratifying to Muir and those who unapologetically supported his recreationalist and preservationist views.[11]

One prominent grazier in the Pacific Northwest loudly scoffed at the

[10] NAS Report on Forest Policy, pp. 18, 21.

[11] Ibid., pp. 18–19; Lawrence W. Rakestraw, "Sheep Grazing in the Cascade Range: John Minto vs. John Muir," Pacific Historical Review 27 (November, 1958): 375; Thomas R. Cox, "The Conservationist as Reactionary: John Minto and American Forest Policy," Pacific Northwest Quarterly 74 (October, 1983): 146.

report. John Minto, a pioneer sheepman who had lived in Oregon since 1844, denied that herds of sheep brought destruction to the forests. As secretary of Oregon's State Board of Horticulture, Minto defended the wool growers of the West Coast against Muir's attacks on sheep grazing. Minto especially raised his voice against the conclusions about grazing in forest reserves reached by the National Academy of Sciences committee. He said that grazing stock in the forests actually prevented grass fires because it eliminated fuel buildup. He charged that the true causes of erosion in the Cascade Mountains were the warm chinook winds, which melted snow rapidly and caused water to flow through poorly drained channels. Also, he contended, open meadows created by grazing retained snow longer than brushy areas that broke up the snow, making it less compact than in the meadows. Minto opposed strong federal control over forest grazing lands and advocated an Australian system of long-term leases with option to purchase. Such a system would encourage private range improvements and conscientious use of the land that would eventually become private property.[12]

When President Cleveland unexpectedly added over twenty-one million acres to the forest reserves on February 22, 1897, voices of protest denounced the entire reservation system. Total reliance on congressional sources suggests a seething reaction in the West against the high-handed appropriation of forest lands based on the recommendations of eastern scientific men. More thorough study of western editorial reaction to the new forest land withdrawal show favorable reception on the part of western urbanites and irrigation interests. Still, western congressmen spoke bitterly about the new reserves, claiming that the western people had not been consulted and that the President listened only to the National Academy of Sciences. Congressman Wilson of Washington asked if the West would "be everlastingly and eternally harassed and annoyed and bedeviled by these scientific gentlemen from Harvard College." Congressman Hartmann of Montana called the proclamation of the lame-duck president, "a parting shot of the worst enemy that the American people have ever had." Congressman Knowles of South Dakota referred to the action as a "villainous order," saying, "We know the 'rotten boroughs of the West,' as the New York World calls us, have little influence with this administration."[13]

---

[12]Rakestraw, "John Minto vs. John Muir," pp. 376–77; R. H. Forbes, "The Range Problem," *Forestry and Irrigation* 10 (October, 1904): 477–78.

[13]As quoted in Ise, *U.S. Forest Policy*, pp. 135, 137; Samuel T. Dana and Sally K. Fairfax, *Forest and Range Policy: Its Development in the United States*, p. 58.

What Fernow had predicted, occurred. The scientific committee's rec-ommendations stirred a reaction in the West, not only among special inter-est groups such as grazing, but in the larger spectrum of public opinion. It created an image of eastern intellectuals dictating to western men on west-ern conservation and resource policies. Such a situation was intolerable and presaged a general attack on governmental forest reserves.

During the last days of the Cleveland administration, western con-gressmen determined to bring the new reserves back into the public do-main. An amendment to the Sundry Civil Appropriations Bill, giving the president authority to modify or rescind any previous executive order creating forest reserves, passed. The entire appropriations bill including this amendment was sent to President Cleveland during the last days of his administration. The president killed the entire appropriations bill with a pocket veto, leaving the government temporarily without operating funds. The protestors would have to wait for the new administration to obtain re-lief from the national forest-reservation proclamations.

To obtain an appropriations bill for government operations, President McKinley called a special session of Congress shortly after his inaugura-tion on March 4, 1897. An amendment to this new appropriations bill by Congress achieved a compromise between anti-reserve forces and those both inside and outside the West who supported an active governmental forest reservation policy. Senator Richard Pettigrew of South Dakota, a former opponent of the reserves and powerful member of the Senate Public Lands Committee, surprisingly sponsored an amendment to the new Sun-dry Civil Appropriations bill remarkably similar to the earlier and much-debated McRae bill. Pettigrew's change of heart probably grew out of his close connection with the Homestake Mining Company, which was eager to exclude as many mineral properties from the forests as possible.[14]

The amendment designated the purpose of the reserves to be for watershed protection and timber production. Mineral and agricultural lands were for the most part to be excluded from forest reserves. In addi-tion, President McKinley, in accordance with the amendment, stated that implementation of the new reserves would be withheld for nine months. The "suspension clause" helped pacify some congressional demands for total rejection of the new reserves. A "lieu clause" allowed those who had

[14] Ise, *U.S. Forest Policy*, p. 137.

taken up land in the reserves to file for lands in lieu of their original claims on other parts of the public domain. The amendment was riddled with similar concessions to western interests, such as the provision that authorized the secretary of the interior to give free timber and stone to settlers, miners, or residents for use as firewood, fencing, and building material and for other domestic purposes. The reserves were to be open to mining and prospecting. Surprisingly, there was no specific mention of grazing or free access by stockmen to forage. The previous condemnations of grazing in the forests had been so pointed and strident that to mention this use at all would have appeared as a total concession to it. Nonetheless, this amendment provided the basis of authority for forest administration for more than half a century. It embraced the principle that resources were for use and gave the power to administer and protect them to the Department of the Interior.

On the surface it appeared that grazing advocates had been left out of the compromise. But one of the phrases of the amendment authorized the secretary of the interior "to regulate [the reserves'] occupancy and use and to . . . preserve the forests thereon from destruction." These few words, although vague, opened the door to grazing in the forests, if the Department of the Interior deemed it advisable and compatible with the safe utilization of resources. The law also authorized the secretary to make rules and regulations governing the uses of the forests, an authority which would later be contested because specific uses were not enumerated in the act. The Department of the Interior, and later the USDA Forest Service, would deem it not only advisable to permit grazing, but also politically expedient for the integrity and expansion of the new government forest lands.[15]

The Granting of Grazing Permission

In response to various petitions from the West and in particular Oregon, less than a month after the passage of the act, the General Land Office issued regulations that in principle permitted grazing (but not sheep grazing) on all forest reserves, provided that no injury should occur to the forests. Sheep grazing would be allowed in the Cascade Mountains of Oregon and Washington. The vacillating tone of the regulations indicated that the office itself was uncertain about the future of grazing on the reserves. Excepting

[15]Gates and Swenson, *History of Public Land Law Development*, p. 569.

the Cascades from the temporary prohibition against sheep probably reflected the influence of the commissioner of the General Land Office,
Binger Hermann, a longtime Oregon politician and friend of the grazing
interests in his state. The office asserted that grazing would be permitted in
the Cascades because ample rainfall in the Pacific Northwest renewed the
range. Although the permission came too late for the grazing season of
1897, it was a further indication that confusion and inconsistency clouded
the issue. The situation continued to be confused when Congress did not
appropriate funds for the enforcement of regulations until 1899.[16]

The tentative position of the department on the grazing question
appeared in the following order issued by the secretary of the interior on
June 30, 1897:

The pasturing of livestock on public lands in forest reserves will not be interfered
with, so long as it appears that injury is not being done to the forest growth, and the
rights of others are not thereby jeopardized. The pasturing of sheep is, however,
prohibited in all forest reserves except those in the states of Oregon and Washington, for the reason that sheep grazing has been found injurious to the forest cover,
and therefore of serious consequence in regions where the rainfall is limited.[17]

More knowledge about the effects of grazing on the forest, herbage,
and watershed conditions was needed by the Department of Interior. Faced
with conflicting reports, testimonies, and petitions from western states, the
Department of the Interior asked the Department of Agriculture to appoint
a botanist to study the question carefully and make recommendations on
the basis of scientific evidence. Clearly, the Interior Department wanted
more than the quick overview offered by the Academy of Sciences.

Frederick V. Coville, a USDA botanist, traveled west in the summer of
1897 to survey the situation in the Oregon and Washington mountains.
Armed with letters of introduction from Binger Hermann, he came into
immediate contact with grazing men upon his arrival in Oregon. One of the
first persons he interviewed was John Minto, who gave him additional
letters of introduction to sheepmen and cattlemen in eastern Oregon. From
the outset Coville noted the difference between the range-sheep industry
and the raising of farm sheep in a heavily settled agricultural region. Because the range land was not fenced, sheep faced constant danger from attacks by wild animals and were attended by a herder. Each herder watched

[16]Rakestraw, "John Minto vs. John Muir," p. 375.
[17]U.S. Congress, House, *Annual Report of the Secretary of the Interior, 1897*, 55th
Cong., 2d sess., 1897, H. Doc. 5, p. 10.

and directed as many sheep as possible, sometimes two or three thousand. Such a grouping was called a "band." Coville noted that the terms *flock* and *shepherd* were seldom heard in the range region of Oregon. The terms were *band* and *herder*.

Coville's extensive report offered more balanced information than the academy's. He spoke of regulating grazing, not abolishing it. He contradicted the earlier report's main assertions regarding the commercial value of the sheep-raising industry to the region, fires caused by herders, and the extent to which erosion problems occurred because of overgrazing. The Coville report concluded that wool clip, mutton, and stock sheep were highly important to the Oregon economy. Wool was one of the three principal crops of eastern Oregon (beef and wheat the other two). The revenues from sheep in one county alone significantly affected the entire economy of the State. Two and one-half million sheep with an annual wool clip of twelve million pounds and valued at $3.5 million could not be dismissed. Even the cattle ranchers who disliked the presence of sheep in eastern Oregon agreed that the exclusion of the sheep from the reserves would be "against the best commercial interests of their communities." They were also aware that sheep excluded from the forests would place additional pressures on cattle ranges during the summer.

Coville deplored the uncertainty surrounding forest reserve policies in the region. Rumors spread that sheep would be permanently excluded from the reserves, leaving sheep owners with little recourse but to oppose the reserves. From his extensive conversations, Coville formed the opinion that if grazing privileges were granted on an equal basis, the reserves would be a public benefit. Without the regulation provided by the reserves, the mountain ranges would undergo intense competition and overgrazing of fragile ecosystems which ultimately harmed all concerned—sheepmen, cattlemen, farmers, and urbanites. Coville proclaimed that "the evils of the present system can be corrected neither on the one side by abolishing the reserve nor on the other side by the exclusion of sheep, without inflicting much more serious evils upon the welfare of the State."

After recommending that sheep grazing be continued in the reserves of Oregon and Washington, Coville went on to sketch a method by which grazing could proceed. His procedures, if adopted, offered protection to forest resources and at the same time allowed use by graziers. He called it "the special tract permit system." The plan provided the foundation for future grazing policies, both those of the Department of the Interior and, later, those of the Forest Service. Each owner, according to Coville's plan, should be granted a permit to graze a specified number of sheep in a designated forage area which the area could support without damage. The grazier would enjoy exclusive and protected grazing rights in his assigned lands. In return he should, by agreement with the government, remain in that area and graze only the specified number of sheep. The agreement would prohibit herders from setting fires and bind them to fight those which were started accidentally.

For the government the chief advantages of the plan were fire-control provisions and a method to protect forage from overuse. For the sheepmen the plan eliminated destructive competition and the annual spring race for the best ranges; as Coville noted, it was "usually to the owner's interest to get all the grass possible without reference to the next year's crop, for he is never certain that he will be able to occupy the same range again." There was a widespread belief that the haphazard grazing system was supported by the sheep owners. In fact, they welcomed a change in government policy which would give them a financial interest in the maintenance of good pasturage. This protection against overuse, according to Coville, would offer the greatest benefit to the industry.

Sheepmen had already attempted through their own organizations to allot grazing areas, but invariably some owners and tramp herders violated agreements. With the authority of the government replacing volunteerism, these problems could be overcome. The Department of the Interior had full power to make land-use regulations within the forest reserves and to enforce them. Coville acknowledged "that while Government undoubtedly wished to handle the subject with the velvet hand of equity there lay beneath it the iron claw of stern authority." The sheep owners could see that errant owners would not be nearly so troublesome to the Department of the Interior as they had been to their volunteer organizations. But how should the range be distributed? By highest bidder or by arbitrary government decisions? After careful consideration, it was decided that the volunteer organizations should parcel out the range through stockmen's associations. The private commission could also serve to adjudicate conflicting applications. These recommendations could then be confirmed by the local forest administration. The 1902 GLO *Forest Reserve Manual* listed this procedure only for issuing sheep permits; cattle graziers had to apply directly to the forest reserve office. Still, everyone realized that the development of tighter controls depended upon Congress to provide for a "forest reserve service and adequate system of administration."

Administering a permit plan for grazing would naturally incur some measure of expense to the government. Coville suggested that the cost of administration could be borne by the sheep owners, who would pay a fee for their permits. Finally, he offered a series of recommendations allowing sheep grazing in Oregon. Coville's report can be seen as one of the most important statements on the pattern of early grazing-control programs in the forests.[18]

As early as July, 1898, the American Forestry Association published a summary of these points, noting that they applied only to the sheep-grazing areas in the Cascade Range Forest Reserve. Different climate and different terrain might dictate altogether different recommendations for regulation, but Coville's was the first comprehensive list to emerge from careful and measured study. Even John Minto commented favorably on the regulations because they definitely opened the forests to grazing.[19]

The 1897–98 annual report of the secretary of the interior reflected the department's response to the Coville report. Controversies surrounding sheep grazing in the reserves superseded all other questions related to grazing. "Next to fires," read the secretary's report, "sheep grazing was found to constitute the most serious difficulty to be considered in administering certain of the reserves." The secretary admitted that the reserved lands were not to be entirely withdrawn from occupation and use, particularly with such an important industry as sheep raising. The secretary still displayed caution when he pledged further efforts to ascertain conditions in a particular region before making final decisions as to the exclusion of sheep.

The General Land Office now undertook to permit grazing in selected forest reserves and referred to it as a "privilege." Forest superintendents, supervisors, and in many cases, ordinary citizens, public officeholders, woolgrowers' associations, fruit growers, and water associations sent reports and petitions to the GLO either supporting or opposing sheep grazing in the reserves. In the face of this deluge of information, the Land Office decided that it would recommend grazing if sheep had customarily grazed

[18] Coville, *Forest Growth and Sheep Grazing*, pp. 8–9, 46, 50, 53–54.

[19] "Regulations for Sheep Grazing in the Cascade Reserve," *American Forestry* 4 (July, 1898): 140–41; Rakestraw, "John Minto vs. John Muir," p. 381.

in the reserve and if the grazing would not endanger the watershed or permanent productivity of the forest. Applications were to be considered from graziers, but only citizens or those who had declared their intention to become citizens of the United States need apply. The applicants must also be residents of the state in which the reserve was located, if they were "to be allowed a grazing privilege in such reserve."

With new grazing applications ready, the General Land Office announced that grazing privileges would be allowed on a limited number of reserves. During 1898 the secretary permitted grazing in only the Cascade Range Reserve in Oregon and the Big Horn Reserve in Wyoming. To some extent these actions represented only a grudging acceptance of the Coville report.

Forest superintendents recommended that a fee be charged for sheep grazing. The charge could vary from forest to forest, but nominal figures such as five dollars per thousand head were suggested. The superintendents pointed out that the Northern Pacific Railroad leased much of its land and gained substantial revenue from sheep graziers. Still, the General Land Office was cautious about taking this step, as there appeared to be no authority in existing law to require payment for grazing privileges. No fees were imposed, but the Land Office called for legislation to authorize the secretary to make reasonable charges for the grazing privilege.

The 1899 report concluded on an uncertain note about grazing's future in the reserves. Admittedly, some portions of the reserves were more adapted to agricultural than forest use. Good grazing lands within the forests created a demand for their use and, if exclusion were practiced, graziers could claim hardship and denial of rights. As long as such lands existed under the forest administration there would be continued pressure from stockmen to enter the reserves with their stock. The Department of the Interior suggested that when a geological survey was completed of the reserves, segregating grazing lands from forest lands, they would "better decide the question of the exclusion of sheep from the reserves; and if it be held that no sheep shall graze in any reserve the agricultural or grazing lands should first be eliminated entirely from the reserve." Here again the intention to protect forests clearly took precedence over concerns for forage cover.

In 1899 the Department of the Interior confused sheep graziers when it withdrew the grazing privilege, claiming that it had been only a "temporary concession." The department believed that the grazing privilege had been greatly abused, "and much damage done." Sheepmen were ousted from the Mount Rainier Reserve in Washington and the Sierra Reserve in California after enjoying a brief season of grazing. This revocation of the privilege, a direct contradiction of the recommendation of the Coville report, appeared to be evidence of bad faith upon the department's part. Lawrence W. Rakestraw explains this vacillation as the result of John Muir's continuing campaign against sheep in the forests. In addition, James Wilson, secretary of agriculture, became convinced in the summer of 1899 that sheep represented a threat to the forest reserves. His conversion to this position probably occurred at a California meeting of the American Forestry Association, where sheep grazing was vociferously opposed. He condemned the permission for sheep grazing in the forests of Oregon and Washington, and "somehow impressed the Department of the Interior with his views, for his suggestion was followed by action." [20]

The partial acceptance of the Coville report for the season of 1898 and then the restrictions in 1899 confused and alarmed graziers, particularly so in the state of Washington. On September 3, 1899, the secretary of the interior ordered two hundred thousand sheep out of the Rainier Forest Reserve. This order came in spite of the fact that the grazing permits ran until September 25. Many believed that the grazing controversy had been settled, but now it appeared that the situation was almost back to where it had been prior to the Coville report. A furor broke out in the Northwest over the question. Grazing interests, with Minto leading the way, naturally supported the use of the forest forage resources, while recreationists, who saw the forests as beautiful preserves, called for further closures to sheep.

Two months later the department, under pressure from Northwest congressional delegations, reversed its order and restored the Coville regulations. John Muir, predictably, was highly critical. He could not believe that his recent friend Pinchot had not stood firmly against sheep in the forests in accordance with the academy's report of 1897. Thus began an antagonism between the two men that did not end until Muir's death in 1913. This occurred after his disheartening battle against the Hetch-Hetchy Reservoir project in Yosemite National Park to provide water for San Francisco. Pinchot and national administrations supported the project until its final approval in 1913. To many, the victory of the forest users in the North-

---

[20] U.S. Congress, House, *Annual Report of the Secretary of the Interior, 1898*, 55th Cong., 3rd sess., 1898–99, 5, vol. 14, pp. xiv, 108, 112, 121.

west grazing controversy of 1899 marked the beginning of a resource policy that paid more attention to the needs of users (like supporters of the Hetch-Hetchy project) than to aesthetic conservationists and recreationist groups.[21]

Even after the return to the principles of the Coville report, sheep grazing was restricted to only a few of the forest reserves. In Arizona powerful sheep organizations continued to push for entrance into the reserves. As in Oregon, local recreationist groups opposed their efforts and allied with cattle and horse raisers as well as with the Salt River Water Users Association. The Black Mesa Reserve, created in 1898, was closed to grazing in 1899, sparking violent protests and defiance of the order. In August, 1899, the Arizona Sheep Breeders and Wool Growers Association reorganized as the Arizona Wool Growers Association with an eastern and western division in the state. The general president and secretary of the western division was E. S. Gosney; Albert F. Potter was secretary of the eastern division.

In January of 1899, Potter and Gosney came to Washington to plead the case of Arizona sheepmen. They visited with officials from the Department of the Interior and with Pinchot, who was now head of the Division of Forestry within the Department of Agriculture. Potter's and Gosney's arguments were so convincing that Pinchot and Coville were again called upon to go West, this time combining their mission. Their task was to perform an investigation in Arizona similar to Coville's Oregon study. In June, 1900, Pinchot and Coville traveled over some of the more remote Arizona mountains accompanied by Potter, the veteran sheepman. Also in their company was Professor E. C. Bunch, representing the Salt River Valley Water Users Association. Lowland irrigators took special interest in the development of policies pertaining to sheep grazing in the higher watershed areas. Of course, Pinchot and Coville were regarded as greenhorns in Arizona, and the sheepmen did not know quite what to expect from these eastern "college boys."

When they moved into the parched country on the first night of their trek through the sheep camps, their fresh water ran low. The water they came upon in an old stock tank was a "stagnant pool of terrible green water." The horns of rotting cattle carcasses stuck out in places. Pinchot

[21] Rakestraw, "John Minto vs. John Muir," pp. 380–82; Linnie Marsh Wolfe, *Son of the Wilderness: The Life of John Muir*, pp. 275–76; Roderick Nash, *Wilderness and the American Mind*, pp. 161–81.

recalled, "We had to drink it or go dry." At the same time, he suspected Potter of arranging this desert country initiation for the visitors. Against their better judgment, both Pinchot and Coville drank with the experienced range hands and thus took a long step toward being accepted by their suspicious companions. They met many of Potter's friends in such places as Moki Spring, Mud Lake, and Lost Camp, all in the general area of the Mogollon Mesa country; Potter proved to be well known among the sheep graziers and a leader in shaping local opinion.[22]

As in the Oregon report, Coville and Pinchot concluded that sheep grazing in the forests should be permitted under supervision. They agreed with Muir and others that sheep could damage a forest terribly, but believed this was the result of overgrazing, and that regulated sheep grazing was preferable to either overgrazing or a complete prohibition. A ban on all sheep grazing might provoke total flaunting of the law, disrespect for the reserves, and strong political pressure for the return of the reserves to the public domain. After all, the large sheep associations in Arizona had never attacked the existence of the reserves, only the prohibition against grazing. Such men could be a source of valuable support in the future.

Potter's capabilities so impressed Pinchot that he persuaded him to come to Washington and head up a grazing branch within the Department of Agriculture's expanding Bureau of Forestry. In October, 1901, Potter moved to Washington. He became the "grazing expert," offering advice to Pinchot and Secretary of Agriculture James Wilson. Potter's service lasted until his retirement in 1920. During that time he became assistant forester and chief of the Grazing Branch in 1907 and associate chief forester in 1910. During World War I he served as acting chief of the Forest Service. Under Potter, scientific studies and recommendations were translated into workable policies on the local level. Coville's studies and Potter's administration of the regulations laid the foundation for the Forest Service's grazing policies. Pinchot said of him, "He was the cornerstone upon which we built the whole structure of grazing control."[23]

As a result of the Coville investigations and the aid of Pinchot in Arizona, the Department of the Interior developed a number of principles by

---

[22] Paul H. Roberts, *Hoof Prints on Forest Ranges: The Early Years of National Forest Range Administration*, pp. 24, 27, 29; Memo for G. P., Jan. 2, 1942, Gifford Pinchot Papers, Series VI, Box 551, Library of Congress, Washington, D.C.; Pinchot, *Breaking New Ground*, pp. 178–79, 181.

[23] Will C. Barnes, "A Pioneer Inspector of Grazing," *Breeder's Gazette* 77 (May 6, 1920): 1233; Pinchot, *Breaking New Ground*, p. 182.

1901 to regulate grazing on the forest reserves. Secretary of the Interior Ethan A. Hitchcock announced that the central idea underlying the regulations would be "cooperation between the Government and the grazing interests." The secretary emphasized that the goal was to bring about the best management in order to produce ultimately an improved range condition. The announcement was an acknowledgment that management and resource use went hand in hand.[24]

In 1901 the secretary declared that under regulated conditions sheep would be permitted in certain portions of the reserves, "where it is shown after careful examination, that grazing is in no way injurious to or preventive of the conservation of the water supply, and that policy it is my purpose to continue." Anyone wishing to reserve forest pastures must obtain a permit, which was granted free of charge. The permits limited the number of animals, set the time of entrance into and exit from the reserves, and designated the district to be grazed.[25]

After Pinchot's visit to Arizona it appeared that the secretary had more concern for water supplies than for the effect sheep grazing had upon forest growth. This policy no doubt reflected the influence and power of Arizona associations of water users who had impressed their views on Pinchot and Coville. In contrast, Coville's Pacific Northwest report paid more attention to forest damage threatened by overgrazing of sheep. As a result of these two studies, sheep grazing was permitted in parts of eight reserves. Cattle were, of course, allowed in all reserves because they never had been as controversial as sheep. Sheep were the symbol of the entire conflict between forest users and forest preservers.

The question of charging for permits had been debated within the Department of the Interior during the previous year. A preliminary regulation issued on April 4, 1900, by the General Land Office stated: "Permits will only be granted on the express condition and agreement on the part of the applicants that they will hereafter pay such reasonable price per head of sheep, goats, cattle, and horses to be grazed within the reserves as the Secretary of the Interior may hereafter require." The attempt to impose this charge, however, was not mentioned in the annual reports of the General Land Office for 1900. The report for the year 1901 showed an amended

[24]Filibert Roth, "Grazing in the Forest Reserves," *Yearbook of Agriculture, 1901*, pp. 337–38.

[25]U.S. Congress, House, *Annual Report of the Secretary of the Interior, 1902*, 57th Cong., 2d sess., 1902–1903, H. Doc. 5, vol. 18, p. 23.

version, dated July 5, 1900. The new version made no mention of grazing fees, but did assert that permittees must comply with all laws passed now or hereafter by Congress relating to the grazing of livestock. The lawyers for the Department of the Interior must have concluded that their authority did not extend to the imposing of grazing fees. Nonetheless, the amended version bound all participants to abide by any future laws passed by Congress, and new legislation could authorize grazing fees.[26]

If the Department of the Interior had remained fast on the fee issue, Pinchot and Coville might have had rough going in Arizona. Their trip was already somewhat controversial inside the General Land Office. The secretary, by asking two Department of Agriculture officials to make the investigation in Arizona, had completely bypassed the General Land Office, which had jurisdiction over the forest reserves. A memo written within the Forest Service in 1942 for Pinchot speculated that there was resentment within the General Land Office because he and Coville had been given these investigatory responsibilities. The memo asked if the commissioner of the General Land Office was irritated that the secretary had turned to Pinchot and the Department of Agriculture for expert advice on how to handle grazing. This alleged animosity may partially explain why grazing was given only cursory mention in the 1900 GLO annual report after appearing conspicuously in the 1898 and 1899 Land Office reports, and why moves to implement a system of grazing privileges came slowly. A few months after Pinchot visited Arizona, E. S. Gosney, president of the Arizona Wool Growers Association, wrote a personal letter to him about the inaction of the General Land Office in initiating a system of grazing permits. Gosney informed Pinchot: "Our stockmen are getting very anxious about grazing on the forest reserves the coming season, this should have been settled before this." [27]

Resource Use and Regulation under the Roosevelt Administration

Events in 1901 sharply accelerated the pace of conservation events in the United States. The assassination of President William McKinley in

[26] U.S. Department of the Interior, *Decisions of the Department of the Interior Relating to Public Lands*, vol. XXX, p. 60 (both paragraphs appear, one dated April 4, 1900, and the other July 5, 1900); Jan. 2, 1942, Series VI, Box 551.

[27] Memo for G. P., Jan. 2, 1942, Pinchot Papers, p. 11; E. S. Gosney to Pinchot [ca. 1901], Forest History Society Archives, Santa Cruz, California.

September placed Vice-President Theodore Roosevelt in the White House. Pinchot called on the new president shortly after Roosevelt's arrival in Washington and even before he moved into the White House. Accompanying Pinchot was Frederick H. Newell, a government hydrographer of ten years. Pinchot and Newell urged the president to support a program of national forestry and irrigation. Roosevelt, who had lived in the West and was devoted to the area, immediately acknowledged the importance of federal resource protection. He asked them to prepare statements on these subjects so that he might include them in his first annual message to Congress. For the next eight years Pinchot remained a confidant of Roosevelt.[28]

True to his promise, Roosevelt's message to Congress in early December contained remarks about the future of forest reserves and the need for nationally supported irrigation and/or reclamation in the West. Pinchot wrote: "T. R. accepted substantially everything we wrote as we wrote it. His message at once transformed Forestry [*sic*] and irrigation into national issues of continental consequence, and started them toward that high degree of public acceptance they achieved before T. R. left the White House." Roosevelt spoke for Pinchot when he said, "The fundamental idea of forestry is the perpetuation of forests by use." He spoke of the usefulness of the forest reserves to mining, grazing, irrigation, and other western interests. He indicated that even westerners demanded protection of the forests and the extension of forest reserves. Pinchot was most gratified with the president's recommendation that the forest reserves be transferred to the Bureau of Forestry within the Department of Agriculture. The current system called for the General Land Office to protect the forests, the United States Geological Survey to map and describe them, and the Bureau of Forestry to provide working plans for their use. Roosevelt believed this prevented cooperation between the government "and the men who utilize the resources of the reserves, without which the interests of both must suffer."[29]

Long, vague, and sometimes contradictory letters passed back and forth between the General Land Office and the forest superintendents on the grazing question. When the GLO superintendent in Colorado advised the exclusion of sheep, Commissioner Hermann, formerly a congressman from Oregon, questioned his judgment and asked him to recon-

---

[28]Philip P. Wells, "Memoirs of the Roosevelt Administration," Nov. 18, 1919, Pinchot Papers, Series VI, Box 2869; Pinchot, *Breaking New Ground*, pp. 188–90.

[29]*Congressional Record*, 57th Cong. 1st sess., 1902, vol. 36, pt. 2, pp. 85–86.

sider. The commissioner suggested that sheep could graze in the open, flat parts of the forest with the understanding that they would be confined to these areas. If they were not, the permit would cease and the sheep would be driven from the entire range. He used the term "restrictive right" to describe the permit privilege that should not exceed the period of a few months. He further proposed that the number of sheep should be limited by setting a "maximum number" for the forest. To avoid the charge of favoritism, the sheepmen themselves were to be asked to name the recipients of permits, since the number of permits would be smaller than the number of sheep seeking entrance to the forest. Hermann wanted the sheepmen to decide among themselves how many sheep each would send onto the range, but the total number would not exceed the safe limit established by the forest supervisor: "In that way it cannot be said that any one owner was discriminated against in favor of another." Hermann attempted to placate local and state interests when he noted that it was "the well-practiced policy" of the department that out-of-state sheep could not have access to reservations in another state. The forest superintendent was asked to provide a marked map to applicants indicating designated grazing areas, so that a full notice of limits for the "proposed privilege" could be understood by all.

Hermann believed he clearly outlined "the restrictive measures" to be invoked if, in the judgment of the superintendent, sheep should be permitted to graze in the forest. In any event the superintendent should telegraph his opinions to Hermann "before a final conclusion can be had." His letter ended with an affirmation of the superintendent's local authority, but suggested that the protection offered by restrictive measures be considered: "In conclusion, let it be understood that this communication is not addressed to you because of any special desire on the part of this office of the Department to permit sheep grazing within your reserve regardless as to consequences, but only in the event that such privilege may be without injury to the reserve, if it is possible that the privilege may be so hedged about and guarded by certain well-defined restrictive measures."[30]

Others complained about the unenforceable grazing regulations in these early years while the reserves were under the Department of the Interior. One forester wrote that the failures of the Interior Department in administering the forests from 1897 to 1905 was caused in large part by

[30] Binger Hermann to W. T. S. May, Forest Superintendent, Denver, Colo., July 14, 1899, Div. R, Book 39, Record Group 49, Records of the General Land Office, National Archives, Washington, D.C.

dilettante rangers and political appointees who failed to take their tasks seriously. Another asserted that no real attempt had been made to estimate carrying capacity of ranges or to promote proper handling of stock.[31] In a 1907 article, Charles H. Shinn, a westerner who had become the supervisor of the Sierra National Forest, commented that the sheep question was the most perplexing one. Although sheep were prohibited from grazing on the reserves, the sheepmen laughed at the rangers. They had copies of the prohibition orders but knew they could not be enforced. In the beginning there was no sheep policy, and the sheepmen could outwit the clumsy efforts of a few rangers to keep them off the reserves. The Basques became particularly adept at knowing the whereabouts of the rangers and how to escape detection. The reserves came into being at the same time that Basque herders were appearing in greater numbers in the western deserts and mountains. In California and western Nevada almost one-quarter million sheep moved annually across the Walker Pass to the Inyo and Mono regions. In increasing numbers the tramp herders, many of them Basques, sought out "the forbidden ground" to feed their sheep. They returned season after season to park and reserve, "and thus learned a profound contempt for unenforced regulations."[32]

The older rangers had to restrain "hotheads" who wanted to "shoot a few sheep" or "hammer the Bascos." The regulations eventually permitted rangers to tie up the herder's dogs, remove the bells from the bellwethers, and scatter the herds over and over again until loss and suffering were inflicted upon the trespassers. Some law-abiding sheep owners decided to quit the business after the establishment of the reserves. They resented foreigners who persistently flouted the law. One complained not only of the Basques but also of the cattlemen who took advantage of early prohibition against sheep. Shinn quoted an acquaintance on this score: "Now here we was puttin' sheep up thar from Crane Valley over Shut-Eye, an' makin' money an' hurtin' noting'. Then comes Uncle Sam an' says no sheep is required. The Bascos keep right on, but the law-abidin' tax-payers like me sells out an' quits. Then they let cattle in on our old ranges. All a put-up game."

Forest rangers and supervisors like Shinn felt that they had an obliga-

[31] Leonard C. Shoemaker, *Saga of a Forest Ranger: A Biography of William R. Kreutzer, Forest Ranger No. 1, and a Historical Account of the U.S. Forest Service in Colorado*, p. 23; Clarence N. Woods, "41 Years in National Forest Administration," typescript, 1943, Box 4, File 18, Federal Records Center of the National Archives, Denver, Colo.

[32] Mary Austin, *The Flock*, pp. 197–98.

tion to explain to disgruntled sheepmen that unregulated sheep grazing could harm the forest and watershed. On the other hand, regulated grazing with fixed, enforceable rules could safely be permitted. Shinn disagreed with many who believed that conservation of the water and the trees in the high Sierra absolutely required the exclusion of sheep from all parts of the mountains. If this were true, the grazing of cattle should also be halted, he charged: "Men who handle their sheep well, keep off the meadows, have small bands constantly moving . . . do not injure the forest so far as very close and constant observation can decide." Shinn concluded that "white sheep away up in the blue brush or eating out fireline in summer weeds, may have a place in forest economics after all."[33]

In November of 1901, Pinchot, now forester in the U.S. Department of Agriculture, termed grazing and irrigation the most important problems facing forest reserves. Pinchot did not yet direct policy; the Bureau of Forestry could only act as advisor to the Department of the Interior. Pinchot's investigations into the grazing question, however, gave weight to his advice. In his articles, which appeared frequently in the *Forester* (forerunner of *American Forests*) and other publications, Pinchot pointed out that in only a few instances did the value of timber taken annually from the forest reserves equal the value of the forage consumed by livestock. Obviously, then, forage resources must be considered in any future forest policies.

In one such article Pinchot wrote that any "adequate" consideration of the grazing question must rest upon three propositions. First, all resources of the forests should be wisely used for the good of the people. The forests' resources were not confined to timber, mining, and watershed. The grasses and the forage plants were also resources of prime importance and should be utilized. Second, because grazing was a local question, it should always be dealt with in the light of local conditions: "Wise administration of grazing in the reserves is impossible under general rules based upon theoretical considerations. Local rules must be framed to meet local conditions, and they must be modified from time to time as local needs may require." Third, overgrazing destroys both the forest and range. Regulation to avoid overgrazing was to the advantage of both forest and grazing interests.

Pinchot reminded his readers in the article that the grazing question

[33] Charles H. Shinn, "Work in a National Forest," *Forestry and Irrigation* 13 (November, 1907): 590–97.

involved more than forests and forage for stock. Other western interests had a stake in the future of grazing policies. Irrigation farmers demanded adequate and protected watersheds for their livelihood. The capital invested in irrigation, in most cases, far exceeded that invested in the range and in range stock. Any threat to irrigated agriculture would be a threat to western prosperity in general. In addition, miners needed both an assured water supply as well as timber on a continuing basis from the forests. The railroads, too, wanted a prosperous West. One interest such as grazing or lumbering should not work against the other varied user interests. Without well-cared-for forests, western economies would suffer.

While Pinchot emphasized the competing interests for the forest resources, he took special notice of the competition within the grazing community itself. In much of the West, the small cattle rancher was extremely hostile to sheepmen. Oftentimes sheepherders completely exhausted the public lands adjacent to the land owned by the small cattle rancher. The small rancher also feared that the large cattle corporations would appropriate the ranges. At least on the question of sheep in the forests, the cattlemen invariably sided with the irrigation spokesmen who called for the exclusion of sheep. Amidst these conflicting opinions and deeply felt antagonisms, the forest officer was faced with difficult decisions, yet was obligated to arrive at "just conclusions." Those conclusions had to arise from a grazing policy based upon regulation and not prohibition, and resting upon cooperation among the user interests themselves.[34]

Eventually, the Department of the Interior began to adopt the type of regulated grazing advocated by Pinchot. In 1902 the secretary of the interior announced that 1,197,000 sheep, and 459,137 cattle and horses were to be allowed into the reserves. Grazing occurred free of charge and with little restriction on time or season, locality, or the movement of stock as long as it was compatible with an economic use of reserve pastures. The department congratulated itself upon helping to keep profitable one of the leading western industries. The 1902 report of the General Land Office made special reference to the office's prior policy on the granting of permits. The report claimed that the principal change in policy was the provision that allowed the forest supervisor to issue cattle and horse grazing permits to reserve residents who owned not more than 100 head of cattle and horses combined. While this may not have been the most significant change,

[34] Pinchot, "Grazing in the Forest Reserves," *The Forester* 7 (November, 1901): 276–80.

considering the earlier provision for a grazing fee, the privilege extended to residents of the reserves is significant.[35]

In a circular issued by the department on January 8, 1902, to explain further the rights of resident settlers within the forests, the word "preference" was used to describe the order in which permits would be accepted; in the late twentieth century the use of the term was still occasionally to be found. The circular stated that stock "of all kinds" would receive preference in the following order:

1. Stock of residents within the reserve.
2. Stock of persons who own permanent stock ranches within the reserve, but who reside outside of the reserve.
3. Stock of persons living in the immediate vicinity of the reserve, called neighboring stock.
4. Stock of outsiders who have some equitable claim.

This official statement established a priority of preference for stock permits in the forests that dominated the policy of administrators for decades to come.

The year 1902 also brought an official endorsement of the practice of permitting the local woolgrowers' associations to recommend who should receive allotment permits. The forest supervisor, however, was the final authority. In return for the power of recommendation, the associations were under obligations to see that all rules and regulations, and terms of the applications and permits were fully adhered to by graziers. The associations were called upon to impose penalties (to be carried out by forest officers) for violations of the initial agreement, such as willful trespass on areas not permited, the setting of fires, or attempting to obtain a permit on false representation. The penalties were a reduction in the number of sheep covered by a permit or the forfeiture of the permit. Representative woolgrowers' associations existed in Arizona, Oregon, Utah, and Washington. They helped determine the allotments in the Black Mesa and San Francisco Mountain reserves in Arizona, the Cascade Range Reserve in Oregon, the Uintah Reserve in Utah, and the Mount Rainier and Washington Reserves in Washington. Qualified associations were not found in New Mexico and Wyoming.

---

[35] U.S. Congress, House, *Annual Report of the Secretary of the Interior, 1902*, 57th Cong., 2d sess., 1902–1903, H. Doc. 5, vol. 18, p.–22.

The Land Office admitted that reliance upon the woolgrowers' associations sometimes caused delays in the issuing of permits. Such consultations took time and investigations made by forest inspectors revealed that too many sheep were allowed in the reserves during the 1902 season and that the number should be materially decreased for the year 1903. Eventually the department initiated rules for access to the private lands within a forest reserve that involved mainly the laying out of stock transits along specified trails across the reserves. Permittees were also required to fight fires (without pay) that broke out in the forests. In this respect, the instructions sent to each forest supervisor directed that it was part of the supervisor's duty "to insist upon parties who have been granted permits within his reserve to do all in their power to prevent forest fires, and also to aid in extinguishing same." More specifically, the instructions stated, "[I]t is not only the party who holds the permit in his name who must render service, but anyone employed by the holder of the permit." These people had to respond to fire call or risk having their grazing permits revoked.[36]

Table 2 shows the reserves in which sheep grazing was permitted, and the number of sheep in comparison with the number of permits issued for 1902 and 1901. The thirty-eight reserves also accommodated the grazing of cattle and horses under a permit system as indicated in Table 3. There appears to have been a large increase in the number from 1901 to 1902; in fact, the number represents the more rigid enforcement of the rule requiring permits on all stock. Therefore, it should not be interpreted to indicate a spectacular increase.

As previously mentioned, in the early years, the presence of cattle and horses on the reserves was not as controversial as sheep. Points of contention arose over the different nature of trespasses committed by the two classes of stock. Cattle, and even horses, grazed without supervision of a herder, but sheep did not. When cattle and horses trespassed upon the reserves, as they often did, the stockman maintained they did so without his knowledge. The sheepman, on the other hand, was directly responsible for the location of his herds at all times because they were under supervision. When sheep trespassed, the owner was legally responsible for the damage.

While the reserves were under the administration of the General Land

---

[36]U.S. Congress, House, *Annual Report of the Commissioner of the General Land Office*, 1902, 57th Cong., 2d sess., 1902–1903, H. Doc. 5, pp. 332–33, 335.

TABLE 2. Sheep Grazing in the Forest Reserves, 1901 and 1902.

Reservation	Number of sheep allowed to enter		Number of permits issued and number of sheep covered			
	1901	1902	1901		1902	
			Permits, number	Sheep, number	Permits, number	Sheep, number
Black Mesa, Ariz.	225,000	150,000	57	176,485	73	147,080
San Francisco Mountains, Ariz.	125,000	100,000	24	124,800	22	99,000
Gila River, New Mexico	225,000	200,000	30	134,320a	44	170,203b
Uintah, Utah	200,000	150,000	87	188,050	76	149,765
Do		50,000c			d	50,000
Cascade Range, Oregon	200,000	200,000	44	166,050	47	188,800
Big Horn, Wyoming	150,000	150,000	54	150,000	78	149,964
Mount Rainier, Washington	250,000	172,000	89	249,713	95	171,466
Washington, Washington	25,000	25,000	6	25,000	8	25,000
Total	1,400,000	1,197,000	391e	1,214,418	443	1,151,278

SOURCE: U.S. Congress, House, *Annual Report of the Commissioner of the General Land Office, 1902*, 57th Cong., 2d sess., 1902–1903, H. Doc. 5, vol. 18, p. 337.

aIncluded 5,840 goats.

bIncludes 11,603 goats.

cAdditional permits not yet issued.

dAbout thirty permits for the additional 50,000 sheep.

eIn 1901, 34 applicants failed to get permits.

Office, the question of unlawful trespass on the forest lands was never adequately addressed. The act passed on June 4, 1897, gave to the secretary of the interior the power "to insure the objects of such reservations," and "to regulate their occupancy and use." If the purpose or objective of a reserve was to insure a continuous supply of timber, protect the water supply of a community; or insure adequate runoff for an irrigation project, grazing could be permitted only when these requirements were met. To insure these

TABLE 3. Cattle and Horse Grazing in the Forest Reserves, 1901 and 1902.

Reserve	Area	Cattle and horses allowed to enter in 1902	Departmental permits, 1902			Supervisor's permits, 1902			Total permits, 1902		Total permits, 1901	
			Number	Cattle	Horses	Number	Cattle	Horses	Number	Cattle and horses	Number	Cattle and horses
Arizona:												
Black Mesa	1,658,880	30,000	71	23,215	1,808	59	1,994	909	130	27,926	99	18,222
Prescott	423,680	1,000	—	—	—	16	557	57	16	614	12	320
Grand Canyon	1,851,520	16,000	11	5,690	578	4	—	215	15	6,483	15	1,021
San Francisco Mountains	975,360	20,000	46	13,900	1,566	57	1,568	915	103	17,985	110	14,675
New Mexico:												
Gila River	2,327,040	50,000	73	44,410	3,154	67	2,077	946	140	50,587	183	45,679
Pecos River	431,040	10,000	67	4,126	355	30	841	139	97	5,461	147	4,602
California:												
Lake Tahoe	136,335	2,500	19	1,875	196	—	—	—	19	2,071	13	1,985
Stanislaus	691,200	10,000	57	9,712	694	—	—	—	57	10,406	39	7,295
Sierra	4,096,000	41,000	238	32,752	1,097	30	1,711	107	268	35,667	180	25,865
Pine Mountain and Zaca Lake	1,644,591	8,000	22	3,180	84	91	2,275	479	113	6,018	20	933
Santa Ynez	145,000	7,500	—	—	—	22	253	124	22	377	12	86
San Bernardino	737,280	3,500	6	1,575	—	8	318	101	14	2,021	18	3,045
San Gabriel	555,520	600	—	—	—	19	306	155	19	461	25	397
San Jacinto	737,280	1,500	5	465	—	18	976	—	23	1,441	16	1,080
Trabuco Canyon	109,920	300	3	85	—	7	220	15	10	320	4	210
Colorado:												
Battlement Mesa	858,240	50,000	162	47,489	1,069	5	415	—	167	48,973	149	46,996
Pike's Peak	181,320	2,500	11	1,965	35	11	780	26	22	2,806	16	1,420
Plum Creek	179,200	5,000	0	2,105	40	24	1,430	77	33	3,652	43	3,915
South Pacific	683,520	25,000	32	9,303	515	37	1,618	69	69	11,505	82	13,808
White River	1,198,080	50,000	176	43,854	1,730	39	1,901	274	215	47,669	154	42,303

Utah:

Fish Lake	67,840	1,000	16	918	52	—	—	—	16	1,000	5	374
Uintah	875,520	10,000	117	9,606	289	2	14	3	119	9,912	60	4,320
Payson	86,400	—	—	—	—	—	—	—	—	—	—	none
Idaho:												
Bitter Root	3,456,000	3,000	—	—	—	22	769	229	22	998	—	—
Priest River, Idaho and Washington	511,160	800	1	14	4	14	286	31	15	335	—	—
Montana:												
Bitter Root	691,200	2,000	4	300	—	6	108	34	10	442	1	400
Flathead	1,382,400	2,500	—	—	—	36	57	266	36	323	39	245
Gallatin	40,320	100	3	100	—	—	—	—	8	100	8	145
Lewis and Clark	2,920,080	15,000	54	7,036	492	17	745	427	71	8,700	52	6,743
Oregon:												
Bull Run	142,080	—	—	—	—	—	—	—	—	—	—	—
Cascade Range	4,492,800	5,000	31	4,462	138	—	—	—	31	4,600	12	1,545
Ashland	18,560	—	—	—	—	—	—	—	—	—	—	—
Oklahoma:												
Wichita	57,120	4,000	14	3,880	35	—	—	—	14	3,915	—	—
South Dakota:												
Black Hills, South Dakota and Wyoming	1,211,680	50,000	13	1,900	293	303	8,986	2,114	316	13,293	166	6,996
Wyoming:												
Big Horn	1,127,680	20,000	182	18,796	1,216	—	—	—	182	20,012	123	14,984
Teton	829,410	3,000	14	1,230	174	24	738	245	38	2,387	32	1,954
Yellowstone	1,239,040	1,000	—	—	—	—	—	—	—	—	—	—
Crow Creek	56,320	637	—	—	—	13	615	22	13	637	—	—
Washington:												
Mount Rainier	2,027,520	6,500	142	6,227	100	16	137	30	158	6,491	94	5,929
Olympic	2,188,800	2,000	1	11	—	6	196	3	7	210	2	129
Washington	3,594,240	5,000	27	1,371	126	12	200	51	39	1,748	—	—
Grand Total	—	459,137	1,627	301,682	15,810	1,015	32,121	8,099	2,642	357,642	1,926	277,621

SOURCE: U.S. Congress, House, *Annual Report of the Commissioner of the General Land Office, 1902*, 57th Cong. 2d sess., 1902–1903, H. Doc. 5, vol. 18, p. 338.

objectives, Congress provided that any violation of the purposes of the Act of June 4, 1897, be prosecuted under the earlier Act of June 4, 1888, that made depredation on public timber lands unlawful.

The act, however, proved unenforceable. The courts held that criminal prosecution for trespass "will not lie to punish a person for such a violation." For example, in *United States* vs. *Blasingame* and *United States* vs. *Camou* (both in 1898) the courts held that "in so far as" the Act of June 4, 1897, "the rules and regulations thereafter to be made by the Secretary of the Interior for the protection of the forest reservations is in substance and effect a delegation of legislative power to an administrative officer," and therefore unconstitutional. As a result, many of the secretary's orders against sheep grazing were defied. Nor did the government have the right to appeal in such cases because criminal violation could not be considered. The decision denied the secretary the right to impose his restrictions under the present law. Beginning in 1899 the U.S. attorney general and the secretary of the interior urged Congress to provide suitable legislation wherein an appeal might be made to higher courts on the basis of criminal violations. In 1903 the secretary of the interior made the following recommendation to Congress: "That every person who knowingly pastures or causes to be pastured any livestock upon public lands of the United States situated within a forest reserve without first having obtained a permit so to do under rules and regulations prescribed by the Secretary of the Interior shall, upon conviction, be punished by a fine not to exceed one thousand dollars, or by both such fine and imprisonment."

Obtaining injunctions against sheep about to enter the forests also proved ineffective. In most instances by the time a court order could be obtained and delivered to the potential violator, the sheep had already invaded the forest and committed the damage that the injunction intended to stop.[37]

The shortcomings of his department's administration prompted the Secretary of the Interior Ethan A. Hitchcock to suggest as early as June 30, 1901, a transfer of the reserves to the Bureau of Forestry within the Department of Agriculture. By 1903, William A. Richards, Roosevelt's new commissioner of the General Land Office, made the same recommendation. (In 1899 Richards had helped arrange for Pinchot's men to provide continuing forestry advice to GLO.) Richards agreed that forest protection was of first

[37] *Annual Report of the Secretary of the Interior, 1903*, 58th Cong., 2d sess., 1903–1904, H. Doc. 5, vol. 18, pp. 24, 25, 28.

importance, but "[f]ollowing closely upon that, however, must come the application of scientific methods in dealing with the many and varied forest problems in connection with the various industries affected thereby." The Bureau of Forestry heartily agreed with these views. President Roosevelt was also convinced.

The bill to transfer the administration of the forest reserves from the General Land Office in the Department of the Interior to the Bureau of Forestry within the Department of Agriculture finally passed Congress on February 1, 1905. Many pressures besides the urgings of the president came to bear to bring about the passage of this legislation. Pinchot was instrumental in organizing two unpaid commissions composed of men in the executive departments to investigate and give opinions. The first commission was the Committee on Scientific Work in the Departments, and the other was the Public Lands Commission of 1903. Both recommended transferring the forest reserves to the Bureau of Forestry not only for the reserves' protection, but also for their scientific administration and management. Under pressure from the president, the commissions, and the recommendations of the Department of the Interior itself, Congress finally acceded.[38] When the Secretary of Agriculture James Wilson received jurisdiction over the forest reserves, he prepared a landmark letter of transmittal, probably written by Pinchot, outlining the administrative duties of the Bureau of Forestry. This letter of instruction governed the spirit and direction of forest administration by the bureau and later the Forest Service for many decades. The letter to Forester Pinchot embodied the utilitarian-conservation principles that Pinchot himself advocated to Roosevelt. With no apologies to preservationists, it stated that "all land is to be devoted to its most productive use for the permanent good of the whole people and not for the temporay benefit of individuals or companies. [All of the resources of the forest] "are for use . . . in a business-like manner."

The secretary recognized that the resources of the forest were varied. He emphasized: "The continued prosperity of the agricultural, lumbering, mining and livestock interests is directly dependent upon a permanent and accessible supply of water, wood, and forage, as well as upon the present and future use of these resources under business-like regulations, enforced with promptness, effectiveness, and common sense." The secretary gave special emphasis to the dominant industry of a particular forest and the

[38] Wells, "Memoirs of the Roosevelt Administration," Pinchot Papers, Series VI, Box 2869, p. 10.

promotion of its interests, writing, "[T]he dominant industry will be considered first, but with as little restrictions to minor industries as may be possible." The principle of utilitarianism, however, should prevail in the use of the resources. That is to say, "where conflicting interests must be reconciled, the question will always be decided from the standpoint of the greatest good of the greatest number in the long run." These were the general principles that were to govern not only the protection of water supplies and the disposal of timber, but also the use of the range. Finally, these principles could be successfully followed only when local forest officers applied them with sufficient authoriy on the local level. These officers must, in turn, be supervised by thoroughly trained and competent inspectors.[39]

The Department of the Interior gave to the Bureau of Forestry the foundations of a general grazing policy. Forage use compatible with the purposes of the forest were the basis of the developing policies. The department formulated its policies by considering expert studies and observations in addition to user opinions and demands, especially as expressed by local stock associations. Many of the enduring terms of range administration of the forest emerged in these formative years. The start of the permit system with preference going first to nearby land owners, then to longtime users, and lastly to itinerants outlined the system for admitting graziers to forest ranges. The enforcement of the policies created by the General Land Office emphasized that admission to the reserves was a privilege granted by the government to stockmen.

The terms *privilege* and *allotment* reinforced the government's contention that stockmen did not possess unlimited rights to graze on the reserves. Similarly, forest administrators spoke of "restrictive right" as opposed to what the stockmen sometimes wished to consider a "prescriptive right." The General Land Office began the designation of "maximum numbers" of stock to be grazed in a forest as it attempted to establish "safe limits" for individual forests. Although the work of the General Land Office pioneered the range policy, the office appeared unable to sustain the bold administrative action needed to give credibility to its policies of range control and management. But to deny the contributions of the Department of the Interior to policy development would ignore the origins of policies ultimately carried out by the Forest Service.

[39] Letter in U.S. Congress, Senate, Doc. 84, 57th Cong. 1st sess., 1902, as quoted in Darrell H. Smith, *The Forest Service: Its History, Activities and Organization*, pp. 33–34.

3

The Forest Service and the Tasks of Management

> The grazing-men of the Forest Service were the shock troops who
> won the West for forestry.
>
> —Will C. Barnes

THE Bureau of Forestry enthusiastically accepted the full administration of the forest reserves in the spring of 1905. Chief Forester Pinchot believed that the agency, under the new name, the Forest Service, could perform three essential jobs: protection, management, and the effective application of scientific research to a wide range of forest problems. Range resources within the forests stood in particular need of these combined services available from the broader authority of the new agency and the Department of Agriculture. Because of the work of Coville, Pinchot, and Potter, a broad outline of grazing policies already existed. The next step was vigorous implementation.

Four days after the bureau's transfer, the secretary of agriculture informed Pinchot that the General Land Office had already set in motion a permit-grazing system for the 1905 season. The secretary authorized the continuation of the program and "whatever plan, in your judgment, will act for the best permanent use of the range." Above all, he noted, the resources demanded protection from trespassers—protection that could offer efficient use of resources. Range lands were to be appraised and divided according to their capacity and the type of stock to be grazed on them. The ranges' "carrying capacity," that is, the stock numbers that could be allowed up to a "maximum limit," would be determined. Efficient management would demand the imposition of a grazing fee to defray the cost of bringing order and protection to the forest grazing lands.[1]

---

[1] James Wilson to the Forester, Feb. 4, 1905, Records of the Forest Service, Record Group 95, Sec. 63, National Archives, Washington, D.C. [hereafter cited as RG 95, NA]; *The*

Albert F. Potter told the American Forest Congress in January, 1905, that grazing regulations must seek to avoid disturbing business by sudden changes in the manner of using the grazing lands. Grazing was not to be radically reduced in total disregard for the economic interest of the grazing community. Regulations were to be adjusted to local needs so that every privilege possible could be allowed on the lands "consistent with their proper care and management." All products of the reserves must be considered. Grazing should be managed in such a way that it did not harm either forests or watershed; farmers and forestry advocates, then, could not demand the end of forest grazing. Speaking to an audience that was somewhat skeptical about the role of grazing in forest management, Potter insisted that lumbermen must respect the right of stockmen to use the forest ranges, just as the farmer should not expect the government to stop grazing or timber cutting, "but must be content to have these things done under a proper system of regulation."

Potter believed that stockmen were beginning to understand that protection of the summer ranges meant better stock and increased profits. In the past season of drought, those who had pasturing privileges brought out fat stock from the forest reserves while stock on the overcrowded public domain ranges suffered and returned much less on investment. From the beginning of forest-reserve management, Potter conceded, grazing presented the most perplexing controversies. Still, he emphasized, there was no difference between the basic principles controlling the use of the forests and those of the range. Just as forest policy aimed to achieve a constant supply of wood and water, so too did range policy seek constant renewal of forage resources. "Overgrazing is just as fatal to the livestock indutry as destructive logging is to the lumber industry," Potter said. He used the word "regulation" to describe policies that would protect the "permanent carrying power" of the range and even increase the number of animals that could be supported.[2]

After it became apparent that the forest reserves would be transferred to the Agriculture Department, Secretary Wilson wished to allay fears in the grazing community about the future course of grazing policies. In

---

Use of the National Forest Reserves (Washington, D.C.: Government Printing Office, 1905), p. 30.

[2] American Forestry Association, *Proceedings of the American Forestry Congress*, Washington, D.C., January 2–6, 1905; U.S. Forest Service, *Forest Preservation and National Prosperity*. Circular no. 35, pp. 22–24.

meetings before livestock associations the secretary assured stockmen that use of the lands would continue and even be accelerated under the future administration of the Department of Agriculture. The main points of agreement, worked out by the department and stock organizations, emphasized that those already grazing in the forest ranges would be protected in their priority of use; that reductions in the number of grazed stock would be imposed only after fair notice; that small owners would have preference over large; that only in rare circumstances would the department seek total exclusion of stock from the forest; and that the policy of use would be maintained wherever it was consistent with intelligent forest management. Finally, some attempt would be made to give stockmen a voice in making the rules and regulations for the management of stock on local ranges through the establishment of forest advisory boards.[3]

In 1905 stockmen suspected that the government had only grudgingly admitted the importance of grazing. Many believed their privileges would be short-lived, fearing that the managers of the forests would become more oriented toward the single purpose of timber management, especially when the professional foresters from the eastern schools obtained secure control over the forest reserves. Ultimately, however, the interests of permittees were also threatened when recreational interests voiced their claims to forest resources and agriculturalists attempted to homestead within the forests. Potter remarked later that, "The outlook for the stockmen at that time was not a very bright one and naturally many felt that the maintenance of the National Forests was detrimental to their interests." Secretary Wilson's mission among the western livestock associations just prior to the transfer was therefore to assure them that their interests would be carefully protected in the future administration of the reserves. Friendly western sources tried to emphasize that regulated grazing would eliminate clashes between cattle and sheep interests; government officials pursued this theme in their meetings with stockmen. Cattlemen felt they would be more protected under a regulated system. But sheepmen saw that regulations could work to their disadvantage because they would not be allowed to compete for the same range against cattle as they could under a more open system.[4]

---

[3] A. F. Potter, "Cooperation in Range Management," *American National Cattleman's Association Proceedings* 16 (1913): 55.

[4] Potter, "Cooperation in Range Management," p. 55; *Walla Walla Evening Statesman*, December 22, 1905, as quoted in Virginia Paul, *This Was Sheep Ranching: Yesterday and Today*.

Much effort had already been devoted to the grazing problem in the forests by the Bureau of Forestry. Potter was appointed grazing expert in 1901 and chief of grazing after the transfer of the reserves to Pinchot's office. The forests submitted their grazing plans and reports to Potter's office. His appointment was obviously Pinchot's attempt to win some measure of acceptance among western stockmen by giving one of their own a key place in the tasks of grazing administration. The presence of Potter as chief of grazing, and Pinchot's attention to the demands of stock interests offered assurance that professional foresters would not subvert the commitment to grazing use in the forests.

Another reassurance was the appointment of several westerners to Potter's staff. W. C. Clos, with a background in animal husbandry and botany, had previously worked in Utah, devoting much effort to the development of grazing procedure. C. H. Adams was formerly in the livestock business. Joe Campbell had been an inspector for the Arizona Territorial Livestock Board. Leon F. Kneipp grew up in Chicago but joined the Forest Service in Arizona. Will C. Barnes, former manager of the Esperanza Cattle Co. in Arizona, was an old friend and former ranch partner of Potter.

Barnes's career included his youthful service as an army telegrapher during the campaigns against the Apache Indians (for which he received the Medal of Honor), his election to the territorial legislatures of Arizona and New Mexico, and his activity in livestock associations (including service as a state livestock official). During his years at the Forest Service, and after his retirement, he also wrote articles and fiction dealing with western history, including an important work on the stock industry, *Western Grazing Grounds and Forest Ranges* (1913). Recalling these days in his *Reminiscences*, Barnes wrote, "Great days were those for the Government Grazing policy; for, say what you will, the grazing-men of the Forest Service were the shock troops who won the West for forestry." [5]

Between the years 1905 and 1906, the policies underwent extensive revisions. By June of 1905 Pinchot's staff developed the *Use of the National Forest Reserves*, or *Use Book*, a small handbook containing directions to forest officers for management of the forest resources, including grazing,

[5] Gifford Pinchot, *Breaking New Ground*, pp. 181–82, 386; Paul H. Roberts, *Hoof Prints on Forest Ranges: The Early Years of the National Forest Range Administration*, pp. 42–43; Will C. Barnes, *Western Grazing Grounds and Forest Ranges*; Will C. Barnes, *Apaches and Longhorns: The Reminiscences of Will C. Barnes*, p. 202.

effective July 1. The handbook listed three classes of grazing permits: class A for those who owned adjacent ranch property; class B for those who owned non-adjacent ranch property and traditionally used the public forest ranges; class C for transient herders who could make no claim to local property ownership. The class C permits came last in preference; A and B permits usually took all of the alloted range. The Forest Service adhered to the principle of "commensurate property ownership" as a condition for receiving forest grazing privileges. The concept of commensurability suggested the ownership by the permittee of enough private ranch land to support the stock during periods when for one reason or another the National Forest was not open to grazing.

The Forest Service's *Use Book* took a far more positive attitude toward the utilization of resources than the Land Office's *Forest Reserve Manual* and used less authoritarian language. On the question of grazing, which was, according to Pinchot, "far and away the bitterest issue of the time," the *Manual* bluntly announced that, "The Secretary of the Interior, in being charged with the proper protection of the forest reserves, has the right to forbid any and all kinds of grazing therein." In a more conciliatory tone, the 1905 Forest Service *Use Book* merely said: "The Secretary of Agriculture has authority to permit, regulate, or prohibit grazing in the forest reserves." The book further stated the objects of grazing regulations to be (1) the protection and conservative use of all forest reserve land adapted for grazing, (2) the best permanent good of the livestock industry through proper care and improvement of the grazing lands, and (3) the protection of the settler and home builder against unfair competition in the use of the range.[6]

Pinchot reported on July 1, 1905, that 7,981 grazing permits had been issued for a total of 632,793 cattle, 59,331 horses, and 1,709,987 sheep for the new season. Although no great changes occurred in the number of stock allowed in this first season under the Forest Service, new allowances were granted where the forage crop was abundant to admit the stock of new settlers and provide for the natural increase of herds previously occupying the ranges. In recently created reserves, livestock already present were allowed to remain without permits. But in some instances where overstocking was apparent and the range deteriorated, reductions in numbers were

[6]Pinchot, *Breaking New Ground*, p. 256; *Use of the National Forest Reserves*, pp. 20–21.

enforced. Generally the moves were moderate, in line with the Forest Service's attempt to win approval by not moving too swiftly or arbitrarily to enforce restrictions.

Permits were issued allowing livestock, especially sheep, to cross the forests as they could in the Sierra and Mount Rainier reserves. This practice facilitated the movement of stock over specified sections of the forests to private grazing lands within the forests or across the mountains. Eventually some of these passageways became designated as driveways and were governed by regulations for that use. In areas where stock became infected with contagious disease, inspectors from the USDA Bureau of Animal Industry examined stock before they were admitted to the reserves. The healthy stock of other permittees were thus protected, and for the most part the practice was welcomed by forest users.[7]

The Implementation of Grazing Fees

Although the Forest Service tried to emphasize the benefits of forest-grazing regulations, the announcement of the intention to charge grazing fees for the 1906 season brought strong protests from stock organizations. Some objections went directly to the White House. It was contended that fees marked a sharp departure from previous policies and a hardship on forage users. Many users apparently welcomed the peace on the range and the exclusion of tramp herders, but saw no need to pay for the service that government-enforced regulations provided.

Despite the criticism from stockmen, the secretary of agriculture defended the fee system to the president late in 1905. He began by telling Roosevelt that the charge for grazing was less than one-third of its actual value, the rent stockmen would have to pay for comparable private grazing lands. The fee schedule called for cattle and horses to graze at 20 to 35 cents per head in the summer season and from 35 to 50 cents for the whole year. For sheep the fee was from 5 to 8 cents for the summer only, and for goats, 8 to 10 cents. A special reduction was to be made for homebuilders near the forests and for small stock owners. In effect, then, a limited number of animals could graze without fee charges. Helping new settlers was of primary importance. In all cases those who were new arrivals and

[7]U.S. Department of Agriculture, *Yearbook of Agriculture, 1905*; U.S. Forest Service, *Annual Report of the Forester, 1905*, pp. 206–207.

owned a small number of stock would be admitted to the ranges unless it was already fully occupied by other small owners.

Range improvements were also to be allowed. These included construction of drift or division fences as long as they benefited forest administration and did not interfere with the use of the range by all who were entitled to share it. Transferring permits from one grazier to another was to be allowed upon presentation of evidence that the sale of the base land was bona fide. The Forest Service would undertake to improve roads and trails and stock watering places and to protect camping places near lakes and streams "for use of the people." Rangers also received instructions to report stock-law violations and help stockmen protect their property from loss by theft.[8]

The secretary was careful to make the president understand that the regulations imposed by the Forest Service did not ignore the small homebuilder near the forests: "It will be evident to you that special effort has been made, not only to give the range greater value to the stockmen than ever before, but also to foster homebuilding and promote the interests of the small owner at every point. Taken altogether, I believe the grazing fee and the regulations as amended to be practical, wise, and right."[9] In reply Roosevelt approved the general policies, especially the effort to keep the grazing lands open to those who lived near the reserves. He acknowledged that to prevent waste and destruction of resources a certain amount of money must be spent to keep the forests usable for stockmen and the public. It was quite justified to obtain part of this money by charging a small fee for each head of stock pastured on the reserves. The policy of favoring the nearby homesteaders received special notice from the president because, as he said, these were men making homes for themselves "by the labor of their hands, the men who have entered to possess the land to bring up their children thereon."

Roosevelt concurred that other occupants of the range should receive a

[8] Pinchot tried to get the fee authorization inserted into the Transfer Bill, but failed. However, it was included in the Agricultural Appropriation Act of Mar. 3, 1905, a month later. He then sought and received a favorable legal opinion on grazing fees from W. H. Moody, the attorney general, but only after speaking personally to Moody and to Roosevelt, who then urged Moody to rule favorably. The ruling was dated May 31, 1905. See Pinchot, *Breaking New Ground*, pp. 270–72; Samuel P. Hays, *Conservation and the Gospel of Efficiency: The Progressive Conservation Movement, 1890–1920*, pp. 59–60.

[9] James Wilson to Theodore Roosevelt, December 20, 1905, Theodore Roosevelt Manuscripts, Presidential Papers Microfilm, Reel 61, Series I.

lesser preference after the small owner and last consideration should be given owners of "transient stock" that the President described as "men who drive great tramp herds or flocks hither and thither." Since they did little to "build up the land" they should not be favored at the expense of the regular occupants, large or small. The system of preferences prevented the herds of nonresidents from destroying the pasturage. Roosevelt believed the policy adopted by the Forest Service was "among the most potent influences in favor of the actual home-maker." He echoed a strong Jeffersonian belief that the small yeoman farmer was the backbone of the republic when he declared: "This is the kind of man upon whom the foundations of our citizenship rest." Forest Service grazing regulations were being translated into social policy. On the other hand, when it came to the public domain lands outside of the Forest Service lands, Roosevelt stood squarely for a grazing lease program, clearly favoring the larger operators.[10]

The fee system that the president endorsed was not imposed without prior study and surveys. As early as 1901, shortly after he came to work for Pinchot, Potter began questioning stockmen about proposed range regulations. He directed some initial inquiries toward the Gila Reserve in New Mexico. He found that the assignment of permanent pasture there would be welcomed among stockmen. If they were given a sort of limited proprietary interest in their ranges through the issuance of ten-year permits, the stockmen's interests would be the same as that of the forester, that is "the care of the ranges by the avoidance of overstocking, erosion, and fire." Small owners desired more guarantees to their ranges and were afraid that in the division of the ranges the large owners would contrive schemes to squeeze them out. Many expressed a willingness to fence their ranges if they could receive a fair allotment when the ranges were divided. By and large Potter found that the small ranchers as well as the large favored government-regulated grazing.

Gila sheepmen, however, opposed fencing of allotments as a means of range division among users, although they fully appreciated that government supervision of grazing also meant protection from cowmen. Understandably, the sheepmen were unsympathetic to his argument that their sheep, being the more competitive grazers, could drive the cowman from the range if fences did not separate cow and sheep allotments. One sheep-

[10]Roosevelt to Secretary Wilson, December 26, 1905, Reel 61, Series I, Theodore Roosevelt Manuscripts; Hays, *Conservation and the Gospel of Efficiency*, p. 63.

man in the reserve, Solomon Luna, advocated admitting a certain total number of sheep to a forest, leaving the numbers to be allowed individual graziers up to the decision of the local sheep association, with no provision for keeping sheep and cattle separate. This plan, while admirable for sheepmen, would be obviously unfavorable to cattlemen. Potter concluded that a just system for both sheep and cattle would require an assignment of a specific area for each allotment and, ideally, its fencing by the stockman, especially the cattlemen. From a larger western survey of 1903, Potter concluded, as he had from the 1901 "Gila Report," that small rental fees would be acceptable, particularly if cattlemen were allowed to fence their ranges on the reserves. Besides recommending the imposition of fees, Potter emphasized four other points in his report to Pinchot in 1903 (1) proper resource use would be allowed; (2) the carrying capacity of the range would determine allotment size; (3) permits would be granted equitably, and (4) regulations would be kept flexible.[11]

The 1906 fee system underlined the protective thrust of forest policies, as the agency sought to finance range administration on the reserves. On the other hand, the Forest Homestead Act of June 11, 1906, encouraged new users of the forage resources. The first, an administrative action, contained "a bit of the strong arm," and the second, a legislative action, seemed to be working at cross-purposes. The fees, many stockmen believed, would deliver the forest ranges into the hands of the large ranchers and force the smaller owners out because of an inability to pay the "grazing tax," as they termed it. But the Forest Homestead Act appeared to be an active effort on the part of the federal government to encourage settlement by the small stock holder and insure his survival as a permanent user of the forest reserve lands. From the beginning these contradictory themes plagued the formulation and implementation of federal forest-range policy.[12]

Immediately, the Forest Service faced a public-relations challenge over the fees. Stockmen insisted that taxation could not be done through administrative fiat—that only Congress could levy taxes. At the American Forest Congress of January, 1906, the secretary of the National Livestock Association spoke of the "peculiar disposition" of the western stockman

[11] Albert F. Potter, "Gila Report" and "1903 Survey," Gifford Pinchot Papers, Series VI, Box 2873, Library of Congress, Washington, D.C.

[12] Jenks Cameron, *The Development of Government Forest Control in the United States*, p. 243.

that made him resent attempts to bind him to ironclad rules and regulations. He emphasized the need to cooperate with the western stockmen, enlisting them as forest rangers and allowing them an advisory role in the administration of policies. He emphasized that stockmen felt they had acquired some moral rights to the ranges "which even the Government should respect." [13]

The same Act of February 1, 1905, which transferred the reserves to the Department of Agriculture, permitted the new Forest Service to charge for resource sale and use and to retain within its budget the money so collected for a five-year period. This authority to retain and use the money collected was withdrawn by Congress in the 1907 appropriations when Pinchot tried to make permanent the provision to allow these fees to be used by the Forest Service for administering the reserves. However, the appropriation was increased. Until 1910 the fees collected for grazing exceeded timber revenues and periodically for a decade thereafter. Pinchot hoped, of course, that the new Forest Service would bring in more revenue than its own cost of administration. The income would come principally from timber harvests and grazing fees. This drive for efficiency may well have been one of the reasons that the Service chose to impose fees so quickly after taking charge of the reserves. The revenue would, in part, make forest administration independent of constant reliance upon Congress for funding. The Appropriations Act of March 3, 1905, also included authority for forest officers to make arrests for violations of regulations, and power to enforce state or territorial laws to prevent forest fires and the enforcement of fish and game laws. The assumption of these new powers, especially the nebulous authority to levy a grazing fee, inevitably caused a backlash out West. [14]

Western sources kept hammering away on the theme that the fee was a tax. One Colorado newspaper said, "There seems to be no adequate reason for imposing a per capita tax or other charge on cattle allowed to graze within the limit of a reserve. Let the sale of timber cover the expense of

[13] Fred P. Johnson, "Advantage of Cooperation between the Government and Live Stock Associations in the Regulation and Control of Grazing on Forest Reserves," in American Forestry Association, *Proceedings of the American Forest Congress, Washington, D.C.*, January 2–6, 1905, pp. 229–30.

[14] *Yearbook of Agriculture, 1900*, p. 96; Pinchot, *Breaking New Ground*, pp. 257–58; Hays, *Conservation and the Gospel of Efficiency*, p. 60.

maintaining the forest, but let grazing privileges be as free as they are on the treeless plains." The so-called Public Lands Convention met in Denver in June, 1907, to denounce the Forest Service's fee system. A stockman's journal, *Ranch and Range*, spoke of the fees as being "taxation without representation" and even talked in terms of western secession. A forest supervisor from Oregon reported that widespread circulation in the press of a letter from Senator Fulton of Oregon, urging stockmen to refuse payment of grazing fees and also to disregard grazing regulations, "caused a great deal of trouble in the forest." He also reported, however, that through "patience and diplomacy" rangers achieved respect for the forest regulations and the payment of fees.[15]

Colorado, however, became a stronger center for protests against grazing fees. Pinchot journeyed to the state in December, 1905, and again in January, 1906, to meet with insurgent stockmen. It appears that he successfully met their arguments against the fees and cooled raised tempers. Cattlemen who had been up in arms against the "tyrant" Pinchot listened to the suave chief of the Forest Service explain the government's position. They failed to offer rebuttals either at the Glenwood meeting with Pinchot in December or at the meeting with both Potter and him on January 29, 1906, at the Brown Palace in Denver. From contemporary accounts it appeared that Pinchot dominated the meetings and "disarmed" the stockmen. The Colorado congressional delegation had already met with President Roosevelt concerning complaints against the fees in December, but they too had been told by the president that the fees could be applied.[16]

After Pinchot's meetings with Colorado stockmen, the question now was, would the National Livestock Association, which was to meet in Denver in early February, accept or oppose the grazing fees? Not only did the association not object to the fees, but it also passed a resolution endorsing them. Immediately, some stockmen protested that fees would work to the advantage of the larger operations and drive the smaller competitors from the field. They further charged that the large livestock interests directed the

---

[15] *Denver Republican*, December 19, 1905, as quoted in G. Michael McCarthy, *Hour of Trial: The Conservation Conflict in Colorado and the West, 1891–1907*, p. 157; *Range and Range*, March, 1907, p. 16, as quoted in Cameron, *Government Forest Control*, pp. 242–43; F. A. Fern to the Forester, Nov. 26, 1907, Sec. 63, Region 2, Dr. 140, RG 95, NA.

[16] McCarthy, *Hour of Trial*, pp. 160–65, 168; Leonard C. Shoemaker, "History of the Holy Cross National Forest," manuscript, Colorado State Historical Society, Denver, p. 57.

organization. But the fact was that many stockmen had been won over to the side of the Forest Service in what two months earlier had threatened to become one of the most severe attacks on government forest control.

The issue of the grazing fee's legality called into question the Forest Service's authority to administer and protect the National Forest lands. Two issues were at stake. The first questioned whether the Department of Agriculture had the right to impose fees under the general administrative order to "regulate the occupancy and use of lands" under the Act of 1897. The second question was also crucial, but less publicized: in order to prevent trespass, especially by cattle, must the Forest Service fence its lands against drifting herds like other property owners according to Colorado law? Both questions demanded settlement if forest grazing administration was to move ahead.[17]

Since the late 1890s, federal courts had disagreed on whether violating regulations imposed by an administrative department constituted a crime. Inevitably, the grazing restrictions were one of the fee regulations being challenged. Major court cases came to federal courts from Colorado and California. Shortly after the Forest Service decided to charge for grazing privileges, Fred Light, who lived near the Holy Cross National Forest, refused to pay fees. He also contended that fees could not be collected on cattle straying into unfenced forests. The government brought suit to compel compliance with fees and to free the forests from requirements to fence lands.

Light argued that he and his wife had pioneered the country. They built a home, raised a family, and developed a herd of five hundred cattle that depended upon the forests for range. The Lights chose their ranch site in a place that gave them access to mountain ranges at a time when no one else claimed them. Everything they had achieved they owed to the use of these pastures. Now the government claimed these lands and, while it allowed grazing to continue, the Forest Service proposed to tax Light's cattle. He did not object that the fees were too high, but he did contend that if the Forest Service possessed the right to set a ten-cent-per-head fee on his cattle, it could eventually impose a confiscatory five-dollar-per-head charge. In addition, if the Service had a right to set the time of year his cattle could come into and leave the forest and the number permitted, it

[17]William Burnet Apgar, "The Administration of Grazing on the National Forests" (Master's thesis, Cornell University, 1922), p. 49.

could entirely prohibit his cattle's grazing at some future time. The lush summer ranges provided the livelihood for his ranch. If the service had the right to prohibit his use of the range either through direct denial or high grazing fees, it could deny his livelihood and destroy his ranching, home, and enterprise.[18] In January, 1909, federal circuit court in Colorado ruled in favor of the government on both the fee and the fencing issue. The *New York Times* called it a decision of utmost importance to the West.[19]

A test case also emerged from the lower courts of California. In November of 1907 the grand jury in the district court for the southern district of the state indicted Pierre Grimaud and J. P. Carajous for pasturing sheep on the Sierra Forest Reserve without obtaining a permit. The indictment concluded that they violated the law of the United States. Their lawyers demurred on the grounds that their actions were not an offense against the United States and, most importantly, "that the acts of Congress making it an offense to violate rules and regulations made and promulgated by the Secretary of Agriculture are unconstitutional, because they are an attempt by Congress to delegate its legislative power to an administrative officer." The court sustained the position of the defendants and dismissed the indictment, ruling against the government. The federal lawyers appealed to the Supreme Court on the basis of the Criminal Appeals Act, which allowed a writ of error where the "decision complained of was based upon the validity of the statute." The law office of the Forest Service deliberately referred to that clause of the Criminal Act (March 2, 1907) in order to place the challenges before the federal courts.[20]

Finally, on May 1, 1911, the United States Supreme Court ruled in favor of the government in both the Light and Grimaud cases. Justice Lamar declared, "From the various acts relating to the establishment and management of forest reservations it appears that they were intended to 'improve and protect the forest and secure favorable conditions of water flows.'" The decision stated that any use of the reservations for pasturage must be subject to the rules and regulations established by the secretary of agriculture. On some reservations range use would be accepted, on others not at all. In all cases such use was to be a matter of administrative detail. "What might be harmless in one forest might be harmful in another,"

---

[18] Roberts, *Hoof Prints on Forest Ranges*, pp. 81–82.

[19] *New York Times*, January 6, 1909; *Denver Republican*, January 6, 1909.

[20] Philip P. Wells, "Federal Control of Water Power," memoir, 1913, Pinchot Papers, Box 2869.

wrote Justice Lamar. It would be impossible for Congress to regulate each forest on an individual basis, he continued. To meet the various local conditions, "Congress was merely conferring administrative functions upon an agent, and not delegating to him legislative power." The secretary had the "power to fill up the details" by the establishment of administrative rules and regulations.

The high court went on to defend the fees by saying they were imposed "to prevent excessive grazing," thereby protecting the resources of the forest from destruction, and to provide "a slight income with which to meet the expenses of management." The court pointed to the Transfer Act of February 1, 1905, which authorized that all monies collected from the sale and use of forest resources should be applied toward the payment of forest expenses for five years. This act had been passed prior to the issuance of Regulation No. 45 that provided for range permits and charges for use. The court concluded its decision by justifying its authority to rule on the matter, stating, "The offense is not against the Secretary, but as the indictment properly concluded, 'contrary to the laws of the United States and the peace and dignity thereof.' " [21]

With the fee system upheld, additional questions relating to fees arose. The court alluded to these questions when it ruled that the fees were for the purposes of limiting grazing and paying the cost of administration. Should these, however, be the sole bases upon which fees were fixed? Within a few years many administrators and members of Congress asked that fees be based upon the cost of forage and established at the rate of the cost to rent similar private lands. Stockmen, on the other hand, saw dangers in this and wished fees set only on the basis of administrative cost or at the least tied to the fluctuating market prices of the stock. The fee controversies did not end with the Supreme Court's decision; in fact, the decision merely opened the door to more complicated issues. Even today attempts to impose fees at market value have been repeatedly frustrated.

The Permit System and Range Classification

The Grazing Branch of the Forest Service authorized forest supervisors to continue the policy of issuing permits according to the three crite-

---

[21] U.S. Forest Service, Range Management Staff, *Court Cases Related to Administration of the Range Resource on Lands Administered by the Forest Service*, pp. 9–18.

ria of preference. The supervisors enforced the fee system by charging according to the number and types of stock entering the forest and for the length of time they used the ranges. From the very beginning Potter emphasized that grazing control was based on a system of decreed numbers. In 1908 Potter made recommendations to local forest officials for estimating grazing capacity. His instructions, along with those of the *Use Book*, became important guides in the tasks of determining grazing land use. The examiner's recommendations should be based upon a close physical observation of the land, water resources, type of forage, climatic conditions, the manner of handling, and a "consideration of the interests involved." This latter point, of course, meant that the local forester should be aware of the economic and political impact of his recommendations upon the local stock industry.

Probably because Potter was from the arid state of Arizona, he determined range capacity first by the proximity of water. The common method of range control throughout large areas of the West had been for local ranchers to secure title to land adjacent to the streams, springs, and lakes. By then denying the use of these sources to stray stock, stockmen often commanded thousands of acres of grazing land without purchasing or possessing title to it. Oftentimes, ranges with excellent forage possessed no watering places for stock. These situations called for such improvements as digging wells or building reservoirs. In some cases the water might be found in deep canyons that could be reached by building trails down the sides to the streams.

The nature of the land had to be considered as well. As a rule the gravelly or rocky pasture lands stood up under grazing better than land with a loose, sandy soil, as they were less subject to serious damage by erosion. The slope of the land was another important feature; level lands with comparatively rolling hills and compact soils were less likely to be damaged by grazing than land with steep slopes, brokenridges covered with loose sandy soil. Hooves of grazing stock tore up such land and removed soil-holding vegetation. Potter classified these lands as critical grazing areas with both pathways and grazing being carefully restricted.

Knowledge of the relative forage value of the different grasses, plants, and brush was necessary for determining range capacity. Potter knew from firsthand experience that the more valuable grasses might be consumed on a range even as the range was covered with coarse, less palatable grasses. An inexperienced range examiner could overestimate the pasture value.

Several varieties of coarse bunchgrass are eaten while young, green and tender, but are not touched when tough and dry. Potter also noted it was well to keep in mind the type of stock to be grazed and their differences in grazing habits. Sheep consumed a larger variety of forage than cattle. They ate many forbs and shrubs which cattle ordinarily did not touch and, since they were herded, they could feed around in little necks and corners of the forest which might be missed by cattle running loose. Sheep required less water than cattle and could be satisfied in the early season by moisture derived from succulent plants. Those portions of the ranges more suitable to sheep grazing than cattle would be so assigned.

The next issue Potter dealt with was how many acres each head of stock would require. Cows and horses could be considered together in making an acreage determination. As a general rule from four to eight head of sheep could be pastured on the range required for one cow or horse. These numbers would vary with the class of range and could be influenced by the manner in which the sheep were handled. The instructions noted that ordinarily good summer range where the feed was mostly on ridges or mesas, rather than in mountain meadows, about twelve acres would be required for each head of cattle or horse per season. On good mountain meadows, though, the area required would not be more than five acres for each animal. In some places where the grass was exceptionally good or improved by artificial seeding, the area could be down to two or three acres per head. On a quite different class of land covered with rocks and shrubs such as manzanita and snow brush, of little value for forage, the area per head would probably be increased to twenty acres or more.

Grazing practices were also a consideration. To protect the range Potter's instructions provided that sheep should be kept moving and not bedded down in the same place for too long. The sheep camp should move every two to three days; otherwise severe damage occurred to the forage and young trees in the vicinity. Admittedly this damage was unavoidable near dipping vats, shearing pens, and other corrals. The forest officers had to impress upon sheep permittees the necessity of handling their bands correctly if they were to retain their grazing privilege. Potter warned that the method of sheep-handling became critical if they were allowed to have breeding and lambing rounds within the forest. If so allowed, they would have to enter earlier in the season than normal. The handling of cattle was also important. Overcrowding of the meadows in early spring was to be avoided because probably one of the greatest damages to summer ranges occurred by cattle tramping out the little mountain meadows early in the season. Cattle should be distributed over the range as evenly as possible and the concentration of large numbers in any particular section guarded against. In salting the cattle, the troughs should be placed in enough different localities to prevent large numbers coming to the same place for this purpose.

Potter probably knew full well that it was easier to write these instructions than to put them into practice in the field. But it was a beginning. The instructions testified to the wide knowledge that Potter possessed about every aspect of the stock-grazing industry, especially its utilization of the western ranges.

Climate was another factor influencing range capacity, and the *average* moisture picture had to be kept in mind in arriving at a safe number to graze the range. An exceptionally wet year could not dictate the admission of excessive numbers of stock onto ranges because they might need that year to recover from previous drought. It also mattered whether the lands had been seen during the early or latter part of the season. Differing climates and terrain affected the length of the grazing season. In the Southwest, snow melted early and the summer ranges were ready for grazing in April. In the Northwest some ranges could not be used until July or August. While Potter preached protection, he also believed in securing the best use of the pasturelands. One method was to allow the stock onto the range at the moment the ground became dry enough to graze while the forage crop was still fresh and in prime condition. For men like Potter and Pinchot conservation and economic use were totally compatible, if not synonymous.

Of course, before making allotments, Potter noted, it was necessary to estimate the present number of livestock using the range. This number could usually be obtained from reliable resident stockmen. Estimates would differ, but a fairly accurate figure could be obtained taking an average of the estimates. Generally it was much easier to know the correct number of sheep occupying a range than it was for cattle. The county assessment roll told a good deal about the numbers. Later forest officers learned that checking the local markets was even a more accurate way to determine volume of cattle on the ranges because assignment rolls usually contained estimates lower than the actual numbers on the range. A good check for sheep was found by adding the local shipping weights of the wool clip and then dividing by the average weight of the fleeces.

Some ranges, especially cutover land or sensitive watershed, required drastic action that might entirely exclude livestock for a few years. For the majority of the ranges, however, all that was necessary was to get them under control. Potter cautioned that in some of the newer reserves care should be taken not to make "sudden changes of industrial conditions," lest the local community become outraged. If overstocking was severe, the numbers should be reduced gradually from year to year and not with one dramatic decision, even at the expense of deterioration. The gradual reductions should occur until the pasturelands' actual capacity was reached and the ranges restored: "By following this policy the good will of the people will be preserved and the object for which the reserve is created finally accomplished." Potter's instructions foreshadowed the Forest Service's participation in programs of range improvements and scientific studies, as it strove to improve range capacity through more utilization and understanding of terrain, forage, soil, and climate as well as the grazing characteristics of stock.[22]

Recognition of a range capacity required the setting of maximum and protective limits on the number of stock individuals and corporations could graze upon an allotment. The limits were adjusted to the total number of animals a forest's ranges could accept. The "maximum limit" was the greatest number any person or firm would be allowed to graze. At first large graziers were permitted to graze their traditional numbers, that number being accepted as their maximum limit, but sometimes it was lowered. Setting "maximum limits" prevented monopolization of a forest's range resource by an individual or a corporation. The "protective limit" represented the number of stock a settler or corporation needed to support a family or operate economically. This was a guaranteed number that varied from user to user. The total numbers could not exceed the total allowed for the forest in each stock category—cattle, horses, sheep, goats, or hogs. The terms *protective limit* and *maximum limit* became common in the communications between Washington and the local forests, as did another word disliked among stockmen, *reductions*.

The service often called upon established permittees to reduce their number to accommodate "new beginners." The established permittees could be asked, if necessary, to reduce to their protective limit. Within

[22] A. F. Potter, "A Few Pointers on Making Estimates of the Grazing Capacity of Lands" [ca. 1908], Pinchot Papers, Box 2873.

forest-grazing districts a protective limit on all permits was attempted.[23] In the case of the dry San Juan Forest in southwestern Colorado, for example, an early protective limit for sheep was set at one thousand head. Potter advised the forest supervisor that permittees grazing more than that number must take reductions the following year. Those grazing less than that number could be allowed renewal without reduction. "When conditions warrant it," he wrote, "persons holding permits for less than the protective limit may be allowed an increase of not more than 20% in any one year." The total number of stock in the forest could not exceed the maximum numbers established for the forest. In making reductions or additions to permits, Potter reemphasized the preferred status of local property owners: "In all cases a preference should be given the owners of improved ranch property located within or adjacent to the Forest and a less reduction made on their permits than is made on the permits of persons who do not own any ranch property and whose equities in the use of the range are based entirely upon having raised stock there during previous years."[24]

Some argued that the protective limit worked a hardship on the stockman who earned his living entirely from stock grazing; large stockmen, especially, often made this assertion. In their view, such a limit on the amount each owner or firm ran, be it 500 or 1,000 head, prevented them from increasing their profit margin and receiving the full rewards they were entitled to from their willingness to work harder. They argued against favoring the small man because they said the small owner could not run a few head with much profit; he could not afford to watch them and had to turn them loose to take care of themselves. Generally, they complained, his cattle were not "blooded" cattle and his stock deteriorated the class of stock of the larger owners through interbreeding.

For all of these reasons many large owners argued that small owners should not be allowed in the National Forests. Understandably, a grazing report from the Stanislaus National Forest in California concluded that people who had these views could not be expected to work in harmony with the Forest Service. The report suggested that, "they are the men who, if there were no National Forests, would in short time monopolize the range without justice to any one. They deserve no consideration further

[23] Robert R. Hill, "Grazing Administration of the National Forests in Arizona," *American Forestry* 19 (September, 1913): 581; Barnes, *Western Grazing Grounds*, p. 217; Roberts, *Hoofprints on Forest Ranges*, p. 47.
[24] Potter to A. A. Parker, San Juan NF, Mar. 16, 1908, Sec. 63, Dr. 23, RG 95, NA.

than is now provided for in the regulations." Thus some saw the Forest Service an instrument of social policy as well as a protector of resources. In various policy statements it appeared to have every intention of righteously pursuing antimonopolistic policies by keeping the forage resource open to the energies of the many and preserving them from the monopoly of the few.[25]

Each year forest supervisors filed an annual report on their forests with the Forest Service headquarters in Washington. The report passed through the district offices, later called regional offices, before reaching the office of the chief forester. The report devoted a special section to grazing and included such items as numbers and category of stock admitted to the forest; their time of entrance and departure, and comments on the attitude of stockmen and their organizations toward the grazing program. In subsequent years supervisors submitted a grazing plan for their forests. The plan was required to show grazing areas, the category of stock to be permitted, access trails to the open grazing area, and any trails across the forest to private grazing lands. Range divisions reflected proposed stock use. Sheep allotment areas, especially, had to be designated. Sometimes the division of the forest into general grazing districts was delayed, but whenever sheep and goats were admitted to the forest, Potter insisted that they be assigned "to a definitely described range."[26]

All things considered, the grazing plan was an effort at land classification representing an early land-use plan for the forest. Table 4 offers a summary outline of a typical supervisor's working plan for grazing.

After his first year in office, Pinchot concluded that range conditions were satisfactory and that stockmen enjoyed a prosperity which gave them confidence in the future. The Forest Service's grazing program was developing a "constituent group" that found security and profit in the government program. Pinchot acknowledged that the collection of fees raised objections, but added that "by firm and considerate action on the part of the Forest Service with the support of the president serious conflict was avoided." Modification in the fees were made which gave settlers with only a few cattle a special half-rate. After this, much of the opposition ceased. The so-called reasonable charges were no more than a token payment on

[25]Grazing Report, 1908, Stanislaus NF, Sec. 63, Region 5, Dr. 94, RG 95, NA.
[26]Potter to Roy Headey, Thompson Falls, Mont., Cabinet NF, Dec. 27, 1907, Sec. 63, Region 1, Dr. 72, RG 95, NA.

the part of the stockmen and nowhere approached the actual dollar value of the forage to stockmen. Still the amount of $514,086.74 collected was significant in terms of defraying the cost of forest administration. Two-fifths came from cattle and horse permits and three-fifths from sheep and goats.

Table 5 lists the number of permits issued in ninety-two reserves in fourteen states and territories before May 1, 1906.

Besides attempting to impose fees and set up grazing districts for more orderly grazing conduct, the management regulations sought to improve the stock quality. The USDA Bureau of Animal Husbandry required all sheep entering the forest to be inspected for scab and other infections. Forest officers ordered infested sheep dipped. In some areas the inspection was extended to cattle. Stockmen saw that cooperation with forest officers and regulations assured the officers' assistance in the enforcement of local livestock laws, which included regulating the grade and number of bulls turned out on the range, and patrolling against rustlers. Local graziers were advised that permits did not relieve them of observing state range laws. A permit to graze animals in the National Forests applied to such lands only. Stock owners were responsible for stock that strayed into private land. In some areas permittees built fences at their own expense around forest land to prevent straying.[27]

Some permits required numerous saltlicks for cattle and on the range. Complaints often arose that stockmen had to salt their neighbors' cattle to keep them from overrunning their own allotments. Checking on proper outlay of salt often consumed many a ranger's work day. Ranchers were reminded individually and in association meetings that failure to salt in accordance with the terms of the permits could make the permit subject to cancellation. In some forests the local association was relied upon to enforce salting and report violators to the service.

As early as 1908 the Grazing Branch office received recommendations that salting be required in the permits. At least five pounds per head was suggested for the summer grazing season. By 1909, requirements for salting the range stock at intervals appeared in the permits. Some forests reported that stock companies and ranchers whose base property was distant from the forest neglected salting while those nearer the forest recognized its value. The permit requirement protected them from the refusal to salt by

[27] Will C. Barnes to District Forester, Missoula, Mont., Apr. 20, 1909, Sec. 63, Dr. 75, RG 95, NA.

TABLE 4. Outline of Supervisor's Annual Working Plan.

(1) General Range Conditions:
    a. Amount of rainfall as compared to previous years
    b. Amount of forage as compared to previous years
    c. Total numbers of stock grazed under permit
    d. Total numbers of stock grazed without permit. Number of owners
    e. General condition of the range at close of season
    f. Areas which were overgrazed and damaged
    g. Areas which were partially or wholly unutilized
    h. Condition of stock at time of entering and leaving Forest
    i. Market conditions, weights, and sales of stock
    j. Matters of general interest concerning welfare of live-stock industry as affected by administration of Forest
(2) Range Divisions:
    a. Proposed changes in boundaries of grazing districts
    b. Proposed division of range between different kinds of stock
    c. Areas to be closed against sheep, goats, cattle, horses, or swine for the protection of watersheds, natural refuges or breeding grounds of game, or camping grounds, or to prevent damage to the Forest
    d. Areas to be set aside for lambing grounds
    e. Establishment of driveways and restrictions in their use
(3) Estimate of Grazing Capacity, Distribution of Stock, Grazing Periods:
    a. Estimate by districts of the grazing capacity of Forest lands, on basis of stock over 6 months old but considering range required for natural increase of that stock
    b. Proposed distribution of stock on range. Reasons for changes in numbers to be allowed on each division
    c. Established grazing periods, changes required. Reasons
(4) Permit Allotment:
    a. General plan to govern approval of applications
    b. Protective and maximum limits
    c. Proposed sliding-scale increases or reductions
    d. Proposed action upon applications of new owners
(5) Enforcement of Protective Regulations:
    a. Quarantine regulations; enforced; to be enforced; required
    b. Counting stock. Methods followed. Results. Proposed
    c. Special restrictions in handling stock; results
    d. Areas closed to grazing to protect reproduction
(6) Live Stock Associations:
    a. Number recognized; degree of cooperation
    b. Methods used in settling controversies and adjusting range disputes
(7) Game Protection:

    a. Conditions in existing State or Federal game refuges or preserves, or in breeding grounds closed to grazing

    b. Enforcement of game laws by Forest officers

(8) Summary of Recommendations:

    a. Number of each kind of stock to be allowed

    b. Grazing periods and fees recommended

    c. Range divisions and distribution of stock recommended

    d. Initiation; continuance or abandonment of term permits

    e. Miscellaneous matters

SOURCE: Annual Report, Beaverhead National Forest, 1912, Sec. 63, Region 1, Dr. 30, Record Group 95, National Archives, Washington, D.C.

other permittees. Correct salting methods attempted to pull the stock away from the water places, according to one ranger: "We pulled the stock back and let them use the outside range for better utilization." Before the Forest Service's salting regulations, some stockmen had placed salt on the ranges, but generally they dumped it only along the creeks and near the springs.[28]

Forest officers joined stockmen in the extermination of predators. By employing hunters to kill wolves and coyotes and utilizing reports from the USDA Biological Survey on the habits of predators, the Forest Service improved its reputation among stockmen. The destruction of these predators, however, brought other complaints that prairie dogs were becoming the greatest menace to the range. The widespread use of poisons was introduced against this rodent.

In protecting game wildlife such as deer and elk, the service found itself caught between the criticism of urban sportsmen and the stockmen who saw game herds as a threat to their forage. If game preserves were located within forests, stock could be prohibited if it deprived the game animals of the forage. By 1918 some urban sporting groups called for fed-

[28] P. L. Lovejoy, Supervisor, Medicine Bow NF, to Hans Olson, President, Albany County Cattle and Horse Growers Association, February 5, 1910, Box 4, Medicine Bow NF Collection, Western History Research Center, University of Wyoming, Laramie; Annual Grazing Report, 1908, Ashley NF, Sec. 63, Region 4, Dr. 62, RG 95, NA; George W. Ring to the Forester, Jan. 3, 1909, Annual Grazing Report, 1909, District 3, Sec. 63, Region 3, Dr. 43, RG 95, NA; "Carl B. Arentson, Forty-One Years of Forest Service Career" (1965), p. 8, Oral History Project, U.S. Forest Service, Region 4, Ogden, Utah.

TABLE 5. Permits Issued in Fourteen States and Territories prior to May 1, 1906.

State or Territory	Cattle and horses			Sheep and goats	
	Number of permits	Number of stock for summer season	Number of stock for year-long season	Number of permits	Number of stock for summer season
Arizona	581	30,096	67,718	87	347,208
California	1,979	132,256	20,529	190	403,088
Colorado	2,774	231,060	8,605	185	420,009
Idaho	385	20,053	531	182	878,550
Kansas	16	3,215	—	—	—
Montana	1,373	93,514	6,862	79	249,908
Nebraska	62	26,806	405	—	—
New Mexico	878	10,274	53,454	234	312,035
Oklahoma	37	884	2,153	—	—
Oregon	915	75,656	1,242	352	1,124,539
South Dakota	433	13,041	—	—	—
Utah	3,376	93,255	294	888	1,148,771
Washington	512	25,520	1,209	108	282,793
Wyoming	772	85,513	2,443	195	591,599
Total	14,093	849,703	165,445	2,500	5,762,200

SOURCE: U.S. Forest Service, *Annual Report of the Forester, 1906*, pp. 16–17.

eral laws to protect game in the national forests. As it was, forest officers merely enforced state fish and game laws. Forest Service personnel met with stockmen more than sportsmen, and therefore officials were not always aware of or sensitive to public attitudes on these questions outside the grazing community. Generally stockmen favored game protection, but only when it did not interfere with their interests. One supervisor in Montana did, however, advise the Forest Service to give more consideration to the forests as a "playground and hunting ground."

At times the Washington office pointedly asked local officers for more information on the condition of wildlife, if reference to it was lacking in the annual grazing reports. Will Barnes complained to the district forester in Missoula, Montana, that one of his supervisors failed to mention the condition of the elk herd that was planted on the forest and to state what effect extending the hunting season had had upon the deer herd. "Both of these matters," he said, "would have been interesting as well as valuable data for future reference." He asked the district forest to call it to the supervisor's attention "in order that special mention of these matters may be included in the next annual grazing report."[29] Forest officials tried hard to harmonize the interests of both wild game and domestic animals. Animals that were neither game nor predators were ignored.

In the category of domestic grazers, hogs represented the least numerous type of stock in the forests. Even during the sharp increases permitted during World War I, the total number of hogs approved for 1917 was only 2,306, down from 4,500 hogs in 1911. The next lowest stock category in 1917, goats, had many times this number, with just under 50,000 on a permit, a drop of 90,000 from 1909, followed by horses with almost 99,000, an increase of 9,000 from 1909. These numbers are of relative insignificance, of course, when compared to the 7,586,034 sheep and 1,953,198 cattle under permit in the peak grazing year of 1917. From the beginning, however, the presence of hogs in the forests caused numerous complaints from forest supervisors. Hogs brought protests about damage to local orchards and gardens. Hog graziers felt this was a "matter between individuals" in which forest officers need not participate. Still, some supervisors reported that the presence of large numbers of hogs retarded the social growth of a community, adding to the cost of gardens and orchards.[30]

In 1908 the supervisor of the Chiricahua National Forest in southern Arizona asked that hogs be prohibited because of problems with them during the 1907 season. His successor in the next year conceded that hogs had been a source of considerable trouble on the forest in the past but regretted that allotments had not been continued because their exclusion caused distress and hardship to settlers. Requests to graze hogs usually came when acorn and other seed corps appeared particularly plentiful in the forests. Many hogs were grazed under the regulation that allowed swine kept for home consumption by settlers within or near the National Forest to graze free. The understanding was that the total numbers of all classes of stock under free permit would not exceed a ten-head limit.[31]

[29] Annual Grazing Report, 1910, White River NF, Sec. 63, Region 2, Dr. 24; L. F. Kneipp to District Forester, Missoula, Mont., Jan. 4, 1910, Sec. 63, Region 1, Dr. 3; Annual Grazing Report, 1918, Helena NF, sec. 63, Region 1, Dr. 4; Annual Grazing Report, 1910, Custer NF, Sec. 63, Region 1, Dr. 4; Will C. Barnes to District Forester, Missoula, Mont., Feb. 2, 1918, Sec. 63, Region 1, Dr. 4, RG 95, NA.

[30] *Yearbook of Agriculture, 1917*, and *1911*; Annual Grazing Report, 1908, Sierra NF, Sec. 63, Region 5, Dr. 94, RG 95, NA.

[31] Annual Grazing Reports, 1907 and 1908, Chiricahua NF, Sec. 63, Region 3, Dr. 43;

Goats also posed problems because of damage to range and forest re-production. Although accused of being opposed to goat grazing, forest officers denied any discrimination against goats. They were merely against the old methods of handling goats which caused damage to the range. Admittedly, study of this class of stock had been delayed, but Will Barnes assured readers of the *Angora Journal and Milch Goat Bulletin* in 1916 that a careful, systematic study of the industry was underway: "I believe we are going to accomplish a great deal for the goat owners and place their business on a better plane than it has heretofore been." William R. Chapline's study on goats from 1915 to 1919 partly confirmed Barnes's promise and showed a willingness to accommodate this animal in the forest. Some forest officials, however, believed that families could do better by grazing cows, but it was recognized that traditions locked some people, especially in New Mexico, into the use of goats.[32]

A successful grazing program required forest officers to understand the local traditions of the people in their district. Officers tried to attend local livestock association meetings "to promote a right understanding of the purposes of forest reserves." These associations in turn sought official recognition from the Forest Service as described under Regulation No. 45 of the 1910 *Use Book* (grazing edition). The regulation on advisory boards reads as follows:

Reg. 45 Whenever any live-stock association whose membership includes a major-ity of the owners of any class of live stock using a National Forest or portion thereof shall select a committee, an agreement on the part of which shall be binding upon the association, such committee upon application to the district Forester, may be recognized as an advisory board for the association, and shall then be entitled to receive notice of proposed action and have an opportunity to be heard by the local Forest officer in reference to increase or decrease in the number of stock to be al-lowed for any year, the division of the range between different classes of stock or their owners, or the adoption of special rules to meet local conditions.

Grazing advisory boards made up of prominent representatives from the organizations could be established for each forest to help formulate local grazing decisions that eventually made up the forest's grazing plan. The

---

A. F. Potter to Secretary of Agriculture, Jan. 11, 1918, Sec. 63, Dr. 45; James Adams to Sec-retary of Agriculture, Sept. 25, 1913, Sec. 63, Dr. 27; Annual Grazing Report, 1915, Black Hills NF, Sec. 63, Dr. 26, RG 95, NA.

[32] W. R. Chapline, *Production of Goats on Far Western Ranges*, USDA Bulletin no. 749, April 30, 1919; W. R. Chapline, interview with author, Reno, Nev., February, 1980; Will C. Barnes letter to editor, *Angora Journal and Milch Goat Bulletin* 15 (May, 1916): 22–23.

board, however, only had the power to advise, not to dictate policy. The local forest advisory boards provided many solutions to local problems that otherwise might have caused serious trouble.

Stockmen were encouraged to present disputes to advisory boards for settlement. By 1912 not one decision made by the advisory board to the Stanislaus National Forest in California was reversed by the Forest Service. More importantly, the supervisor of the Stanislaus forest understood that as stockmen realized forest officials were taking their recommendations seriously, "they immediately [took] more interest in bettering grazing conditions and in seeing that the administration of the business runs more smoothly." Livestock associations often performed the role of "company unions" for the Forest Service by supporting its policies and complying with regulations in return for concessions allowing certain stockmen to purchase and absorb smaller allotments or needed range improvements.[33]

On the other hand, some forest supervisors suspected that strong local stock organizations wished to dominate the advisory boards in order to impose "an absolute monopoly." From Wyoming came the report that the members of the Sweetwater Association believed "the Service is absolutely bound to conform in all respects to their wishes." The supervisor conceded that the service wished to cooperate as far as possible with these associations, but they must be informed "that the Advisory Board is not recognized as a dictator of Forest business, but simply as a medium whereby matters affecting stock and Service interest may be discussed, and disputes settled more effectively." Here again the forest officer reflected the service's opposition to grazing monopolies on its lands and a general dedication to carrying out governmental policy against such movements. Generally forest advisory boards did not play a large role in setting policies. Often they did not exist on forests and many times were not much encouraged.[34]

Large Grazing Interests vs. the Small Landholder

Government land policy also tried to promote small landholder settlement on verifiable agricultural lands in the forest. The Forest Homestead Act of June 11, 1906, opened National Forest lands to agricultural settle-

---

[33] U.S. Forest Service, *Annual Report of the Forester, 1906*, pp. 15–18; U.S. Forest Service, *Use Book: Grazing, 1910*, p. 13; Annual Grazing Report, 1912, Stanislaus NF, Sec. 63, Region 5, Dr. 113, RG 95, NF; Lawrence Rakestraw, "History of Forest Conservation in the Pacific Northwest, 1891–1913," (Ph.D. diss., University of Washington, 1955), p. 238.

[34] Annual Grazing Report, 1908, Shoshone NF, Sec. 63, Region 2, Dr. 40, RG 95, NA.

ment, offering 160 acres of land free to actual settlers after a residency period. The definition of "agricultural land" within the forests quickly became a disputed point. D. C. Beaman, in an article about the national forests, complained that "Czar" Pinchot arbitrarily changed the description of agricultural lands in the 1908 *Use Book*. Whereas the 1907 *Use Book* had said that homestead claimants were required to "live upon and cultivate or graze lands" embraced in their claims, the words "or graze" were eliminated from the 1908 volume. "Is there any officer," asked Beaman, "other than Mr. Pinchot, who would thus assume to change the policy of the land laws according to his fancy?"[35]

Officially the Forest Service maintained that room for newcomers to the grazing community was made by reducing the number of stock that large owners were allowed to graze. This overt policy of favoring small landowners brought pressures on the Washington office to ease regulations for some large concerns. Senator Warren of Wyoming (called "the greatest shepherd since Abraham") wanted more pasturage for his livestock company and got it. Potter felt obliged to write the Cheyenne National Forest in 1910 that Senator Warren had requested additional sheep grazing for his company. Potter carefully suggested that it might be possible to increase the number of sheep under permit if it could be done "without interfering with the rights of prior users or damage to the watershed." Potter suggested that any small permits that were not renewed during the summer be given to the Warren Livestock Company.

In response the supervisor held a conference with the manager of the company. The manager protested that "the little men wanted the whole country and the Forest Service was helping them to it." The supervisor reported that the manager did not accept the idea "that the small man getting a start in the foothills was entitled to more consideration than a large outfit." Nevertheless, the Cheyenne Forest supervisor was put on notice to pay more attention to the interests of Warren Livestock Company. Later in the year the supervisor reported that the forest officers took great care to prevent small livestock permittees from straying onto allotments of the Warren Company.[36]

[35] D. C. Beaman, "The National Forests and the Forest Service," *Irrigation Age* 23–24 (November, 1908): 10.

[36] Potter to Supervisor, Cheyenne NF, (Mar. 1, 1910); P. L. Lovejoy, Supervisor, Cheyenne NF, to Assistant District Forester, Apr. 10, 1910; Lovejoy to District Forester, October 20, 1910, Medicine Bow Collection, Box 10, Western Research History Center, University of Wyoming, Laramie.

Another indication that the Forest Service was not consistent in its alleged support of small landholders was evidenced in its many rulings against sheep interests. H. G. Merrill, supervisor of the Santa Barbara National Forest in California, claimed that the Forest Service practiced "an unconscious and unwitting discrimination against sheep and goats." On some forests the majority of the stockmen were cattlemen and many rangers themselves had worked as cowboys. Their experiences often influenced the local decisions about use of resource "even though there is no intentional discrimination." These statements lend support to those sheepmen who asserted that the reason for the decline of the sheep industry in the western part of the United States lay primarily with the coming of Forest Service regulations on sheep grazing.[37]

Regardless of differences among competitors for the grazing lands, the Forest Service maintained that it pursued policies to strengthen the entire grazing community. During the 1909 grazing season the forest ranges carried (as of June 30) 7,680,000 sheep, 1,491,000 cattle, 90,000 horses, 4,500 hogs, and 140,000 goats, all increases over the previous year. Increased applications caused a per capital reduction for sheep and goat raisers, however. Most significantly, more than 27,000 individuals and concerns held permits for grazing. Small permittees and their animals outnumbered the large permit holders. Five-year permits were issued on twenty-six forests, nineteen more than in 1908. There were forty-six forest livestock advisory boards. The one million dollars collected in fees was less important than controlling ranges for "the healthy upbuilding of communities," said the Secretary of Agriculture in his annual report of 1909. Grazing fees were fixed with an eye to meeting only the costs of administration and not to raise revenue. A charge comparable to the rental of private land was not considered because "such a commercial policy . . . would have meant sacrifice of an opportunity to promote the public welfare in the best way." To have charged stockmen the full value of their privilege would have worked against the new settler and the small owner and would have led to range monopoly. If such monopoly had occurred, grazing policy would not have been doing "its share toward building up stable communities of independent American citizens."[38]

Range managers from the beginning of government range administra-

[37] H. G. Merrill, Supervisor, Santa Barbara NF, Grazing Plan, 1911, Sec. 63, Region 5, Dr. 93, RG 95, NA.

[38] "Report of the Secretary of Agriculture," in *Yearbook of Agriculture, 1909*, p. 92; U.S. Forest Service, *Annual Report of the Forester, 1909*, pp. 23–25.

tion to the present have conceded that the basic problem of range management is handling people, not stock. In its early years the Forest Service undertook range regulation amidst a climate of hostility and suspicion. One of the first steps taken by service personnel in a community was to seek cooperation of ranchers and local stock organizations. If no organization existed, forest officers encouraged their formation in order to facilitate communication and cooperation. These groups were mostly welcomed by growers in the difficult decisions of alloting grazing privileges, developing grazing plans, and in promoting range improvements. By the year 1909, forty-six stock associations had received official recognition from the Forest Service, and many others had been recognized on an informal basis. Advice and consultation could be sought from these associations on a regular basis, as well as possible support for Forest Service policies.[39]

Reports coming from local forests indicated that stockmen who were originally hostile had changed attitudes during the 1907–1909 period. "Where a year or two ago," said one report from Colorado, "dissatisfaction, discontent, and grumbling against the Service existed on every hand, now the majority of the stockmen appear to be favorably inclined." Its author, James A. Blair, supervisor for the White River National Forest, cautioned that his report should not be interpreted as indicating that all stockmen were in sympathy with the service. But he did believe that at least half were now willing to cooperate where earlier an overwhelming majority were "strenuously opposed."[40]

The growing acceptance of the grazing control program rested in no small measure on Washington's reliance upon information provided by local forest officers. As information on the ranges with accompanying recommendations was received from local forests, the Grazing Branch determined the numbers of stock to be grazed in each stock category. For example, in January, 1909, Potter authorized ten thousand head of cattle and horses and one hundred thousand head of sheep and goats on the Absaroka National Forest in Montana. His order set the grazing season to begin on May 1 and to close on October 31. On a map sent to Potter's office, the

[39] Forest Service, Region 1, History Project, John F. Preston, "Early Days in the Forest Service," vol. 3, November 20, 1962, p. 191, Oral History Project, U.S. Forest Service, Region 1, Missoula, Montana; Overton W. Price to Secretary of Agriculture, Nov. 29, 1909, Sec. 63, RG 95, NA.

[40] James A. Blair, Supervisor, White River NF, Meeker, Colo., Annual Grazing Report, Dec. 16, 1909, sec. 63, Region 2, Dr. 24, RG 95, NA.

forest was divided into four general grazing districts, with changes subject to his directions. The Washington Office was assured by local forest officials that all stock would be excluded from an area one mile in width along the boundary line of the Yellowstone National Park.[41]

The grazing section of the annual report from each national forest usually addressed the following subjects: (1) general grazing conditions; (2) range divisions accompanied by map; (3) driveways for stock and some explanation of the steps taken to avoid harm to other forest resources, such as trees; (4) range allotments; (5) commentary on the livestock associations and their willingness to cooperate; (6) condition of stock grazed on the forest compared with those grazed outside; (7) recommendations (8) the grazing period for various categories of stock, particularly cattle and sheep, and any yearlong permits granted; (9) estimated annual cost of running stock; (10) report on efforts to keep accurate count of animals allowed in the forest under permits; (11) stock mortality; and (12) range improvements through cooperation, predator control, identification of poisonous plants, or experimental reseeding. From forests that had little or no grazing the reports were naturally brief; in 1909 the forest supervisor in Minnesota reported, "I have never submitted a grazing report for this forest as there is nothing in the line of grazing carried on here at all." [42] On the basis of these reports, which were also reviewed in the district (regional) offices, the Grazing Branch could offer criticisms and recommendations for future action or praise the work in progress.[43]

In some cases the coexistence of government and private land in a forest called for special agreement between the private land owners and the Forest Service to implement an effective controlled-grazing plan. Private land owned by individuals often broke up solid blocks of forest lands in a checkerboard pattern making it almost impossible to control grazing practices or to contain roving stock. This condition existed in the Palouse Division of the Coeur d'Alene National Forest in Idaho. The forest encompassed more than 60 percent private land, much of which belonged to the Potlatch Lumber Company. When a large company owned the lands it was far easier to make an amenable agreement on a general grazing program.

[41] W. B. Greely to Potter, January 5, 1909, Sec. 63, Region 1, Dr. 26, RG 95, NA.

[42] G. E. Marshall to District Forester, Missoula, Mont., Dec. 28, 1909, Sec. 63, Region 1, Dr. 29, RG 95, NA.

[43] C. K. Wyman, Supervisor, Beaverhead NF, Annual Report, 1908, Sec. 63, Region 1, Dr. 28, RG 95, NA.

The companies often had their own grazing rental program and sought agreement with forest officials on a division of the forest, one part of which they would administer in grazing matters. Such divisions relinquished all grazing rights by the company in one portion of their land while the service gave up grazing rights to the government land embraced in another area.

These trades simplified grazing administration both for the company and the service. Later, however, the service realized that the low fees it charged for grazing discouraged such agreements. The checkerboard arrangement of government and railroad sections or other private lands presented serious obstacles to proper grazing administration until a division agreement could be made. Preferably, the service should retain control of the entire range and turn over its share of the receipts to the railroad in order to simplify administration. But until rates reached what the railroad charged for grazing on a commercial basis, such an arrangement could not occur. The fee question did not simply involve charges to stockmen; it affected many aspects of range management policies and practices.[44]

The Forest Service made exceptions to its general rules for the grazing of Indian stock. Reservation Indians received free grazing where stock numbers were small and the products were consumed entirely by the Indians. Their stock was allowed into the forests without permit and without charge. Some tribes after all assumed that earlier treaties guaranteed them grazing rights on the forests. In return, the Indian agent was required to attempt to see that all forest regulations were met and to secure the assistance of local tribes in fighting forest fires. This ruling avoided the difficulty, as one report put it, "of making them understand the reason for paying grazing fees." In forests where these concessions were allowed, a tradition of Indian use had already existed. Their uninterrupted use of the lands was to be encouraged with as few complications as possible.[45]

Stockmen often listed fewer livestock than they actually grazed in order to pay lower fees. W. H. B. Kent, supervisor of the Garcés National Forest in the Southwestern District (Region), complained against these "excess counts": "I am strongly opposed to settling these cases by again

[44] W. G. Weigle to the Forester, Jan. 18, 1909, Sec. 63, Region 1, Dr. 28; Annual Grazing Report, 1914, Gallatin NF, Sec. 63, Region 1, Dr. 30, RG 95, NA.

[45] Potter to Assistant Forester to District Forester, Denver, Colo., Jan. 18, 1909, Sec. 63, Region 2, Dr. 21; Overton Price to Secretary of Agriculture, Jan. 8, 1909, Sec. 63, Region 2, Dr. 5; Edward G. Miller, Grazing Report, October 23, 1913, Sec. 63, Region 3, Dr. 48, RG 95, NA.

requesting them to apply for the proper number. It seems to me the Service should back up its own action and handle these cases as trespasses. . . . There are many stockmen here who do pay on the proper number and they are naturally and correctly indignant at the well-known cases of those who do not. This is a matter of grave reproach to the Service—and justly so." He strongly recommended that the supervisor be instructed to refuse to approve applications that consistently listed fewer animals than the number actually being grazed. Such permits should be revoked, stock removed, and fines imposed.

Someone in the district forester's office wrote in the word *no* in the margin of Kent's report before it went on to Washington. Six weeks later, in early January, 1910, George B. McCabe, USDA solicitor and temporary acting forester, said that he could not agree with the marginal note made on the supervisor's report, "but instead approve[d] Mr. Kent's recommendation." He added that the integrity of the grazing regulations could not be maintained "except by enforcing them fully and properly." When the supervisor knows, McCabe said, that an applicant is running a greater amount of stock than his permit shows, the owner should be informed either to amend the application or be faced with immediate removal and the charge of trespass.[46]

Counting of the stock on the range, conducted annually, was one of the first tasks of the ranger administering grazing controls. In the Lemhi Forest in Idaho young ranger Carl B. Arentson remembered that in this early period he counted cattle during the winter while they were on the home ranches. This method proved accurate because most ranchers wintered their stock on their home pastures; only in the spring did they move their stock to the public forest ranges. Their ranch pastures could then be used for raising winter feed. However, one rancher in Arentson's district made it known that the number of cattle on his ranch was none of the Forest Service's business. "He didn't want any tenderfoot ranger on his ranch counting his stock," Arentson said. The ranger postponed a visit to that ranch until he devised a plan.

One morning Arentson went to the post office and picked up the man's

---

[46] W. H. B. Kent to the Forester, Nov. 10, 1909; George B. McCabe, to District Forester, Jan. 8, 1910, Sec. 63, Region 3, Dr. 45, RG 95, NA. Pinchot had been fired January 7, and Potter was out West on an inspection trip. Secretary Wilson named McCabe, the department solicitor, to the post until Potter's return. Henry S. Graves became the new Forester on February 1.

mail and then proceeded to his ranch. "I tried to time my trip," said the ranger, "so that McGovern would have his cattle strung out on the feed yard at the time of my arrival. I was fortunate. I was able to ride across his feed yard with a string of cattle on each side and up to his back yard where he was loading hay." After giving the rancher his mail and exchanging pleasantries that included congratulating the man on the quality of his stock, Arentson turned around and rode away. "There was no discussion of any counting," the ranger recalled, "but, of course, McGovern knew that I had counted his cattle as I rode in and out." From his experience Arentson found that large owners usually applied to the forest for allotments of less stock than they actually owned. The smaller owners, on the other hand, trying to make provisions for increased herds, applied for more stock numbers than they had available to place on the range.[47]

When the Ballinger-Pinchot dispute brought the dismissal of Pinchot as forester in January, 1910, the possibility of extending a grazing regulatory system to millions of additional acres on the public domain died. (Pinchot had openly criticized Secretary of the Interior Richard Ballinger because of the latter's liberal coal leasing policies in Alaska. President Taft could not tolerate this public criticism of a cabinet member and promptly fired Pinchot. Grazing expert Alfred Potter almost became Pinchot's successor, but in the end Yale forestry professor Henry S. Graves obtained the appointment.) Despite the disruption in leadership caused by the Ballinger-Pinchot affair and the abrupt halt of plans to extend grazing administration to areas of the public domain, the grazing regulatory system remained secure within the Forest Service. The benefits of forest grazing administration were becoming widely recognized. From Montana came testimony from cattle dealers that stock coming out of the forests were in better condition than similar stock kept on the public domain. They weighed from fifty to one hundred pounds more and brought from two dollars to five dollars more per head on the market. Also from Nebraska came reports that cattle shipped from the North Platte National Forest sold for a higher price than did any other cattle shipped from western Nebraska. Forest-grazed cattle were undisturbed on their own range throughout the season. They had plenty of grass, salt, and water. On the unregulated public lands, herds mixed together and were chased about and in constant turmoil as owners cut out their branded cattle. They also did not have their own watering

[47] Carl B. Arentson oral history, pp. 5–6.

places or salt. On the national forests the supervisor encouraged permittees to build and maintain drift and division fences, windmills, wells, and reservoirs. "Each permittee is then working for his own interests and at the same time developing the range," wrote one supervisor.[48]

Some administrators, however, worried that stockmen were becoming too cooperative, too devoted to making improvements on the range. Improvements built in partnership, such as fencing or watering facilities, gave rise to the question of whether stockmen were gaining "prescriptive rights" to the rangeland designated in their allotments. The improvement accomplished either independently or in cooperation with the service represented an investment in property. Would the permittee be able to retain his permit long enough to regain this investment, and if the service decided he must leave this allotment, would he have a right to sue in defense of his investment and thus assert a "prescriptive right" over that section of the range?

Some forest officers conceded that these fears might be purely imaginary, but nonetheless the concern was there because such improvements could ultimately threaten Forest Service authority over the land and the entire management program. In addition it was probably unwise for the service to do much in the way of improvements because, as one officer said, "Where the Service does a large amount of range improvement there is danger of going too far and inducing the graziers to depend upon us to an extent which is neither wise nor desirable." The proper procedure appeared to be for the service to make the improvement itself and then rely upon stockmen for maintenance. If the service did all the work, the stockmen in effect would be receiving subsidies. The economic stability of the grazing community would be threatened if these subsidies or services were suddenly withdrawn by a change in government policies.[49]

Another danger to grazing policy was the widely held attitude that a stockman "owned" his permit. Forest officials warned local supervisors that efforts in several communities to have permits recognized as a property right, subject to sale or transfer, might seriously undermine the proper administration of the forest. Very early on, the Forest Service took the

[48] C. W. Hudson, Annual Grazing Report, 1909, Madison NF, and Nebraska Allowances, North Platte NF, 1908, Sec. 63, Region 1, Dr. 4, RG 95, NA.

[49] Pamphlet from Hayden NF, Wyo., 1909, Forest History Society Archives, Santa Cruz, California; Will C. Barnes, "The Forest Service and the Stockmen: Cooperation with a Big 'C,'" *The Producer: The National Livestock Monthly* 1 (June, 1919): 5–9; Annual Grazing Report, 1909, Kaibab NF, Sec. 63, Region 3, Dr. 29, RG 95, NA.

position that a permit to graze was a personal privilege obtained from the secretary of agriculture, and only the secretary retained the right to grant, withhold, or revoke the permit at his discretion. To regard the permit as a permanent property right was misleading to future buyers and to local bankers who might be persuaded to pay a higher price for permitted stock or lend money against this declared "asset." By 1916 it was a common practice for bankers to inquire about grazing privileges when making livestock loans. Often the holding of a permit determined whether or not a rancher could obtain a loan.[50]

In practice the sale of permits did occur, despite the official protestations of the Forest Service that no such value could be guaranteed or endorsed by the government. One of the advantages of having a permit was the enhanced value attached to livestock and ranch property upon its sale. The annual grazing reports from the forests in the period from 1910 to 1912 noted that permittees placed a premium of at least five dollars per head upon stock through which a permit was secured. Similar additional value accrued to ranch property when sold on the open market with grazing permits attached. Grazing privileges added as much as 25 to 33 percent to sale prices of properties. Often the existence of these privileges was the crucial factor in the sale. Small landholders were not the only ones who attempted to sell permits. Larger and older stockholders resented having to give up part of their ranges in order to accommodate newcomers to the forest who qualified for class A permits. These older stockholders had come to regard portions of the range as their private land and felt that if it were to be relinquished, it should be done under terms of sale. Their custom of selling grazing rights was "still very real in spite of our administration," said the grazing report from the Stanislaus National Forest in 1914.[51] Forest Service officers, while not wishing to recognize these practices, accommodated them by transferring permits to the new owners of property either in stock or land.[52]

On occasion the maximum-number rule also caused problems in the

[50] F. A. Silcox, Associate District Forester, to Supervisor, Deerlodge Allowance for 1911, Sec. 63, Region 1, Dr. 29; Annual Grazing Report, 1916, Rio Grande NF, Sec. 63, Region 2, Dr. 35, RG 95, NA.

[51] Annual Grazing Report, 1914, Stanislaus NF, Sec. 63, Region 5, Dr. 113, RG 95, NA.

[52] Annual Grazing Report, 1916, Helena NF, Sec. 63, Region 1, Dr. 31; Annual Grazing Report, 1917, Beaverhead NF, Sec. 63, Region 1, Dr. 7; Annual Grazing Report, 1912, San Isabel NF, Sec. 63, Region 2, Dr. 36, RG 95, NA.

transfer of permits. By purchasing stock and lands of other permittees, individuals or concerns could not automatically increase the number of their stock. They were limited by the maximum allowable number for individuals or firms in that forest and the rule that permittees who did not run stock to their protective limit were given the first opportunity to increase their numbers. Under the permit system, so-called "lease stock" appeared on the forest ranges, especially in Utah. The permit holder leased his stock to a second party, who handled them in the forest. In many instances the Forest Service recognized this practice but made no attempt to cancel or reduce numbers because the permittee was not managing his own stock but had turned it over to a "lessee."[53]

After the passage of the Stockmen's Homestead Bill in 1916, permits were in greater demand on the public range outside of the forests. The legislation allowed 640 acres of public domain land to be claimed by stock enterprisers, which meant reduced public grazing lands and a heavier demand for preferential grazing privileges in the forests. Although forest grazing officials cautioned that permits should not be viewed in terms of dollar value, use of the permits in this manner indicated acceptance of the grazing program as an ongoing institution that even bankers acknowledged in making loans. Often ranches were purchased not for the value of the ranch, but for the advantages of the permits that went with the ranch.[54]

Besides its obvious financial advantages, the forest grazing program received wide acceptance because of its benefits to stockmen in establishing reliable procedures for the distribution of range resource. If reports from the forests can be relied upon, it is evident that stockmen trusted forest officers to settle range disputes that individuals or even private stock associations failed to handle. As one supervisor said, "They have become accustomed to our methods, have accepted them and now realize that the Forest Service has come to stay."[55] Another concluded, "We have been able to make real advancement in range management, utilization of forage and other matters of vital importance to the community." Some forest officers

[53] F. A. Silcox to Forest Supervisor, Absaroka NF, Dec. 20, 1910, Sec. 63, Region 1, Dr. 111; Acting District Forester to Supervisor Ashely NF, Allowance Permits for 1915, Sec. 63, Region 4, Dr. 69, RG 95, NA.

[54] Annual Grazing Report, 1917, Beaverhead NF, Sec. 63, Region 1, Dr. 7, RG 95, NA.

[55] Annual Grazing Report, 1915, Leadville NF, Sec. 63, Region 2, Dr. 32, RG 95, NA; Mrs. Louise Marvel Oral History Project (1968), p. 7, U.S. Forest Service, Region 4, Ogden, Utah.

acknowledged that radical feeling against the grazing program had died down "and we seem to be on good terms with our worst enemies." [56]

The local forest officers, from the viewpoint of Washington were sometimes on *too* good terms with the stockmen. Washington feared that the officers were not critical enough of the local community and too reluctant to carry out all the grazing regulations if it meant risking unpopularity in the community. This belief might be quite true if the supervisor stayed in a forest for more than ten years. As Grazing Assistant Barnes wrote to Potter in 1915: "When a supervisor has been on one forest for ten years he can't help but get into ruts, pick up local differences and prejudices, and generally get the point of view of the local resident rather than the broad view which a supervisor should take of his work." [57]

Local officials did not live independently of their community. Their children attended the local schools, families participated in social affairs, and friendships grew. If forest policies were popular the officials' acceptance in the community was easy, but if policies became unpopular their life could become strained. No wonder accommodation was more often the case after long residence in an area.

As demand for forest range increased prior to World War I, the fee issue again threatened to disrupt friendly relations between stockmen and the Forest Service. Some grazing officials concluded that the growing demand required higher fees. At the same time, both Forest Service policies and government land policy continued to encourage more numerous permit applications from many new, small property owners. Previously, the small livestock owner was practically prohibited from utilizing the ranges adjacent to his lands because they were stocked to the utmost by larger owners. Forest-grazing regulations reduced the threat of stock straying into the herds of large owners and virtually guaranteed the availability of range each year without the fear of a large outfit sweeping in to use it. [58]

Pressures from the smaller settlers and some fraudulent claims obtained through the Homestead Acts of the twentieth century had the inevitable effect of expanding the number of stock in the forests. It was always

---

[56] Annual Grazing Report, 1916, Sheridan, Mont., Sec. 63, Region 1, Dr. 14; Annual Grazing Report, 1912, Sopris NF, Sec. 63, Region 2, Dr. 31, RG 95, NA.

[57] Annual Grazing Report, 1916, Coconino NF, Sec. 63, Region 3, Dr. 51, RG 95, NA; Barnes to Potter, Aug. 16, 1915, U.S. Forest Service Range Management Office Files, Arlington, Virginia.

[58] *Yearbook of Agriculture, 1914*, p. 80.

difficult for those already present on the range to make room for new-comers. The enlarged Homestead Acts not only encouraged private acqui-sition of the public range but also indirectly increased demands for forest-grazing permits as public range land became more scarce. These pressures plus the general success that the service experienced in making the forest range permit system workable and profitable for participants all meant one thing—increased numbers pressing toward and into the forest boundaries.[59]

By the Forest Service's own admission, a decade after it assumed con-trol of the forests there was more than a 50 percent increase in the number of animals utilizing forest ranges. There was also more forest range as ad-ditional lands had been added to the system. Better utilization of existing ranges was being achieved. From the service's viewpoint, it had proved that under systematic management the value of grazing land could be restored and increased. Heavier animals could be produced even with increased numbers, and "[the]se lands can be improved faster in use than in idle-ness." By 1914 the secretary of agriculture cited the request of many stock-men that the department's system of grazing regulation be extended to the public range outside of the national forests as proof that stock were flour-ishing under the constructive administration of the Forest Service. Al-though the total area of the 160 national forests was about a million acres less than in 1913, about 38,000 more cattle and horses and 347,000 more sheep and goats were under permit. All this meant, according to forest offi-cials, that carrying capacity of the range was increasing under better man-agement, especially in the areas of distributing and handling stock.[60]

In view of the heightened demand for forest range, some local forest supervisors recommended an increase in fees. Higher fees could be accom-panied by a guarantee that the new rate schedule would remain in effect for five or ten years. At the end of that period new adjustments would be made "in accordance with demand for range and conditions at that time." Others believed by 1916 that "the time was ripe to place the fees on a commercial basis." The fee program had been accepted as a permanent fixture in forest administration, and the industry was recognized as having a permanent place in the "land classification work" in the forests. Quite clearly, how-ever, the suggestions that fees be raised to a commercial level was because

[59] Annual Grazing Report, 1911, Tusayan NF, Sec. 63, Region 3, Dr. 48, RG 95, NA.
[60] *Yearbook of Agriculture, 1914*, pp. 16–17; "Grazing for Eleven Million: Livestock Increases on National Forests," *American Forestry* 20 (1914): 436–37.

of the heavy demand for range and the general acceptance of the benefits of the range-allotment control program.

Increased fees appeared to be one solution to the proliferation of permit demands from small users. Since such operators were marginal at best, increased fees could serve to discourage them and prompt others to fail in uneconomical ventures. While on the one hand Forest Service and government land policy encouraged small stock holders, on the other, forest officers experienced problems from constant demands from new and small stockmen. Many concluded that it was time to curb the growing demands, not through an official change of policy, but rather through the more subtle method of making it more expensive to run stock in the forests.[61]

Still, in both word and deed, the social policies of opening and preserving opportunity for the small stockmen persisted in the Forest Service's grazing policy. However noble the social goals of improving local communities, the policy served in some instances to lay the foundation for conditions of overgrazing. One investigation suggests such overgrazing occurred in the Manti forest in Utah, where the Mormon village pattern of small landholding reinforced the policy and encouraged Forest Service personnel to issue many small permits without enough offsetting reductions. Official publications of the Department of Agriculture celebrating the increase in small stockholder permits and use cited the Manti forest as an outstanding example. Years later this same forest was criticized for the overextension of permits to small users that resulted in deteriorated range and erosion problems.[62]

Before World War I, government policy encouraged and built up the production of livestock by small farmers in the Manti forest. "When the Forest was created the ranges were practically monopolized by the large herds," read a 1914 report of the Department of Agriculture. But because of the new forest-range policies, some ranges became almost entirely occupied by stock farmers in the nearby valleys where farm units averaged thirty-eight acres. Every year the forest received applications from new settlers to graze from one to ten head of cattle. To make room, the larger owners were continually reduced.

[61] Supervisor's Annual Working Plan for 1916, Colorado NF, Nov. 15, 1915, Sec. 63, Region 2, Dr. 12; Supervisor's Annual Working Plan for 1916, Jefferson NF, Nov. 15, 1916, Sec. 63, Region 1, Dr. 13, RG 95, NA.

[62] *Yearbook of Agriculture, 1914*, pp. 79–82; Charles S. Peterson, "Small Holding Land Patterns in Utah," *Journal of Forest History* 17 (1973): 9–10.

This forest was probably an extreme example. It exemplified how official policies, local customs, and forest officials acting in sympathy with community values could promote the interests of the small grazier at the expense of range protection. Higher grazing fees might offer a solution to growing pressures to expand the number of grazing privileges. The fees could eliminate uneconomical graziers without many of the difficult personal and political decisions involved with individual reductions.

The Forest Service moved to implement modest fee increases for the grazing season 1917. At the same time, it braced itself against a possible storm of angry protests that it hoped would follow proper administrative channels. As Grazing Assistant Barnes wrote to one local forest, he did not want "a deluge of protests from small stockmen seeking to prevent increases through political pressure instead of presenting arguments to the department against it."[63] Before the increased-fee rate could prompt a response from stock operators, World War I intervened in April of 1917. Higher wartime stock prices and increased allowable stock numbers in the forests overshadowed the issue of slightly increased fees. Stockmen were delighted with the high prices and greater access to forest ranges in this time of war emergency. Clearly modest increases in fees did nothing to reduce numbers of stock at a time when the war virtually threw open the gates of the forests to almost everyone. The result was a damaged resource.

While some officials looked to increased fee rates to control the pressure of stock numbers, studies were underway in the new field of range science to learn more about range renewal and carrying capacity. As one forester said, many of his decisions had been based only on "chance, approximations, and guesses." The time was at hand when the service required a body of scientific work to support its range resource-use decisions.

[63] Barnes to Supervisor, Cabinet NF, Thompson Falls, Mont., Jan. 19, 1917, Sec. 63, Region 1, Dr. 13, RG 95, NA.

4

The Science of Management

Such expressions as "range was overgrazed but not permanently injured" must be supported by that permanent sample plot to show whether inferior and unpalatable species are displacing it.
—John H. Hatton

RATIONAL use and management of range resources by a government agency required a detailed knowledge of the rangelands. Although stockmen had long relied upon their own observations and experience to judge their ranges, professional managers needed more than a stockman's advice. The rule-of-thumb guesses of the early range managers had to be replaced by knowledge rooted in tests, experiments, and intensive analysis of the resulting data. The Forest Service needed a research arm to fulfill Pinchot's boast that it could competently manage and protect all of the forest resources. An accumulation of a body of knowledge for application to range grazing problems required time, effort, and above all, money. The depleted condition of the forest ranges after the turn of the century demanded not only reductions in stock grazing, seasonal limits, and arrest of chronic trespassers, but also the broader approach of protective management. Programs of protection could not rest solely upon the authority of government land ownership and orders from distant Washington. Officials had to be able to demonstrate convincingly to users on the basis of scientific tests that overgrazing had caused severe damage and that remedial action was necessary. The results of these on-range tests would help to create a climate of acceptance for those steps needed to restore forage, protect watersheds, improve grazing capacity, and apply better methods of stock handling.

Ordered, useful knowledge about western resources constantly challenged government and private enterprise in the nineteenth century. During the earliest explorations of the American West, trappers, military men, missionaries, and emigrants reported on the rich grasslands of the Great

Left: Albert F. Potter, Grazing Chief, Forest Service, 1905–10. (*Courtesy, Forest Service*) *Right*: Leon F. Kneipp, Grazing Chief, Forest Service, 1910–15. (*Courtesy, Forest Service*)

Left: Will C. Barnes, Grazing Chief, Forest Service, 1915–28. (*Courtesy, Forest Service*) *Right*: Christopher E. Rachford, Director of Range Management, Forest Service, 1928–36. (*Courtesy, Forest Service*)

Left: Walt L. Dutton, Director of Range Management, Forest Service, 1936–54. (*Courtesy, Forest Service*) *Right*: Charles A. Joy, Director of Range Management, Forest Service, 1954–60. (*Courtesy, Forest Service*)

Left: William R. Chapline, Director of Range Research, Forest Service, 1920–52. (*Courtesy, Forest Service*) *Right*: Clarence L. Forsling, Assistant Chief of the Forest Service for Research, 1938–44. Forsling was an early grazing researcher and earlier headed the Intermountain and the Appalachian Forest experiment stations. (*Courtesy, Forest Service*)

Staff of the Forest Service Grazing Branch, Washington, D.C., March, 1924. Branch Chief Will C. Barnes is seated left of center, and Assistant Branch Chief Christopher E. Rachford is seated second from right. *Standing, left to right*: William A. Dayton; L. C. Hurtt; Clarence L. Forsling; D. A. Shoemaker; William R. Chapline, chief of the Office of Grazing Studies; and I. Tidestrom. (*RG 95, NA*)

Left: A Forest Service ranger points out a sign designating the center stock drive-way for sheep herds on the Malheur National Forest near Lakeview, Oregon, October 21, 1930. This open woodlands of big ponderosa pines is east of the Cascade Mountains. (*RG 95, NA*) *Right*: Sign showing separation of sheep and cattle allot-ments near an allotment fence on Valley Creek on the Stanley-Cascade Road, southern Idaho. Challis National Forest, July 1940. (*RG 95, NA*)

A typical sheep herder on the Chelan National Forest, Washington, September, 1915. (*RG, 95, NA*)

Cattle grazing in the upper Ruby Valley summer range, Montana, January, 1940. This photograph was taken during filming of the movie *Blessings of Grass*. (*RG 95 NA*)

Sheep belonging to A. H. Brailsford of Hagerman Valley, southern Idaho, at Horse Creek near U.S. Highway 93. Forest officer Robert S. Monahan and L. "Del" Dickinson, Lowell & Miller sheep commission representative from Denver, count ewes as they are returned to the summer range from sorting corrals. Sawtooth National Forest, July, 1940. (*RG 95, NA*)

Ewes and lambs grazing in aspen-bunchgrass vegetation on the Uncompahgre National Forest, Colorado. (*RG 95, NA*)

Second-weed-stage condition in Gold Center Meadow, Whitman National Forest, eastern Oregon, July 23, 1941, comprises a mixture of California bromegrass, yarrow, *Potentilla gracilia*, *Cares athrostachya*, and annual weeds. (*Courtesy, Forest Service*)

Big Hollow west of Richfield, Utah, being prepared for planting with crested wheatgrass, mountain bromegrass, and smooth bromegrass by a large disc plow. Note the heavy sagebrush growth. August–September, 1945. (*Courtesy, Forest Service*)

Typical meadow erosion along a stream in Broder Meadow, Sequoia National Forest, California, July, 1941. (*Courtesy, Forest Service*)

Good grass growth following erosion control in Bear Valley, Modoc National Forest, northern California, July 16, 1942. (*Courtesy, Forest Service*)

Grazing plot fenced in 1941, illustrating how an overgrazed area can be brought back to grass by protection for a few years. Buckhead Mesa, Tonto National Forest, Arizona, August 19, 1947. (*Courtesy, Forest Service*)

Cattle watering at a tank installed on Custer National Forest, Montana, August 4, 1948. This was a new improvement on a fifteen-mile cattle and horse allotment. (*Courtesy, Forest Service*)

Plains and mountain meadows. Explorers Lewis and Clark, Zebulon Pike, and Stephen Long made some of the first observations. Pike and Long referred to much of the land as a "great American desert," unfit for white settlement. Later trappers and mountain men such as Jedediah Smith recognized the possibilities of the western country for various agricultural and stock enterprises. Missionaries like Father De Smet, Jason Lee, and Henry Spaulding wrote encouraging letters about western resources and sent plants to collectors in the East. John C. Frémont wrote of the "bucolic" nature of the land from the Great Salt Lake to the front of the Wasatch Mountains. Richard Henry Dana in *Two Years Before the Mast* described the rich cattle-hide and tallow products of pastoral California in the 1830s.

Edwin Bryant, leader of a California-bound emigrant group in 1846, described a high, secluded, verdant mountain valley in the Sierra that would eventually become a part of a national forest:

> We reached the summit of the gap that afforded us a passage over the mountain, about eleven o'clock, and descended a long and very steep declivity on the other side, bringing us into a small, oval-shaped and grassy valley, with faint spring branch of pure cold water running through it. This hollow is entirely surrounded by high mountains. The soil is rich, and the grass and other vegetation luxuriant. The impersonations of romance and solitude could scarcely find a more congenial abode than this beautiful and sequestered spot.

The Pacific Railroad surveys of the 1850s conducted by the War Department compiled not only information about possible rail routes to the Pacific, but also information on the resource characteristics of the land and life it supported. These reports hoped to determine the most feasible route to the Pacific for the "Iron Horse"; in the process it provided some the earliest environmental reports. Botanical studies in America were absorbed in the tasks of collection and identification as the first step in knowing the flora of these new lands. The various United States geological surveys after the Civil War also promoted collection of flora and fauna.[1]

Early studies of the range by the Department of Agriculture addressed general questions of overstocking, range depletion, stock disease, insects, and poisonous plants. In 1868, a few years after it became an independent

---

[1] William H. Goetzmann, *Exploration and Empire: The Explorer and the Scientist in the Winning of the American West*, pp. 247–49; Edwin Bryant, *What I Saw in California*, p. 199. The valley (Dog Valley), now in the Toiyabe National Forests, was denuded by overgrazing before being acquired by the Forest Service in the 1930s. Dog Valley became an example of many of the problems of meadowland restoration.

department, the Division of Botany was created to provided a more concentrated effort in plant labeling and classification. After the establishment of the Bureau of Animal Husbandry in 1884, the tick controversy in studies related to Texas fever pointed out the need for firsthand observation and experiments rather than mere speculation about the origins of the disease. At first, bureau scientists refused to believe, as many stockmen on the scene contended, that Texas fever was transmitted by ticks. Much to the embarrassment of the bureau, subsequent experiments proved stockmen correct. By the mid-1890s the Department of Agriculture established the Division of Agrostology to combat western range depletion with a substantial fifteen-thousand-dollar congressional appropriation for grass and forage-plant investigations.

In 1901 the Divisions of Botany and Agrostology were combined into the Bureau of Plant Industry, the studies of which encompassed forage plants, reseeding in limited tests, and grazing impacts. These studies bore more directly upon the economic impact of plant culture. Just before the creation of the Forest Service, the investigations by the Department of Agriculture into sheep-grazing problems in eastern Oregon and the Southwest involved the department directly in the range situation on the forest reserves. As the Forest Service assumed the duties of grazing administration, a range-research program became a top priority.[2]

The objective of range research was the application of scientific principles to rectify range problems. In 1907 the Forest Service, in cooperation with the same Dr. Coville of the Bureau of Plant Industry, began a basic study of sheep grazing on the ranges. These projects involved experiments in developing coyote-proof pastures, grazing in dense timber, and "camping" or bedding down sheep. Very early came the application of deferred and rotation grazing. Experiments showed that delayed grazing late in the season gave the seed crop time to mature. With plants well headed out, seeds would be trampled into the ground, giving them a necessary cover for a high rate of germination. Rotation grazing divided the range into five or more sections, allowing one section to remain unused each year. Careful observations in Oregon showed that ranges recovered more rapidly under the deferred system.

Grazing-capacity studies relating to particular range types were begun

[2]T. Swann Harding, *Two Blades of Grass: A History of Scientific Development in the U.S. Department of Agriculture*, pp. 150–51; "The History of Western Range Research," *Agricultural History* 18 (1944): 129.

in northeastern Oregon in the Wallowa National Forest by James T. Jardine of the Department of Agriculture, in cooperation with Coville. When the Forest Service set up an Office of Grazing Studies three years later, Dr. Coville continued as a consultant. Studies of ecological processes, also in the Wallowa National Forest, in plant communities and the impact of grazing on plant species occurred under the direction of Arthur W. Sampson. Again in cooperation with the Bureau of Plant Industry, artificial reseeding experiments with various forage species were conducted. Primarily these experiments were directed toward cattle and sheep use of the forest ranges, but an early study by John H. Hatton also examined the problems of Angora goat grazing on chaparral range in the Lassen National Forest.[3]

In 1910, to coordinate and promote range research and the collection and use of technical range management information, the Forest Service established the Office of Grazing Studies, naming Jardine as its director. The office received official approval from the secretary of agriculture in late 1911. Special arrangements were made for the office to be headquartered in Washington, D.C., from November 1 to March 31 and in Ogden, Utah, from April 1 to October 31 of each year, but for some reason, perhaps budgetary, this arrangement never was achieved. Once in office Jardine launched a grazing "reconnaissance" of specific forest ranges. In later years this job was called "range survey" or "range-resource inventory." The range reconnaissance did more than observe the conditions of the ranges. Ultimately the survey hoped to find a simple, reliable method for empirically (visually) rating the condition of the range and also for determining whether the range was improving or deteriorating. The goal was to provide a stronger factual basis for improved range management on the areas covered.[4]

The range reconnaissance became a systematic survey that collected field data for final compilation in the office. One result of the field work was a map classifying the grazing lands into vegetation types. The map showed location, acreage, topography, amount and character of vegetation, condition of the range, available watering places, and cultural features. On

[3] Work Projects Administration, History of Grazing Papers, Collection 8, Box 16, Fd. 9, Utah State University Library, Logan; A. W. Sampson, "Natural Revegetation on Rangelands Based on Growth," *Journal of Agricultural Research* 3 (November, 1914): 93–147; A. F. Potter, "Grazing Experiments on the Federal Range Reserves," *American Sheep Breeder* 36 (February, 1916): 74; James T. Jardine, "Improvement and Maintenance of Far Western Ranges," *American Sheep Breeder* 38 (August, 1918): 498.

[4] Potter to Secretary Wilson, December 28, 1911, Sec. 63; "Special Authorizations for Various Purposes, 1905 to 1912," Sec. 3, RG 95, NA.

the basis of these data, grazing-management plans were written and periodically adjusted for discrepancies. In the early years when there were no universities or colleges teaching range management, it was necessary to use capable students, preferably with a botany background, to conduct range reconnaissance under careful supervision.

Beginning in 1911 each reconnaissance party consisted of a chief and, usually, three assistants. If topography permitted, each member of the party covered the equivalent of three "sections" (three square miles or 1,920 acres) each working day. Each man started the day from a specific section corner of an area which had been completed the day before. He would follow the section line for three miles in a straight line, observing the vegetation on each side for a quarter of a mile. He would type in the boundaries of each type observed and describe the plant composition and its actual utilization. If necessary for accurate observation, he would go away from the section line, usually leaving a marker, at right angles into the vegetation type far enough to record reasonably accurately the type boundary as noted on the ground, the composition of the vegetation, all evidence of grazing of individual species, and other essentials. The density of the herbaceous and other grazeable vegetation for each range type was recorded on a record sheet on a scale from 1 to 10, with 10 being a full complete density (only on fully productive moist meadows in excellent condition) and 1 being very poor condition (one-tenth or less of the ground surface covered). The important grasses, herbs, and shrubs were listed by percentages in the total plant cover. For each type, notes relating to soil, utilization of specific species, and other pertinent information were also recorded. By the end of the day, reconnaissance people had each mapped a total of three sections of land—three-fourths of three sections and one-fourth of three other adjoining sections.

According to William Ridgely Chapline, for many years chief of the Division of Range Research, reconnaissance work was a well-planned undertaking, requiring trained personnel in charge of each party and effective training of assistants at the start of each year's work. During the evening, each field observer checked his type lines, density estimates of adjoining types on his maps, and the major plant species listed on each type against those of the adjoining observer. If there were major differences, they were usually checked in the field by the chief of the party. On rainy days and often on Sundays, the field records were assembled for range allotments with calculated forage-acre values for types. In addition, a collection was made of every plant found on the forest being covered. For each plant a form was filled out relating to the characteristics of the location where it was collected, the soil, the topography, and evidence of use by animals. Such data were not ordinarily analyzed during the field work, but the information proved helpful later in developing published material on range plants.

Range reconnaissance differed from range inspection. Range inspection concentrated on analysis of a specific allotment, and its purpose was to discover weaknesses in the current management plan and recommend solutions. The inspection was most useful in fixing adjustments that must be made either upward or downward in the number of stock grazed. Although the service admitted in 1910 that many years would be required to reconnoiter the ranges of the national forests, range inspections served to correct errors and problems in specific management plans. Above all an inspection would produce a field map showing the relationship of the allotment boundaries to the topography. Much of this information was contained on overlays showing allotment boundaries, number of stock within each, acreage with acres per head of stock, and permittee's name.[5] By learning the carrying capacity of certain range types through continued observation, the capacities of similar ranges could be estimated. The central problem was whether a range was being overstocked. In those early years, it was believed, the condition of the stock could indicate an overstocked or overgrazed range. Depleted ranges seldom produced fat cattle. Later it was realized that this could not be the criterion for testing an overgrazed range, because there were instances when such ranges temporarily continued to produce fat stock.[6]

The Forest Service's push for scientific knowledge about its range resources came at a time when the world of plant science was engaged in new and sophisticated theories about the origins and growth of plant associations and related soils. The research efforts of the Forest Service's Grazing Branch attempted to utilize the latest theories in vegetative development.

[5] James T. Jardine and Mark Anderson, *Range Management on the National Forests*, USDA Bulletin no. 790, August 6, 1919, pp. 75–76, 82; "History of Western Range Research," p. 132; R. E. Bodley, "Grazing Reconnaissance on the Coconino National Forest," *Nebraska University Forest Club Annual* 5 (1913): 77–78.

[6] David G. Kinney, "General Range Condition, 1911," Missoula NF, Sec. 63, RM, Region 1; Donal Johnson, "Grazing Report Gila National Forest, 1912, Sec. 63, RM, Region 3, Dr. 45, RG 95, NA; Will C. Barnes, *Western Grazing Grounds and Forest Ranges*, p. 244.

Primarily concerned with plant succession, researchers attempted to blend range-management practices with prevailing notions about plant growth, formation of plant communities, and reproduction. The idea of succession in plant communities would be central to a general theory of ecological succession that touched all living forms in the forest.[7]

The Universities of Chicago and Nebraska were the leading centers in the United States conducting investigations into vegetational processes. Scientists working in these schools built upon European investigations of the late nineteenth century that developed a concept of plant associations moving through developmental stages to a climax formation. While Europeans pioneered these theories, American botanists were still collecting, describing, and cataloging the plants of an unexplored continent. By the turn of the century, however, Professor John Merle Coulter at the University of Chicago and Professor E. E. Bessey at the University of Nebraska produced studies on vegetational processes. Their students, particularly E. F. Clements, who studied with Bessey, became leaders in the study of plant succession. Clements developed the quadrat method of quantitative study of plant associations that the Forest Service later adopted as a factor in its research. By sampling forage and counting different plant species in protected plots over a period of time, quantitative data could be obtained that would indicate the stage of the plant association in the successional process.[8]

Clements was the first American credited with giving systematic form to the phenomenon of "dynamic ecology" or succession in plant associations. He suggested that a community of plants passed through a cycle of development similar to that of the life of the plant itself. That is to say it struggled to survive in the beginning, but took hold and grew strong. At the end of its growth cycle, it died just as a vegetational community in a climax condition died out and was replaced by another life form. These principles guided the performance of early research experiments. By counting the various species of grasses and forbs in sample plots, an estimate could be made of the vegetal composition and the value of its edible plants for grazing. Through an analysis of species composition, an understanding of the

[7]Charles Elton, *Animal Ecology*, p. 21; Ronald C. Tobey, *Saving the Prairies: The Life Cycle of the Founding School of American Plant Ecology, 1895–1955*, p. 70.

[8]James C. Malin, *The Grassland of North America Prolegomena to Its History with Addenda*, pp. 7–8; Richard Overfield, "Charles E. Bessey: The Impact of New Botany on American Agriculture," *Technology and Culture* 16 (April, 1975): 162–81.

seral stage in the successional process could be determined. Strictly from the viewpoint of range science, the amount of grazing allowed should be gauged according to the availability of forage provided by a particular successional stage of vegetation.[9]

One of Clements's most productive students was Arthur W. Sampson. In 1912 Jardine, Coville, and Sampson helped organize the first experiment station (first called the Utah Experiment Station and later the Great Basin Experiment Station) devoted mainly to range research on the Manti Forest near Ephraim, Utah. Sampson remained there as director of the experiment station until 1922. His numerous publications eventually led to his appointment as professor of range science at the University of California, Berkeley, in 1923. His work, *Range and Pasture Management* (1923), was the finest comprehensive textbook in the field and won him the reputation of "father of range science."

In articles written in 1917 and 1919, Sampson related the idea of plant succession to effective range management. In these works he referred to progressive development of a simple, sparse vegetation into more complex, abundant forms. Sampson believed that progressive development (*re-vegetation*) "may be greatly expedited by cropping the herbage in such a manner as to interfere as little as possible with the life history and growth requirements peculiar to the different successional plant states."[10]

If, however, factors adverse to progressive development intervened— that is, overgrazing—the vegetation, according to this view, would revert eventually to a "first weed stage." Erosion accompanied this process until the soil was practically carried away, leaving the "pioneer stage" of soil formation—bare rock, algae and crustaceous lichens (Fig. 1). A change of plant cover down the scale from the more complex to the more simple and primitive was termed "retrogression, retrogressive succession, or degeneration."

[9] Malin, *Grassland of North America*, pp. 162–81; Paul T. Tueller, "Secondary Succession Disclimax and Range Condition Standards in Desert Shrub Vegetation," in *Arid Shrublands: Proceedings of the Third Workshop of the United States/Australia Rangelands Panel*, Tucson, Ariz. March 26–April 5, 1973, p. 57; W. R. Chapline, "Range Management History and Philosophy," *Journal of Forestry* 49 (September, 1951): 635; Frederic E. Clements, *Plant Succession: An Analysis of the Development of Vegetation*; Frederic E. Clements, "Ecology in Public Service," in *Dynamics of Vegetation*, pp. 246–78.

[10] Arthur W. Sampson, "Succession as a Factor in Range Management," *Journal of Forestry* 4 (May, 1917): 593–96; Arthur W. Sampson, *Plant Succession in Relation to Range Management*, USDA Bulletin no. 791, August 27, 1919, p. 6.

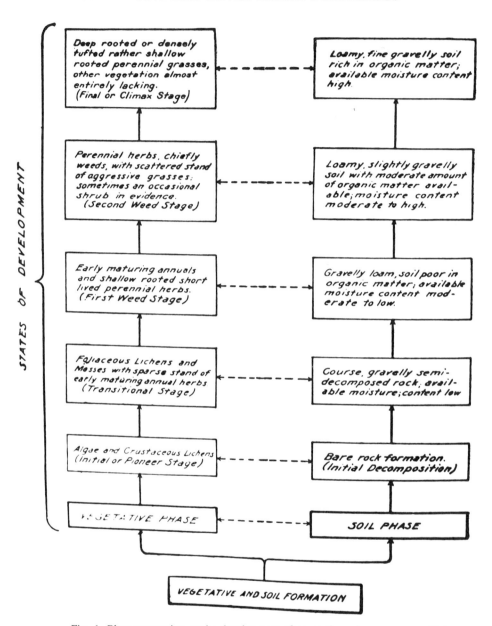

Fig. 1. Plant succession or the development of vegetation where grass constitutes the climax or subclimax type. Source: Arthur W. Sampson, *Plant Succession in Relation to Range Management*, USDA Bulletin no. 791, August 27, 1919, p. 4.

A working knowledge of plant succession could assist in judging what was overgrazing or undergrazing. Grazed animals could then be moved safely toward maximum carrying capacity and "the herbage cropped on the basis of a sustained yield." Cropping the herbage should be done in a manner that would not interfere with the maintenance of a desired successional stage. Range managers armed with this knowledge about the composition of the range vegetation and its successional stages could help promote "progressive succession." They could better determine, on the basis of the life history of the various plant species, the season of grazing with reference to the time of seed maturity and other factors required for good range management. With this knowledge, correct grazing practices could attempt to maintain a range in a stable subclimax stage over long periods of time. These practices would afford optimum grazing levels (later investigations will suggest the system allowed too much croppings of the forage) and prevent the range from developing less desirable vegetation. Most often overgrazing moved the range into a brush condition as stock destroyed the ability of grass to compete with brush.[11]

The concept of classifying range conditions as advocated by Jardine was studied even earlier than 1911. Attempts to judge range condition emerged in the studies of J. G. Smith in the *Yearbook of Agriculture* of 1895, David Griffiths' study in 1903 of Washington, Oregon, and Nevada ranges, and E. O. Wooten's study of the New Mexico range in 1908 for the New Mexico Agriculture Experiment Station. In the early range-survey maps in 1911, range condition was indicated to be either satisfactory or unsatisfactory. "Unsatisfactory" referred to those ranges producing less than their capability. Sampson classified conditions into four broad stages of plant succession in his 1919 article. The four stages, as he described them, were (1) the wheat-grass consociation (subclimax stage), (2) the porcupine-grass–yellow-brush consociation (mixed grass-and-weed stage), (3) the foxglove–sweet-sage–yarrow consociation (second or late weed stage), and (4) the ruderal–early-weed consociation (first or early weed stage). These stages for the range under study corresponded roughly to the more modern condition classifications of excellent, good, fair, and poor. In 1950 Chapline noted that when range surveys first began in 1911, unsatisfactory ranges were shown by "cross-hatching" on early survey (then called "range-reconnaissance") maps. Chapline wrote that Sampson's ideas

---

[11] Sampson, "Succession as a Factor in Range Management," pp. 593–96.

about plant succession in relation to range management "brought the close interrelation of ecological processes to range deterioration and restoration to the fore." [12]

The concept of ecological succession implied that plants react to their surroundings "and in many cases drive themselves out." Theories of plant succession laid the foundation for a general theory of ecological succession that was eventually adopted by wildlife managers because it appeared to hold true for wildlife habitat as well. Ecological succession, however, was sometimes held up and prevented from reaching a natural climax by the intervention of outside factors. In these more frequent situations it was common to refer to the stage at which it stopped as a sub-climax. Ultimately, the quadrat method attempted to confirm through statistical analysis of plant composition the condition and the direction in which succession was moving. Observers needed to know whether more valuable perennial grasses were increasing in numbers or decreasing as compared with the less valuable annual grasses and forbs. [13]

In 1911 the Office of Grazing Studies expanded into regional offices. Charles F. Fleming, Alfred E. Aldous, Lynn H. Douglas, and Robert R. Hill respectively took charge of the offices in the Pacific Northwest, Intermountain, Rocky Mountain, and Southwestern regions. All of these men learned range reconnaissance from Jardine on the Coconino forest in the spring of 1911. The reconnaissance became the main work of these regional grazing-study offices. Later were established an office in California, with Fred D. Douthitt in charge, and the Northern Rocky Mountain office in 1915, under Homer S. Young. Jesse L. Peterson took charge of the Pacific Northwest in 1913 after the transfer of Fleming to the Northern Rocky Mountain Region. Offices of regional studies promoted the implementation of uniform grazing practices by adjusting them to special regional needs. [14]

Determining the economic values of plants for grazing was coordi-

[12] W. R. Chapline to Marion Clawson, September 18, 1950, Sec. 63, Box 637, RG 95, NA; Sampson, *Plant Succession in Relation to Range Management*, p. 7; Tueller, "Secondary Succession Disclimax and Range Condition Standards," p. 60.

[13] Elton, *Animal Ecology*, p. 21; James A. Malin, review of *Range Management: Principles and Practices*, by Arthur W. Sampson, in *Scientific Monthly* 74 (May, 1952): 308–309; F. E. Egler, "A Commentary on American Plant Ecology," *Ecology* 32 (1951): 673; Tobey, *Saving the Prairies*, pp. 110, 143.

[14] "History of Western Range Research," p. 32; W. R. Chapline, "First Ten Years of the Office of Grazing Studies," *Rangelands* 2 (December, 1980): 223–24; W. R. Chapline, interview with the author, Reno, Nevada, March, 1980.

nated by William A. Dayton, who headed a program to handle range-plant collections from the field and the development of a Forest Service range-plant herbarium. The Bureau of Plant Industry and the U.S. National Herbarium at the Smithsonian Institute assisted in formal identification of plants so that a uniform system could be established. The identification of poisonous plants and recommendations for their eradication were given a high priority. Erosion and its relation to grazing were first studied by Robert V. R. Reynolds on the Manti forest in central Utah. Will C. Barnes produced an important study on stock-watering places in 1914. General management studies concentrated on methods for handling sheep, cattle, and goats. The goals of these studies were more efficient utilization of the range, prevention of damage to forage, and protection of forest and watershed resources.

Jardine and Mark Anderson's study *Range Management on the National Forests* brought together the basic principles of range management in light of the advances of range science and the assessment of resources. It was recognized as the "range bible" and modified the management procedures as originally outlined in the grazing section of the Forest Service's *Use Book*.

From these studies Jardine developed the open system of bedding sheep. The bedding-out system required herdsmen to return their stock to a designated bedding area each night, but they were not to stay in any one place more than three nights. In addition to offering greater protection to forest and forage growth, the system provided greater security against predators. As early as 1915 the Forest Service was recognized as the national leader in range research. In that year the responsibility for range research was transferred from the Bureau of Plant Industry to the service. The wider scope of the assignment yielded studies relating to climate and plant growth and range management in semi-desert ranges, notably the Jornada and Santa Rita experimental ranges in southern New Mexico and Arizona.[15]

After Jardine's resignation from the Office of Grazing Studies in 1920 to head the Oregon Experiment Station, W. R. Chapline took the post. In 1925 the research duties were placed under the Branch of Research. The administrative operation of the Office of Grazing Studies, relating to range

---

[15] "Jack Albano's Forest Service Career," p. 5, Oral History Project, U.S. Forest Service, Region 4, Ogden, Utah.

reconnaissance and development of range-management plans, remained in the Branch of Grazing. Funds for these projects represented about two-thirds of the funds allotted to the Office of Grazing Studies in 1925, when Chapline transferred to the Branch of Research for the major purpose of expanding range research. In 1935 a Division of Range Research expanded research in the area, including additional range erosion and range watershed studies. In 1937, the Division of Forest Influences was established, combining forest and range watershed studies.[16]

At times the Forest Service was asked to mediate disputes over range-research problems. In 1915 the Public Health Service and the Bureau of Entomology became involved in a dispute over the presence of ticks on sheep. The Health Service maintained that sheep destroyed ticks because their heavy wool coats prevented penetration by ticks. The Entomology Bureau said that was not so and that sheep would perpetuate the ticks by acting as hosts to them. When asked for an opinion, Forest Service officials retreated from the controversy. Potter wrote the district (regional) forester in Montana, "The injecting of the Forest Service into the matter would merely be in the shape of a peace maker, if I may put it that way, and I question if our overture for peace would be received in the right spirit." Controversies over applied science among government bureaus often did little to advance the quest for scientific truth about a problem. In this instance both Potter and Barnes agreed that the service best stay clear of the controversy unless ordered to participate.[17]

Working with some of the scientific men also posed early challenges to administrators in the Forest Service. Barnes, who viewed himself as a practical cowman, complained of the temperamental natures of the scientists who worked on range problems when he first headed the Branch of Grazing. In some frustration Barnes commented to Potter in 1915, "Confound these scientific chaps anyhow with their temperamental weakness. I'd rather be a plain cow puncher individual without temperament or brains." On the other hand, Barnes knew the value of research workers in developing better methods of handling stock and for assessing range productivity and condition. He pushed for more appropriations to extend

[16]Chapline, "Range Research in the United States" [ca. 1942], Division of Range Research, Forest Service, USDA, Box 5, Fd. 10, Work Projects Administration, History of Grazing Papers, Special Collections Library, Utah State University, Logan.

[17]Potter to District Forester, Missoula, Mont., January 26, 1916; Barnes to same, January 6, 1917, Sec. 63, Region 1, RG 95, NA.

range-survey work. As he was quick to point out, the Grazing Branch turned into the U.S. Treasury almost as much money as did timber sales ($1,130,500 compared to $1,175,000 in fiscal year 1915), but got only one-sixth of the money necessary to carry on the work. The return in increased fees, he pointed out, justified the work because such surveys usually resulted in the more efficient use of the range by greater numbers of stock.[18]

By the 1920s administrators of range research emphasized that innovations and new methods in range or livestock management must meet "the acid test of practical economy." Theories had to be supported by practical observations and results. As John H. Hatton, assistant regional forester for Region 2 emphasized: "Such expressions as 'the range was overgrazed but not permanently injured' must be supported by that permanent sample plot to show whether a given palatable species is going to hold its own, or whether inferior and unpalatable species are displacing it." Certainly, Hatton contended, stockmen would understand how it would be more profitable to graze in a manner that preserved the basic forage crop. The figures demonstrated that more profits were to be made by following the suggestions made by the Forest Service in its frequent publications related to "improved methods in range management."[19]

The work of the research offices could demonstrate additional economic results through their program for the identification and eradication of poisonous plants. The market value of one large cow or steer was equal to the cost of hoeing out ten acres of larkspur, about the only method of dealing with the menace other than identifying its presence and keeping stock away from it. Range plant identification was an essential project if knowledge of forage values—their advantages and disadvantages—were to be widely known.

By 1913, *American Forestry* announced that grazing lands studies on the National Forests, as part of a comprehensive plan to determine the grazing value of every acre, had resulted in the collection, identification, and determination of economic value of six thousand specimens of range plants. The studies were to help decide which class of stock was best suited for individual ranges. The work of identification established a uniform collection method. Local forests were directed not to render information on

[18] Barnes to Potter, March 23, 1915, and May 17, 1915, U.S. Forest Service Range Management Office Files; U.S. Forest Service, *Annual Report of the Forester, 1915*, p. 2.

[19] John H. Hatton, "Economic Results of Improved Methods of Grazing" [ca. 1924], Box 5, Fd. 15, Work Projects Administration, History of Grazing Papers.

plants until they had been identified through the Forest Service's Washington office. Plants were to be collected in accordance with instructions in a Forest Service leaflet dated April 5, 1909: *Suggestions for the Collection of Range Plant Specimens on National Forests*. All specimens, it said, were to be collected in triplicate. One was to be retained at the local office and two sent to the district office. From the district office one was retained in the district herbarium and the final one forwarded to Washington for identification.[20]

By 1915 the Forest Service's Office of Grazing Studies became the leading governmental agency in the field of range research. By the time of World War I, the office had attempted to provide some factual and empirical answers in seven general areas where knowledge was needed, if the ranges were to be properly managed:

1. Opening and closing dates for grazing to harmonize range readiness with nutritional requirements of livestock
2. Determining of grazing capacities of western range types
3. The basis of determining whether forage cover and soil were improving or deteriorating
4. Deferred and rotational grazing practices to permit seed maturity and root system growth for the survival of perennials
5. Improved methods of grazing sheep and goats in open and quiet herding; also new procedures for bedding herds in different locations each night
6. Better management of cattle through well-placed watering and salting sources
7. Elimination of damage to timber reproduction from grazing and other forest resources.

Research into outdoor public recreation had not yet begun, but concern for game animals and the impact of domestic grazing on their food resources was already becoming a point of contention between recreationists and the grazing interests.[21]

[20]Jardine and Anderson, *Range Management in the National Forests*, fig. 2; District Forester to Supervisor, Uinta NF, Provo Utah, December 1913, Sec. 63, Region 4, Dr. 87, RG 95, NA; Bodley, "Grazing Reconnaissance on the Coconino National Forest," 77; A. E. Aldous, *Eradicating Tall Larkspur on Cattle Ranges in the National Forests*, Farmers' Bulletin no. 826; "The Forest Service in 1913 and 1914," *American Forestry* 19 (January, 1913): 26.
[21]Chapline, "Range Management History and Philosophy," p. 636; R. S. Campbell, "Milestones in Range Management," *Journal of Range Management* 1 (October, 1948): 6.

In response to numerous studies with controlled experiments and statistical tables, many old range men still insisted that most of these questions had already been met in one way or another through experience and intelligent guessing. Reliance upon the "college boys" and some of their hybrid-research leaders seemed to them a needless expense involving time-consuming procedures and doubtful experiments. Still, in order for its officers in the field to administer with confidence and professionalism, the Forest Service needed to make decisions rooted in information derived from objective, scientific study. Whether these decisions concerned the reduction of stock numbers on the range, when to allow entry in the spring, or where to build watering places for stock, the professional manager could speak much more authoritatively if he could show that "studies have been conducted." On the basis of this research, decisions could be made in the interests of professional management of the forest and its resources. If the administrators of the range were to professionalize themselves and their tasks, they needed a body of knowledge from which they could derive authority.

In the long run, knowledge gained through field investigations would prove more acceptable to the resource users in the stock industry than the mere authority of Forest Service uniforms, laws, or administrative orders issued from Washington. Range science was the unspoken but necessary source of authority for aggressive range-management policies. Until 1927 there were fewer than forty fulltime forest range research and technical workers in the Forest Service in any given year. Range research doubled in the next two years, however, with the passage of the McSweeney-McNary Forest Research Act in 1928, and expanded thereafter to meet needs in the stock industry and public land management.

5

The Challenges of War and Peace

The man who is accorded a privilege of exclusive use of land or
material for commercial profit shall pay the public in proportion to
the value of what he receives.

—*Annual Report of the Forester*, 1916

TEN years after its creation, on the eve of World War I, the Forest Service
could boast of its commitment to the small ranchman and the economic use
of the forage resources. The impending war, however, subordinated these
goals to that of increased stock production. During the 1916 season, stockmen suffered in the West because of a small hay crop and a cold, extended
winter. The bad weather reduced agricultural production throughout North
America, and the war effort rightfully stressed the importance of food production to offset the previous year's bad harvest in both America and
England.

To meet the war emergency the chief forester ordered supervisors to
make available every acre of grazing lands for the greatest possible utilization. The newly formed War Finance Board extended money to local
banks, which, in turn, made loans to stockmen to increase their herds.
Livestock buyers from Chicago sent out information encouraging ranchers
to expand, citing both patriotism and profits. With most ranges already
overstocked, the addition of extra stock under "temporary permit" came
as a staggering blow to conservation efforts on the ranges. In some areas
where ranges were already carrying large numbers, the temptation to expand the permitted stock was resisted. But most forest supervisors accepted the message from the government that "full utilization" was "of extreme prime importance." The following figures show the marked increase
in 1917 and 1918 in the number of stock grazed on the national forests:

	Cattle	Sheep
1916	1,758,764	7,843,205
1917	1,953,198	7,586,034
1918	2,137,854	8,454,240
1919	2,135,527	7,935,174[1]

The war brought a flush of patriotism to forest administrators as they sought to mobilize the resources for the allied cause. Four days after the United States' declaration of war, Regional Forester Ferdinand A. Silcox wrote that the war would probably be the most expensive one in the nation's history, and the Forest Service should insure that no natural resource in the forests should be ignored. Cattlemen should be allowed the privilege of grazing their normal number of cattle in order to utilize the forage that might go unused by homesteaders lacking the capital to place such large numbers into those areas. Other foresters reiterated this desire to graze as many stock as possible, but without sacrificing future range interests. The task challenged forest personnel to supervise the proper distribution of stock and to see that they were confined to such portions of the range during the various seasons as justified by the cycle of forage growth. A plan of "double utilization" emerged for the maximum use of forage. Cattlemen were called upon "to give way" on their present prejudices against sheep and join in a program that would allow both cattle and sheep to use the same ranges.[2]

To increase the number of stock on the reserves, the Forest Service issued a series of permits that, it was stressed, were only a temporary privilege. The service continued, however, to restrict the issuance of grazing permits to aliens. It was policy not to issue new permits to aliens or to

[1] Paul H. Roberts, *Hoof Prints on Forest Ranges: The Early Years of National Forest Range Administration*, p. 121; Leon F. Kneipp, "Land Planning and Acquisition, U.S. Forest Service," Regional Oral History Office, Bancroft Library, University of California, Berkeley, p. 75; A. F. Potter, *National Wool Grower* 7 (May, 1917): 26; Grazing Report, Klamath National Forest (February 8, 1918), Sec. 63, Region 5, Dr. 98, RG 95, NA; U.S. Forest Service, *Annual Report of the Forester, 1917, 1918,* and *1919,* pp. 177–78, p. 187 and p. 192, respectively.

[2] F. A. Silcox to the Forester, April 10, 1917, Sec. 63, Region 1, Dr. 13; L. F. Kneipp to Supervisor, Uinta NF, Provo, Utah, "Permits for 1918," Sec. 63, Region 4, Dr. 87; Smith Riley to Supervisor, Routt NF, Permits for 1918, Sec. 63, Region 2, Dr. 36, RG 95, NA; Will C. Barnes, "The Call: An Echo of the War from Distant Forest Depths," *Breeder's Gazette* 74 (December 19, 1918): 1120, 1165, 1196.

allow increases even when they owned commensurate ranch property and were below the protective limit. It was argued that aliens were not drafted into the army and should not be allowed to compete with citizens for the use of the nation's natural resources. Even aliens who had filed intentions to become citizens were denied permits.[3]

The Forest Service's directives were not met with universal approval; local supervisors as well as regular users were alarmed at policies allowing more stock on some divisions than their estimated grazing capacity. In Montana the emergency increase was accompanied by an abnormally dry season that reduced the forage crop by about 10 percent. At the end of the 1918 grazing season the supervisor of the Helena National Forest reported that the entire war emergency program caused the forest to be grazed too closely, citing as evidence the number of stock forced to leave the forest before the close of the grazing period. The supervisor called for a considerable cut in the allowances for 1919 to prevent permanent damage; the general conditions of the ranges, he believed, were already from 10 to 20 percent below normal. Other supervisors believed that the government had lost sight of the purposes for which the forests were created: "All of these people who have been encouraged to buildup grazing preferences may later seriously interfere with the protective and silvicultural development of the forests," said the supervisor of the Nez Perce National Forest.[4]

Some recreationists also feared the extension of grazing to the national parks in the war crisis. Mrs. John Dickinson Sherman, chairman of the Conservation Department of the General Federation of Women's Clubs, said that if such grazing was permitted, the enemy would have succeeded in destroying some of the natural beauty of the United States. She recalled the fight to save Yosemite National Park from the devastation of sheep and asked for the full use of national forest grazing lands before using national parks. Equating recreation values to wartime necessities, she asserted that the strength of the nation rested largely on the mental attitude of the people. The right mental attitude grew out of wholesome recreation in the outdoors, especially in places of scenic beauty. Grazing in national parks

---

[3] "National Forest Receipts Increase," *National Wool Grower* 7 (August, 1917): 58; Annual Working Plan, 1918, Sopris NF, November 13, 1917, Sec. 63, Dr. 14, RG 95, NA.

[4] John Hatton, "Grazing in National Forests Likely to Be Increased in 1918," *Denver News*, January 1, 1918; Supervisor's Annual Working Plan, grazing chapter, 1917, 1918, Helena NF, and Supervisor to District Forester, "Allowances, Nez Perce NF, 1919," Sec. 63, Region 1, Dr. 13, RG 95, NA.

would discourage such outdoor recreation, she feared. In defense of the parks, Mrs. Sherman concluded, "Such places as national parks help us to maintain our strength and courage and to gain a clearer vision of the problems and emergencies of life." In only a few short years similar arguments would be used in favor of developing the recreational potential of the national forests to the detriment of the grazing interests.[5]

In the years to follow, forest grazing officials would often point to the wartime measures as a significant setback in range resource protection. Many explained the continued deterioration of the range by attributing it to the wartime excesses. Some suggest, however, that the measures were only an acceleration of a process well underway. Grazing figures do show a continued increase in the number of stock in the forests from 1905 (although the additional land added to the system must be taken into account). As one critic wrote: "World War I represents a milestone rather than the conclusive event in the lengthy story of rangeland abuse." Range deterioration occurred with pioneer settlement and continued on into the twentieth century, grazing control programs notwithstanding.

The Department of Agriculture in 1919 made the doubtful claim that national forests produced "material increases" in both meat and wool supplies for the war effort. The department asserted that the number of animals was increased without overgrazing the forests. The conclusion was that under regulation the productivity of the forest ranges was rising and that of the public range outside the forests was deteriorating. The department attempted to justify the wartime effort and the methods of forest range regulation while calling for similar regulations to be extended to the remaining unappropriated public domain. Later assessments of the wartime experience with the range took much the opposite view. They not only criticized the overgrazing during the war, but also refused to accept it as the only reason for deteriorated forest ranges. Overgrazing was a convenient explanation, they contended, used by the Forest Service to explain shortcomings, whereas the real reason probably lay with the hesitancy of the service to exercise its powers to protect the resource against the stock industry. It should be noted that the increased number of stock during World War I and the expenditure of resources did not yield the expected additional

[5] Mrs. John Dickinson Sherman, "National Parks in Danger of Invasion," clipping from a Pennsylvania newspaper, Jan. 10, 1919, Natural Resources and Conservation Section, Denver Public Library.

meat production from the forests. The animals that emerged from some overgrazed forest lands were thin and poorly fed. Not only were the results harmful to the forage resource, but they were also ineffective for stock production.[6] Clearly the wartime policies and their significance were interpreted by the Forest Service, the Department of Agriculture, and future critics of grazing policies to justify their particular viewpoints. Later the Forest Service would use these wartime statistics in both meat and wool production to prevent a similar overuse of the ranges during World War II.[7]

After eighteen months of expansion, the stock industry, like other segments of American agriculture, faced the cruel realities of overinvestment. The markets evaporated and prices fell; only indebtedness and expenses continued. The impact of the postwar agricultural depression from 1919 to 1921 forced many stockmen in both cattle and sheep to sell for whatever price dealers would offer. Many stockmen went bankrupt. For forest officials the end of the war meant enforcing downward adjustments, the end of wartime permits, and increased pressure from stockmen for continued access to cheap grazing lands. The Forest Service opened new forest lands (bought under provisions of the 1911 Weeks Act), in the Appalachians from Pennsylvania to Alabama. Now it had an opportunity to spur progressive methods of handling livestock in the Southeast. Between the years 1923 and 1928, however, the region reported a steady decline in the numbers of cattle and horses under permit:

1923	6,909
1924	5,749
1925	4,508
1926	2,799

Earlier a comparison of the grazing fees on the Shenandoah forest with those charged on privately owned range showed the Forest Service fee to be higher than that charged by the adjacent ranges. This may have contributed, along with the general economic difficulties of the stock industry

[6]Daniel R. Mortensen, "The Deterioration of Forest Grazing Land: A Wider Context for the Effects of World War I," *Journal of Forest History* 22 (October, 1978): 224–25.

[7]U.S. Department of Agriculture, *Yearbook of Agriculture, 1918*, pp. 29–30; W. R. Chapline, "Range Management History and Philosophy," *Journal of Forestry* 49 (September, 1951): 635.

in the 1920s, to the decline in numbers grazed on eastern and southern forests.[8]

Because of the worsening economic picture in the West, many stockmen sold out to larger interests, thus consolidating land holdings and permits. The effects of the war and the following economic crisis crushed many of the smaller operators and those speculators who plunged deeper into the business on the high tide of wartime expansion and demand. The elimination of permit holders did not automatically mean a reduction in the number of animals in the forests. It merely opened the opportunity for the remaining users to request increased protective limits. After the war the service tried to pursue more ardently the anti-alien policies initiated during it. In 1920 it announced that permanent preferences to all noncitizens were revoked. Although temporary permits were issued for 1920 to soften the impact, no permits would be issued to aliens afterwards. In addition, those holding the temporary permits where reductions were ordered had to take the established reduction plus a further one of 20 percent. After 1920, noncitizens would not be considered for permits unless there was clearly an excess of range after satisfying the demands of citizens.[9]

During the war forest officers overlooked some poor methods of handling stock in favor of achieving increased numbers. In the postwar years these officers were directed to enforce regulations more stringently. In a speech delivered in Ogden, Utah, to local officials, Potter emphasized that grazing permittees must be prepared to handle their stock according to the plans which the service had by observation and experiment found to be practicable.[10] The clear message was that the deliberate, "heavy" stocking (forest officials did not use the term *overstocking*) of the ranges now required stockmen to adopt progressive measures in handling their sheep and cattle or face inevitable reductions in many forests. Local forest officials often complained, however, that many of the small stockmen were particularly difficult to convert to progressive methods of handling stock. There-

---

[8] Will C. Barnes, "New Grassland in the Southeast," *Breeder's Gazette* 77 (April 15, 1920): 1–7; Evan W. Kelly to the Forester, May 26, 1928, and Clinton G. Smith to Supervisor, Monongahela NF, February 13, 1922, Sec. 63, Region 7, Dr. 634, RG 95, NA.

[9] *Lake County Examiner* (Lakeview, Oregon), July 29, 1920, pamphlet in Forest History Society files, Santa Cruz, California.

[10] Grazing Report, 1918, Harney NF, Sec. 63, Dr. 29; R. H. Rutledge to Supervisor, Gallatin NF, October, 1919, Sec. 63, Region 1, RG 95, NA.

fore, stringent measures were required to accomplish full utilization of the forage. In one area, the Arapaho National Forest in Colorado, the supervisor announced that if the stockmen refused to comply with instructions, the forest would be opened up to other users who promised more cooperation.[11]

Despite the difficulties with some small stockmen, many forest officials reported that small men realized more than ever before the benefits incurred in the conservative use of the forest range. They believed their survival could be attributed to "the Forest Service's policy of the little man first." In the Missoula National Forest, for example, approximately 80 percent of the stockmen living in or adjacent to the forest were dependent upon forest range. The overcrowded conditions of the range in many instances necessitated rigid application of regulations to avoid disputes among users. Still, complaints were surprisingly few considering the number of permits issued. In the case of disputes, it was believed essential "to build up for the Service a reputation for absolute fairness and impartiality." Permittees were encouraged to come directly to the district supervisor's office to air their problems instead of confronting each other. If the users could be sent away in a friendly state of mind, wrote the supervisor, the way would be paved for more "harmonious future relations . . . the only way to handle a group of users whose individual interest are so often in conflict."[12]

Grazing Fees Again Become an Issue

By 1919 it was estimated that grazing privileges increased the selling price of ranches by as much as one-third; as one supervisor stated: "There is no doubt whatever, that every waiver of grazing preference carries with it in the minds of both seller and buyer, a distinct monetary value." As long as the value was not explicitly stated officials felt that they could not act to revoke privileges because they had been given a value equivalent to property. But the service was fighting a losing battle to keep permits from assuming value in the commercial grazing community. It did not wish to officially recognize their values because the holder might then claim a per-

[11]Annual Grazing Report, 1920, Arapaho NF, December 9, 1919, Sec. 63, Region 2, Dr. 7, RG 95, NA.

[12]John W. Spencer, Annual Working Plan, November 22, 1919, Sec. 63, Region 2, Dr. 12; Supervisor's Annual Working Plan, 1919 (December 1, 1919), grazing chapter, Nez Perce NF, December 1, 1919, and Supervisor's Annual Working Plan, 1919, Missoula NF, December 22, 1919, Sec. 63, Region 1, Drs. 13, 14, RG 95, NA.

manent possessory right over the use of the forest range. If such rights could be claimed, the service would be, in effect, giving away public property.[13]

After favorable court decisions, general and modest fee increases occurred from 1909 to 1912. Substantial increases in the years 1915–16 and 1917–19 raised grazing revenues to about three times the cost of administration. The rates increased to averages of about eleven cents per month for cattle and three cents per month for sheep. Formerly, rates had served more as a symbol of the service's authority over grazing lands than as a source of revenue, although the income was significant.[14]

In 1916, as it imposed a higher rate schedule, the service referred to the possibility of raising rates to a level comparable to the charge for the rental of private grazing lands of similar quality ("comparable value" rates). The 1916 *Annual Report* pointed out that grazing privileges sometimes cost three times as much on private, state, and Indian lands. As the demand for grazing lands increased, it became clear that stockmen using the national forest ranges enjoyed special advantages over those who must pay for range on a competitive basis. The report also acknowledged that values increased in commercial transactions if ranch and stock property enjoyed forest privileges. The Forest Service now indicated a belief that "the man who is accorded a privilege of exclusive use of land or material for commercial profit shall pay the public in proportion to the value of what he receives." During this same year the Forest Service undertook the first comprehensive study to determine fair compensation for range use in comparison with similar private land ranges. As a result, cattle-grazing fees were increased for 1917 by 12 to 20 cents per head; similar increases were ordered for both 1918 and 1919. The minimum of 40 cents per head set in 1915 was raised to 60 cents, and the maximum of $1.50 was continued. Sheep fees were set at one-quarter of these rates. Pressure from Congress for much greater increases soon prompted an even more far-reaching study after the war.[15]

[13] Supervisor's Annual Working Plan, 1919, grazing chapter, Nez Perce NF, Sec. 63, Dr. 13, RG 95, NA.

[14] Jenks Cameron, *The Development of Government Forest Control in the United States* pp. 333–34.

[15] U.S. Forest Service, *Annual Report of the Forester, 1916*, p. 158; "The History of National Forest Grazing Fees," (1939), Sec. 63, Dr. 579, RG 95, NA; W. L. Dutton, "History of Forest Service Grazing Fees," *Journal of Range Management* 6 (November, 1953): 393–98.

In 1919, Congress began pressing for rates to be raised to market rental value; some congressmen muttered about forest ranges being maintained as a subsidy for stockmen. The grazing fees of many forests were barely one-half of what states and private owners asked for similar privileges on their land. It was difficult for local rangers to justify this situation. It was true that stockmen were put to some extra expense in complying with Forest Service regulations, but, as one Montana official argued, better range and grazing conditions offset that expense.[16]

Some cattlemen even admitted to foresters that the fees were "ridiculously small." Low fees caused overgrazing, fencing of the open range as stockmen sought commensurate property to qualify for a forest privilege, and general overall pressure on the forest ranges. Fees charged below reasonable levels became subsidies to the stockmen who were fortunate enough to secure summer range in the forests. By World War I, Congress provided that a percentage of fees collected would be returned to local governments for school and road funds. When the service gave stockmen range below cost, it deprived the general communities of money which should be theirs under the road and school fund provisions. Many ranchers leased their own lands under private contract and then applied for a national forest lease. The low fees promoted instability and constant pressure for more permits. Still, the Forest Service was hesitant to raise the fees dramatically in 1919 because of its having granted five-year permits that very year to stock operators. Although the service generally agreed that fees should be raised to market value for the privilege, it was reluctant to disturb the present agreements with stockmen. It did not wish to be accused of bad faith in extending those agreements. In addition, the service felt that values were too inflated in the West to justify hasty increases. To counter pressure from Congress in 1919 that an immediate 300 percent increase be imposed, the Forest Service proposed a comprehensive study of the range values in western states. The objective of the study would be to determine a fair basis of compensation and method for estimating value. Also, the traditional foresters became alarmed that heavy stocking of the forest ranges threatened the timber resources. The retirement of Potter in 1920 signaled an end to the power within the Forest Service of grazing interests, which Potter had

---

[16]"Purpose of the White River National Forest," (December 20, 1916), p. 6, Region 2, RG 95, Federal Records Center, Denver; Supervisor's Annual Working Plan, 1917, grazing chapter, R. E. Bradley, Gallatin NF, October 31, 1917, Sec. 63, Region 1, Dr. 15, RG 95, NA.

always defended and promoted, and the advance of more conservative forestry practices that saw great danger in ever-increasing numbers of animals in the forests. The conservatives expressed interest in lowering animal numbers, halting the issuance of permits to new grazing applicants, and raising grazing fees. Access to forest grazing resources, especially for the little man, was drawing to a close.[17]

How should range values be determined? Should the fee be tied to the market price of beef and lamb on the hoof or to the fair-market value of land rental, or should it be opened to competitive bidding? Only the largest stock outfits favored competitive bidding. Fair-market value was the Forest Service's choice. After the study, new fees could be put into effect when the five-year permits expired in 1924.

The plan for an appraisal of range values was approved by the secretary of agriculture in November, 1920. Conducted by Christopher E. Rachford of the Grazing Branch, the report undertook to determine the fair market value of the approximately thirty-six thousand grazing allotments on the basis of their accessibility, the quality of their forage, their water resources, the cost of handling livestock, losses in handling livestock, and any other factors that affected the value of the individual grazing allotment. The survey also included a study of rental value of private rangelands near the national forests. Forest Service leadership contended that rental value paid for rangelands in private ownership, fairly compared with national forest rangelands, was the best basis for determining what national forest ranges were worth as rental properties.[18]

Forester Colonel William B. Greeley, testifying before Congress in 1925, suggested that the question of whether forest users should be charged the same for government grazing as the private owner obtained from rental property was probably a separate question from that of the true market value of government grazing lands. Still, whatever fine distinction existed between the two questions, they were closely related. The method by which comparable fees was determined ultimately set a rental figure for

[17] Allowances, 1918, Jefferson NF, Sec. 63, Region 1, Dr. 16, RG 95, NA; Dutton, "History of Forest Service Grazing Fees," p. 394; James T. Jardine, "Efficient Regulation of Grazing in Relation to Timber Production," *Journal of Forestry* 18 (March, 1920): 367–81; Patrick C. West, *Natural Resource Bureaucracy and Rural Poverty: A Study in the Political Sociology of Natural Resources*, p. 57.

[18] William Voigt, Jr., *Public Grazing Lands: Use and Misuse by Industry and Government*, p. 59.

government lands. The real question was: Should stockmen pay comparable rental prices? One of the most telling arguments in favor of this position was that Forest Service range administration provided the benefits of regulation in arbitrating disputes, patrols against rustlers, salting and bull regulations, and rules against itinerant sheep bands, all of which helped to improve the range and grazing conditions. For these services stockmen should be at least required to pay at a rate they would rent similar private lands.[19]

Spokesmen for the stock industry denounced the idea that national forest grazing land was worth as much as grazing on private lands. They believed that the grazing regulations, combined with requirements to help fight forest fires, justified a lower fee than private land rental. An editorial in the *National Wool Grower* reported the dissatisfaction arising from the management of stock according to rules laid down by agencies who had not financial interest in the lands. The editorial stated that the national forests were created solely to conserve timber and protect watershed, not to return revenue to the federal treasury. It pointed out that in 1919, Forest Service income from grazing fees was $2.6 million, while income from timber was only $1.5 million. Instead of raising grazing charges, the government should be looking to raise the prices for timber, it suggested. It further expressed the hope that the remaining public domain would be sold or given away in homesteads so that it could be in private hands, on the tax rolls. The editorial did not, however, suggest the abandonment of the national forest system.[20]

Several reasons emerged for the demand of higher fees. Congressional forces from the Midwest, and the Forest Service itself, were not insisting that public grazing lands make money from grazing, but they charged that as things stood the Forest Service provided a subsidy to western stockmen that midwesterners could not approve. Second, the low rents for the grazing privilege encouraged small stockmen to take homestead lands to make themselves eligible for a permit under class A status, thus increasing the number of permittees in the forests for what amounted to speculative purposes. If property ownership were tied to the permit privilege, the value of

[19] "History of National Forest Grazing Fees" (1939), Sec. 63, Dr. 579, RG 95, NA; Dutton, "History of Forest Service Grazing Fees," p. 394.
[20] *National Wool Grower* 10 (March, 1920): 23.

the stock and the ranch property would increase. This type of speculation would continue unchecked until such time as fees were raised to a point where the grazing privileges were issued at fair-market value, rather than as a gift from the government to stockmen.[21] From the point of view of the Forest Service, increased fees would (1) relieve the service of the charge of subsidizing western stockmen, (2) curb the demand for more permits, and (3) offer greater stability in range management.

The report that Christopher Rachford compiled first sought to survey the value of millions of acres of private land used for stock-grazing purposes throughout the West. The law of supply and demand ruled the rangeland values as stockmen competed from year to year to profit from their operations by estimating possible investment according to projected stock prices. According to the methods outlined by the Rachford team, the prices set for these lands under a free-market system could be taken as true value. Private range values could then be used as a basis for determining the value of national forest range. At the outset of the study it was recognized that only selected parcels of private rangeland comparable to national forest lands should be used in the study. The values were to be calculated on the basis of *average* rental values over a period of years. The study was conducted throughout the western states.

The wide fluctuations in prices for similar rangeland from locality to locality caused Rachford to recommend against basing fees upon strictly local values. Such a policy would have created greater inequalities in fees between forest and individual ranges than even a flat-rate system. The collected data were applied instead to a larger regional area. The regions were designated by similar accessibility, transportation, market, and general range conditions. Sometimes the area included a group of forests such as in the Blue Mountains in Oregon, or an entire state, as in the case of California. In most instances the figures covered a period of ten, and in some, fifteen years. In the process of accumulating the data, conferences were repeatedly held with all supervisors and others in charge of the work. The conferences focused on the available private land data and the "comparative rating" of national forest ranges.

Making adequate comparisons between national forest land and private land demanded standardization of methods. Grazing land was classi-

[21]Charles L. Wood, *The Kansas Beef Industry*, pp. 90–91.

fied as ideal, good, fair, and poor, with a carrying capacity assigned to each class for the four classes of stock—cattle, horses, sheep, and goats. Water availability, topography, accessibility, range improvements, losses of livestock, costs of handling stock on lands, and Forest Service restrictions were also considered in making the comparisons of Forest Service lands with private lands. Users were consulted in nearly four hundred meetings throughout the West. The study eventually yielded a fairly complicated rate schedule that varied from forest to forest. Cattle and horses were given the same rate. Similarly, sheep and goats had an identical rate.[22] Table 6 gives the scale of "appropriate fees" as determined by their range appraisal report.

The new fee structure appeared in the revised range manual of 1924 and was scheduled to take effect on January 1, 1925. But Secretary of Agriculture Henry C. Wallace announced that no increased fees would be imposed until the livestock industry recovered from its depression. In response, Senator Robert N. Stanfield of Oregon launched a hearing by a subcommittee of the Senate Agricultural Committee into the fee system and general administration of rangelands by the national forests. Stanfield represented Oregon stock interests and his own stock business, which had previously clashed with the Forest Service over permits. The committee's investigations began in Washington and moved to locations in the West. From the beginning Stanfield revealed his intention of publicizing dissatisfaction with the service and general users' objections to the Rachford recommendations. Drought and market conditions had devastated many cattlemen. With these problems and a determined western leadership, the Forest Service faced a challenge to its grazing administration similar to the first years of the program. The new challenge was united, determined, and carefully organized by the stock industry.[23]

As the first witness before the committee, Chief Forester Colonel Greeley emphasized the need to raise rates to a commercial level in line with the pricing policies for other forest resources. He could not agree with Senator Stanfield that low rates were acceptable because the ranchers had pioneered the areas and therefore deserved special privileges. At the same time that the secretary of agriculture suspended the implementation of the

[22]C. E. Rachford, "Range Appraisal Report," November 5, 1924, Sec. 63, Box 89, RG 95, NA.
[23]Herbert A. Smith to Pinchot, June 10, 1925, Pinchot Papers, Box 2844, Library of Congress, Washington, D.C.

TABLE 6. Recommended Scale of Appropriate Fees per Head per Month, 1924.

	Cows and Horses		Sheep and Goats	
	Max.	Min.	Max.	Min.
District 1				
Absaroka	$0.30	$0.10	$0.08	$0.02
Beartooth	.30	.12	.08	.02
Beaverhead	.30	.12	.07	.02
Bitterroot	.30	.08	.06	.01
Blackfoot	.20	.08	.04	.01
Cabinet	.30	.10	.05	.01
Clearwater	.20	.08	.05	.01
Coeur d'Alene	.25	.03	.04	.01
Custer	.20	.10	.04	.01
Deerlodge	.35	.05	.10	.02
Flathead	.20	.08	.05	.01
Gallatin	.35	.15	.08	.03
Helena	.35	.15	.10	.04
Jefferson	.30	.14	.08	.03
Kaniksu	.30	.05	.03	.01
Kootenai	.20	.08	.04	.01
Lewis and Clark	.35	.14	.08	.02
Lolo	.15	.08	.04	.01
Madison	.35	.14	.09	.04
Missoula	.30	.08	.06	.02
Nezperce	.30	.03	.09	.02
Pend Oreille	.30	.15	.04	.01
Saint Joe	.20	.14	.04	.01
Selway	.12	.05	.06	.01
District 2				
Arapahoe	$0.27	$0.21	$0.08	$0.075
Bighorn	.29	.25	.08	.07
Blackhills	.19	.15	.055	.045
Cochetopa	.25	.13	.07	.04
Colorado	.27	.23	.075	.07
Grand Mesa	.20	.18	.08	.07
Gunnison	.27	.19	.08	.07
Harney	.18	.15	.055	.045
Hayden	.28	.26	.08	.07
Holy Cross	.27	.23	.075	.07
Leadville	.27	.21	.08	.07
Medicine Bow	.27	.23	.08	.07
Montezuma	.28	.20	.08	.065

TABLE 6. Continued.

	Cows and Horses		Sheep and Goats	
	Max.	Min.	Max.	Min.
Nebraska	.12	.11	—	—
Pike	.27	.18	.08	.07
Rio Grande	.27	.24	.08	.07
Routt	.28	.18	.08	.07
San Isabel	.27	.16	.06	.05
San Juan	.29	.25	.08	.07
Shoshone	.27	.22	.08	.07
Uncompahgre	.27	.19	.07	.04
Washakie	.25	.12	.07	.04
White River	.28	.14	.075	.065
District 3*				
Apache	$1.81	$0.32	$0.045	$0.03
Carson	1.56	.84	.0375	.02
Coconino	2.18	.29	.0475	.01
Coronado	1.89	.36	—	—
Crook	1.76	.38	.03	.0125
Datil	1.63	.31	.035	.02
Gila	1.76	.34	.0325	.01
Lincoln	1.74	.40	.0325	.01
Manzano	2.21	.25	.0425	.0125
Prescott	1.88	.51	.0475	.02
Santa Fe	1.44	.84	.0325	.02
Sitgreaves	1.57	.49	.0375	.0175
Tonto	1.65	.54	.0375	.035
Tusayan	1.88	.43	.0375	.01
District 4				
Ashley	$0.27	$0.24	$0.055	$0.055
Boise	.18	.16	.0475	.045
Bridger	.17	.17	.035	.035
Cache	.27	.19	.0575	.04
Caribou	.23	.18	.055	.0525
Challis	.17	.10	.04	.025
Dixie	.37	.32	.085	.08
Fillmore	.35	.19	.08	.06
Fishlake	.37	.16	.08	.0525
Humboldt	.18	.17	.0575	.055
Idaho	.18	.09	.045	.02
Kaibab	.25	.10	.06	.025

TABLE 6. Continued.

	Cows and Horses		Sheep and Goats	
	Max.	Min.	Max.	Min.
La Sal	.29	.25	.0775	.045
Lemhi	.17	.15	.045	.04
Manti	.24	.22	.085	.085
Minidoka	.21	.17	.0575	.055
Nevada	.16	.12	.05	.0375
Payette	.16	.10	.0475	.035
Powell	.34	.19	.075	.0725
Salmon	.16	.06	.05	.015
Sawtooth	.20	.18	.05	.045
Targhee	.26	.16	.055	.0325
Teton	.17	.17	—	—
Toyiabe	.15	.10	.05	.05
Uinta	.36	.30	.0825	.07
Wasatch	.37	.29	.0625	.055
Weiser	.18	.18	.0475	.0475
Wyoming	.19	.18	.045	.045
District 5				
Angeles	$0.29	$0.25	$0.095	$0.09
California	.30	.27	.10	.09
Cleveland	.28	.27	.0925	.09
Eldorado	.32	.27	.105	.095
Inyo	.31	.24	.1025	.09
Klamath	.30	.23	.10	.085
Lassen	.31	.25	.105	.095
Modoc	.31	.25	.10	.095
Mono	.32	.24	.1175	.085
Plumas	.31	.26	.195	.095
Santa Barbara	.30	.28	.10	.095
Sequoia	.31	.21	.105	.075
Shasta	.31	.26	.10	.095
Sierra	.31	.21	.0975	.07
Stanislau	.31	.25	.11	.09
Tahoe	.31	.26	.105	.095
Trinity	.31	.34	.105	.08
District 6				
Cascade	$0.23	$0.22	$0.065	$0.06
Chelan	.19	.12	.06	.05
Columbia	.20	.15	.075	.06

TABLE 6. Continued.

	Cows and Horses		Sheep and Goats	
	Max.	Min.	Max.	Min.
Colville	.20	.17	.03	.02
Crater	.30	.16	.0725	.05
Deschutes	.18	.11	.0675	.01
Fremont	.29	.20	.075	.06
Malheur	.27	.25	.12	.08
Mt. Baker	.20	.19	.03	.02
Mt. Hood	.27	.20	.075	.05
Ochoco	.27	.15	.12	.07
Olympic	.20	.19	.03	.02
Rainier	.20	.11	.075	.06
Santiam	.23	.22	.065	.06
Siskiyou	.23	.09	.075	.04
Siuslaw	.23	.09	.075	.04
Snoqualmie	.20	.19	.03	.02
Umatilla	.27	.17	.12	.08
Umpqua	.23	.22	.075	.01
Wallowa	.27	.20	.12	.08
Wenatchee	.20	.17	.075	.06
Whitman	.27	.21	.12	.06

SOURCE: U.S. Congress, Senate, *Hearings Pursuant to S. Res. No. 347*, 69th Cong., 1st sess., 1926, pt. 1, vol. 246, pp. 31–32.
*Cattle fees per head per year; sheep fees per head per month.

higher fees, he authorized lower rates on allotments where the report found rates higher than comparable private rental. Colonel Greeley estimated a loss of revenue from this decision at almost $150,000 in 1926 alone. He complained that when the service appealed to stock organizations for help in determining the accuracy of range reappraisal figures, it received only objections to the principle of the increase.[24]

By the mid-1920s, in spite of the uproar over fee increases, stockmen

[24]Cameron, *Development of Government Forest Control*, p. 339; "The History of National Forest Grazing Fees" (1939), Sec. 63, Dr. 579, RG 95, NA; Dutton, "History of Forest Service Grazing Fees," p. 394; U.S. Congress, Senate, Committee on Public Lands and Surveys, *Hearing Pursuant to S. Res. No. 347*, 69th Cong., 1st sess., 1926, part 1, vol. 246, p. 100.

obtained either lower fees or a continuation of their past "reasonable fees." In addition, the Forest Service put into effect ten-year permits to stabilize the grazing business on the national forests. For the moment, primarily because of the ongoing Stanfield investigations, the stock industry seemed to have won everything it demanded from the keepers of the forest range: low fees, long-term permits on designated areas that could be fenced, and a curb on distribution to make room for new applicants. Some ranchers obtained "exemption limits" that exempted them from reductions if their operations were totally devoted to stockraising. Some large ranchers received non-use permits allowing them to graze less than their permit stated without losing the right to the larger number. The ten-year permits did contain the proviso, however, that the secretary of agriculture could make a new determination of the fee schedule in 1927. Understandably the Department of Agriculture moved cautiously in the face of the outcries from the stock industry and a move on the part of Senator Stanfield to curb the authority of the Forest Service over grazing administration. While the secretary of agriculture agreed to yet another fee study, the service had to muster strength against westerners like Senator Stanfield and others who planned bills to give local stock associations authority over forest range matters. Ultimately the bills sought private property rights on the ranges.

At the suggestion of the Forest Service, Secretary William Jardine agreed to appoint an independent investigator to study the Rachford fee recommendations. Dan D. Casement, a well-known stock buyer from Manhattan, Kansas, was appointed to review the Rachford findings and report his conclusions by the end of 1926. Although the Casement review was perhaps not welcomed by strong advocates of increased fees within the service, it was hoped that a new study from a representative of the stock industry would serve to quiet protests against the increased fees that most likely would be ordered in 1927. Still the question of how increased fees could contribute to the stability of the range persisted. As it maintained in recommending a review of the Rachford fees, the Forest Service was committed to no set schedule of fees but only to stability of the industry.

The illusory goal of stability was reinforced with long-term permits, but a central cause of the range instability was the possibility of ever-increasing demands by property owners for forest permits. The 1920 *Yearbook of Agriculture* posed the questions: "How can stability be reconciled with further development? And how can we be fair to those already in the business while giving a square deal to new men equally entitled to the benefits of the public resource?"[25]

From the regional offices came letters expressing uncertainty about how much consideration to give to increased numbers of class A applicants. As the public range was homesteaded under the Stockmen's Homestead Bill of 1916, the smaller land owners who had traditionally used this range turned to the forests for grazing privilege. These new demands were made at the expense of the B permits of longstanding preference. The new arrivals were also in a position to take advantage of the range improvements made over the years by the B permittees. It distressed forest administrators to disturb these longtime users of the forest to accommodate new demands from small users who, on the average, applied only for ten head of stock but probably intended to run more than authorized.[26]

Will C. Barnes spoke to these problems on January 19, 1921, in an address before the National Wool Growers' Association in Salt Lake City. The audience, composed mainly of large sheep owners, were concerned with the Forest Service's attitude toward the demands of small owners for more permits and the general lowering of the protective limits. Barnes acknowledged that many small farmers requested permits for only twenty sheep. "I know this looks like small business to many of you larger owners," said Barnes, "but it is a condition—not a theory—which we are studying." The overall reductions made on larger users to accommodate these men were critical to those who were in the "sheep business as a business by itself." Still, Barnes maintained that the small farmer should be given every opportunity to have an additional source of income to his little farm: "I am sure we would be going against the general public sentiment in this matter if we refused to recognize the claims of these men." Then he added doubtfully, ". . . up to a certain limit." The Forest Service would make a judgment on what constituted a reasonable number of stock for any one man to operate. This judgment would also take into consideration whether the applicants wanted privileges for legitimate grazing purposes or speculative purposes to enhance the sale of property.

[25] West, *Natural Resource Bureaucracy*, pp. 59–65; Subcommittee on Public Lands and Surveys, *Hearing Pursuant to S. Res. No. 347*, pp. 156–57; U.S. Forest Service, *Annual Report of the Forester, 1922*, p. 28; *Yearbook of Agriculture, 1920*, p. 319.

[26] C. C. Reid to District Forester, January 2, 1920, Colville NF, Sec. 63, Region 6, Dr. 111; Tahoe NF, Annual Grazing Report, 1921, Tahoe NF, Sec. 63, Region 5, Dr. 113, RG 95, NA.

Barnes admitted that the service found it easier to deal with a few large permittees grazing the maximum number of stock each rather than a larger number of small permittees. Grazing administrators in the Forest Service found large users enforced more supervision over their stock, obeyed regulations more willingly, "and in every way [made] ideal users of National Forest range." Barnes admitted that field men administering grazing policy saw the impracticality of a continued policy of reductions on larger operations to accommodate newcomers. The Forest Service would suffer an economic loss in further and smaller subdivisions of grazing preferences. To honor every request for a grazing privilege on the basis of adjacent land ownership would create instability and chaos in forest grazing administration and an uneconomical use of the ranges.

Stockmen, too, held strong opinions about redistribution. Richard Dillon, a representative of the Colorado Stock Growers' Association, asserted that once a forage resource had been leased in connection with commensurate and dependent ranch property, it passed from any power of further redistribution by the federal government. Only when a higher and more valuable economic use could be demonstrated, were grazing rights to be amended. Later, in an article lambasting Chief Forester Greeley, Dillon declared, "Redistribution of grazing rights is pure socialism." [27]

By moving in the direction of commercial rates for grazing privileges, higher costs could discourage pressure for increased use by more permittees. The fees themselves could work against a social policy that had become burdensome and downright uneconomical. But some large users also objected vociferously to increases, failing to see that they might ultimately lead to stability and reduced demand from small users. In reaction to the proposals of the Rachford report, the National Wool Growers' Association in late 1923 approved the following resolution: "That we are unalterably opposed to the plan of commercializing the public domain lying within the National Forest. That it is un-American in principle and contrary to the long-established policy of our government. That it is unnecessary to make profits out of the necessity of the frontiersman." [28]

[27] Will C. Barnes, "Sheepmen on the National Forests," *National Wool Grower* 2 (February, 1921): 22, 33; Richard Dillon, "Comes Now the Plaintiff," *The Producer* 5 (April, 1924): 5–9; Richard Dillon, "Policy of Peasantry," *Saturday Evening Post*, June 19, 1926, pp. 58, 60.

[28] "Higher Grazing Fees Result of Re-Appraisal," *The National Wool Grower* 13 (November, 1923), pp. 13–15.

Clearly larger users wanted protection from further reductions caused primarily by new landowners, but not in the form of higher grazing fees. They wished for a simple reversal of longstanding forest policy on this issue. They could not speak too loudly for this position, because it would appear that they stood only for the monopolization of the grazing lands by the large interests. Their cause would be popular neither in Congress nor among the growing recreation forces who viewed grazing suspiciously and as a threat to plentiful game, camping areas, and summer homes in the forest. By 1920 it was announced that the service would not authorize local forests to pay for advertising to notify the public of the availability of grazing permits. The grazing program, it was hoped, would assume a lower profile in forest affairs.[29]

Unfortunately the controversy over fees brought the grazing issue to the forefront of public affairs. Congress introduced bills to give stockmen more authority over their allotments and curb the management powers of the service. The most threatening bill was the so-called Stanfield Grazing Bill introduced by Senator Stanfield in January of 1926 after extensive subcommittee hearings throughout the West in the spring and fall of 1925. The committee was the same one that had conducted the famous Teapot Dome investigations, which exposed the scandal surrounding Secretary of the Interior Albert Fall and his dealings with William Dohoney of Sinclair Oil Company.[30]

The intent of the committee very early in its hearings appeared to be to indict Forest Service policies. Prior to its arrival in a community, Senate members of the committee solicited citizens to testify against increased fees and protest arbitrary acts upon the part of forest officers. From his position in Washington, Assistant Forester Barnes noted that the committee was giving Greeley "merry Hades" in the Southwest. Barnes claimed that Senators Ashurst and Cameron deliberately insulted him at a banquet in Phoenix. In the local Arizona newspapers Senator Ashurst denounced the system of departmental government, and said the Forest Service was an example of bureaucracy run wild. Some of the southwestern press reacted against the committee's attack on the Forest Service: "The senator (Ashurst) knows just as well as do the general run of sheep and cattlemen that

<hr>

[29] NA, RG 95, Sec. 63, Region 2, Dr. 28, A. S. Peck, District Forester to Supervisor Cochetopa NF.
[30] *Miami Evening Bulletin* (Arizona), June 8, 1925; *New York Times*, August 9, 1925.

the greatest disaster that could happen to the stock industry would be the throwing open of all national forests as free public grazing grounds to all comers."

The Eastern conservationist press also struck back at the publicity generated by the committee against the Forest Service and accusations by Senator Rufus King of Utah that federal ownership of the public lands was comparable to the dead hand of the Church in the Middle Ages.[31] The *New York Times* called for the attacks to be checked and referred to western senators as resisting the "march of civilization, which has overrun the prairies and the ranges and is now invading the forests."[32] "Civilization," for the *Times*, meant ordered, regulated, and efficient use of resources with the recognition that the forest should also include recreational uses.

The *Saturday Evening Post* included an article by Chief Forester Greeley, who referred to the handful of stockmen and their leaders who were attacking the basic policy that governed the forest ranges. He condemned the demand by stockmen that grazing rights be confirmed by laws as an attempt to secure special privilege for a few users who would then have the right to sell these privileges at high prices. Greeley pointed out that the Department of Agriculture had always recognized the rights of prior users of grazing lands. "It has never, however," he declared, "been able to sanction the claim to a vested right of property interest in the forage. On the contrary, it has regarded that conception as absolutely inimical to the principles of conservation."[33]

In reply to some of Greeley's statements, the editor of *The Producer: The National Livestock Monthly*, ran a letter from E. L. Potter, a professor of animal husbandry at Oregon Agricultural College, who charged that despite Greeley's defense of the Forest Service's attempts to keep the forests open to new graziers, the service was doing everything in its power to prevent the dividing up of the ranges among homesteaders and other newcomers. He said Greeley wanted to exclude those stockmen who demonstrated no ability to handle stock properly and who could not stay in the business profitably. He deplored the attack of the chief forester on the stock

[31] Barnes to Philip Wells, June 1925, Pinchot Papers, Box 2875; *Arizona Republican*, June 11, 1925; *Albuquerque Morning Journal*, October 3, 1925.

[32] *New York Times*, August 28, 1925.

[33] William B. Greeley, "The Stockmen and the National Forests," *Saturday Evening Post*, November 14, 1925, pp. 10–11, 80, 82, 84. George F. Authier, "Both Sides of the Range Controversy," *American Forests and Forest Life* 31 (December, 1925): 715–17.

industry and especially his "misrepresentation" of the service's policies and actions.[34]

While the outspoken debate over the purposes of the committee surfaced in the eastern and western press, Senator Stanfield became involved in political trouble in his home state of Oregon. His difficulty did not grow out of his aggressive stand against the Forest Service and public grazing policies, but over an incident in Baker, Oregon, that resulted in his arrest for drunkenness and disorderly conduct. Those events occurred in September, 1925, at a time when Stanfield's name was much in the news concerning his committee's activities. This incident doubtlessly contributed to Stanfield's defeat in the primary election the following April and probably served to discredit his proposals in Congress to curtail Forest Service authority over grazing matters.

In the meantime, Stanfield continued his attacks on federal land ownership, declaring that the federal government had confiscated the public lands. Stanfield maintained that the federal government's only function in land policy was to hold the public lands in trust for the states. "I admit," he said, "that the government should have the administering of the lands, but it should be for the benefit of the states."[35] Stanfield was especially critical of the conservationist publication *American Forests and Forest Life*, claiming it to be nothing more than the "mouthpiece of Mr. Greeley."

Although the methods of the committee might be termed heavy-handed, many western stockmen believed that the hearings and especially the work of Senators Stanfield, Oddie, and Cameron forced important concessions on policies and fees from Chief Forester Greeley.[36] On January 22, 1926, the Department of Agriculture issued the memo "New Grazing Regulations on National Forests." The regulations made three significant concessions to stockmen. First, the previously authorized ten-year permit assumed the full status of a contract between the stockmen and the Forest Service. It could only be revoked because of violation of terms. Second,

[34] E. L. Potter, "Takes Issue with Colonel Greeley," *The Producer* 7 (December, 1925): 17–18.

[35] *Baker Herald* (Oregon), September 14, 16, 1925; *Portland Oregonian*, September 22, 1925; *Baker Democrat* (Oregon), December 4, 1925.

[36] Tasker L. Oddie to William Blattner of Winnemucca, Nev., August 10, 1925, and Vernon Metcalf, Secretary, The Nevada Land and Livestock Association to Oddie, March 27, 1926, Tasker L. Oddie Papers, NC-6, Nevada Historical Society, Reno.

although individual grazing allotments and further distribution of grazing allotments were encouraged, further distribution of grazing privileges was generally suspended. Distribution was to be kept to a minimum, particularly in regions where it might harm the most economical production of livestock and use of ranch lands dependent upon national forest ranges. Third, the department reemphasized the role of local grazing boards. These boards could represent a single national forest or a group of national forests, with one member representing the Department of Agriculture and other members selected by grazing permittees. Their primary purpose was to settle grazing disputes either among permittees or between a permittee and the Forest Service. In addition, the boards' advice would be consulted, in developing grazing policies. The forest supervisor's decisions would prevail still over the board's, but these decisions might now be appealed within the Forest Service and to the secretary of agriculture himself.

To explain these new regulations, the service sent carefully worded letters to senators and congressmen from the western grazing states. Acting Forester Leon F. Kneipp explained that under the new regulations the term permits issued in 1924 would be far less subject to reductions; in some areas where it was deemed uneconomical, reductions would be completely abandoned. Reductions would not be carried out where they would seriously affect the operations of established permittees without accomplishing any great amount of good. In addition, new and stricter standards for commensurate property would come into effect to make it more difficult to obtain class A permits. In the case of the sale of ranch or stock property the old instructions had provided that a 10-percent reduction in permits would be made in sales of both the ranch and its stock (20 percent when either ranch property or stock was sold). The new instructions made reductions subject to the judgment of the forest supervisor, with surplus numbers to be applied to class A permits. The revised regulations spelled out the desirability of establishing individual allotments with designated boundaries wherever conditions allowed.[37]

Despite these policy concessions to users, Senator Stanfield introduced a comprehensive grazing bill in late January, 1926, to force the Forest Service into full retreat on its grazing policies. Under the new bill, the permit agreements would not only assume the status of term contracts, as

[37] Leon P. Kneipp to Oddie, February 8, 1926, Oddie Papers.

the Forest Service had already conceded, but also acknowledge the stock-man's vested right in the grazing lands used under the permit. This recognition would remove the ever-present threat of permit revocation by the service. By recognizing a vested right, the bill, in effect, gave away government property to the stockmen. In addition, under the Stanfield bill the advisory boards would establish grazing policies and be under control of local stockmen. Final authority would not rest with the secretary of agriculture, but with local boards.[38] The bill also authorized the creation of grazing districts within the public domain under the control of local users instead of the Department of Agriculture.

To prevent passage of the Stanfield bill, Colonel Greeley and the Forest Service formulated a new bill that was introduced through Senator George Norris of Nebraska (S. 3698). It incorporated many of the features of the Stanfield bill by recognizing grazing as a function of the forest resources and extending semicontractual rights to the ten-year permits. The bill also endorsed the principle of reasonable charges on a stable basis to protect stockmen from a strictly commercial charge or one based on competitive bidding. This bill completely placated the western senators; in fact, it became known as the Greeley-Stanfield bill. It appeared that Greeley had caved in to most of the demands of the industry in return for the recognition of the legitimate retention and administration of forest grazing lands by the Forest Service. Conservationists were assured, however, that although grazing was recognized, grazing was to be considered subordinate to the development and utilization of other resources such as timber and water.[39]

Greeley hoped that the new bill would "head off" attempts to eliminate grazing from the forests. He recalled that following the Pinchot-Ballinger controversy, millions of acres of grazing lands had been eliminated from the national forests and placed in the unregulated public domain on the grounds that the service had no specific lawful authority to administer grazing lands. This occurred under an agreement between the

---

[38] F. A. Phillips and W. A. Stewart of the Cattle and Horse Raisers' Association of Oregon to Stanfield, January 18, 1926, Oddie Papers; Robert N. Stanfield, "The Rights of the Shepherds: Definite Status for Public Land Grazing Vital to Prosperity of West," *National Spectator*, April 10, 1926, pp. 3–4.

[39] Stanfield, "Rights of the Shepherd," p. 4; "The Grazer and the Government," *Outlook* 142 (April 14, 1926): 556–57; Tom Gill, "Stanfield Grazing Bill Is Dehorned," *American Forests and Forest Life* 32 (April, 1926): 203–204.

secretaries of the interior and agriculture. It was precisely this type of future attack on the forests that Greeley hoped to avoid in the new bill's recognition that grazing administration was an official duty of the Forest Service on the national forest lands.[40]

Not everyone welcomed the Greeley bill, however. Gifford Pinchot considered the Greeley bill a terrible mistake: "It imperils the principle of the highest use, in the long run, for all national forest lands." He warned that the bill undercut the preference for the homesteader and small ranchman in the forests and laid "a foundation for reducing grazing fees under political pressure."[41]

Pinchot's remarks echoed the sentiments of Phillip Wells, one-time chief law officer in the Forest Service under Pinchot. A memorandum from Wells charged that the Greeley bill would establish what amounted to grazing easements in the national forests and abandon the preference of the independent small rancher in maintaining his home and working his land and stock himself, "which in the past made the Forest Service a shining example in the dispensing of social justice." Wells claimed the bill enthroned organized stockmen in a place of power that belonged to the Forest Service as the representative of all the people and the steward of the people's property.[42] Wells moved to have Senator Norris of Nebraska introduce another bill, S. 3885. Under the new Norris bill, fees were to be established by the secretary based on the "prospective value of the forage." The measure safeguarded the forests along strong conservation lines and defined at some length the position of grazing as an activity on the national forests.

The second Norris bill was not considered before the adjournment of the congressional session by June 1. After all the public display both in the West and in Washington, no legislation would be forthcoming from Congress to significantly alter the Forest Service's grazing administration. The greatest changes came in the "New Grazing Regulations" issued by the Forest Service in January, but even these did not address the smoldering issue of fees that had sparked all of the congressional interest in the grazing question in the first place.[43]

[40] W. B. Greeley to S. T. Dana, December 27, 1926, Pinchot papers, Box 2875; "Grazing," *Outlook* 94 (February 12, 1910): 321–22.

[41] Pinchot to Potter, May 6, 1926, Pinchot Papers, Box 2875.

[42] Memorandum on Greeley's Bill, April 1, 1926, Pinchot Papers, Box 2875.

[43] Will C. Barnes, "Grazing Legislation," *Service Bulletin* 10 (April 26, 1926): 7; Pinchot to Henry S. Graves, June 8, 1926, Pinchot Papers, Sec. 4, Box 261.

The Impact of the Casement Report

The release of Dan Casement's report came in late 1926. Although Casement was closely associated with the livestock industry, he condemned neither the Rachford report nor the Forest Service. He did, however, recommend a general reduction averaging 25 percent from the increased rates proposed by the Rachford study. The downward revision was necessary because grazing land values had fallen. Casement believed that commercial rates were ultimately desirable and that these levels could be achieved over a four-year period beginning in 1927. He foresaw gradual increases, compared to the sudden increases of the Rachford study, as necessary to achieve the commercial level. An editorial in *American Forests and Forest Life* proclaimed that the report left little to be said in defense of the claims asserted by powerful stockmen: "Whatever glory certain western stockmen may . . . have gathered to themselves from their unsuccessful attempt last winter to foist upon the American public specious grazing legislation will be abruptly dimmed by the report of Dan D. Casement." [44] Casement was critical of the Grazing Homestead and Forest Homestead acts, as both pieces of legislation had failed to benefit settlers and made more difficult the administration of national forests. He reported: "Only in very exceptional instances has it benefited the true home-seeker even in the slightest degree, while it has seriously hampered the operations of establshed permittees on the forest and has heavily handicapped the work of the Forest Service in handling the grazing problem." He also directed criticism at the conduct of stockmen during the recent committee investigations:

I think it exceedingly unfortunate that the stockmen of the West permitted the presentation of such unrepresentative and extravagant demands relative to forest grazing as were submitted to the Senate Subcommittee on Public Lands at Salt Lake last year. This ill-advised action was harmful to their own interests, since it quite excusably aroused the resentment and protest of that part of the public most intent on safeguarding the principles of conservation. It is in my opinion equally to be regretted that the prevailing tone of the record of the subcommittee's hearings held last summer throughout the West is so severely critical of the Forest Service. Plainly the permittee with a grievance against the Service received greater consideration and a more sympathetic hearing from the committee as a whole than were accorded the great majority of forest-users who entertained and, in a few instances only, read into the record favorable and far more representative views. In consequence, the hearings appeared to be directed toward a destructive rather than a constructive pur-

[44] "The Casement Report," *American Forests and Forest Life* 32 (December, 1926):

pose; and this, I think, was clearly reflected in the forest section of the original Stanfield bill, which was the outgrowth of them.

Casement supported the view that the low fees charged in the past gave advantage to permittees over those not holding the privilege. Those not using the forest system outnumbered permittees by three to one or more. Many permittees asserted that this advantage was neutralized by handicaps placed upon them in the use of the forests. Casement did not accept this argument, saying that because no protests had been voiced by the unpermitted stockmen it had little real bearing on the case. What he did believe was relevant to the case was the rising demand for permits at the prevailing low rates. Demand exceeded the availability of forage. These circumstances complicated administration and menaced the user "with the dreaded threat of distribution." This danger, he acknowledged, was to a large extent eliminated through the longterm permits now issued by the Forest Service.

Casement's recommendations for increased fees had as their ultimate purpose greater stability in the industry, and the early termination of the period of uncertainty and transition from which it has long suffered. In his opinion the acceptance of the increased fees by the industry might, in the long run, promote a lower cost of grazing on the forests. With the additional income from fees, Congress might be more easily persuaded to make appropriations for range improvements: "More fences and water development would contribute largely to the proper conservation of the forests, to their greater usefulness, to the profits of the permittee, and to government revenues derived from grazing." He believed permittees would cheerfully pay increased fees if they could be assured that those fees would go to range improvements. From this standpoint, opposition to increased fees was "an absurd and short-sighted policy." After recommending that the revised rates be placed in effect gradually over a period of four years, from 1927 through 1930, he suggested that in the subsequent years fees for forest grazing be related to prices paid for products of the ranges and "vary from year to year proportionately therewith." Casement concluded that he believed his plan offered represented a permanent settlement of the fee question and efficient use of the forest forage resources.[45]

743–44; Report by Dan D. Casement to the Secretary of Agriculture, June 30, 1926, Sec. 63, Dr. 144, RG 95, NA.

[45] "The Casement Report," *The Producer* 8 (December, 1926): 9–12.

Even after the general settlement of the fee issue with the presentation and adoption of the Casement report in 1926, the service continued to face many of the complaints about the administration of the grazing lands that surfaced in the recent Senate hearings. Nevada stockmen, for example, forced a restudy of rates in their state beyond the Casement report and extracted from the secretary of agriculture a further rate compromise.[46] Assistant Forester Barnes now referred to Regulation G-8, which was adopted for the purpose of giving the district forester authority to meet special conditions where the distribution of grazing privileges had reached a point beyond which it would be uneconomical to continue. He emphasized to district foresters, "It is quite true that stability in range allotment will often preclude the possibility of the admission of new owners, and it is difficult if not impossible to assemble small areas of range into new allotments." He said that number of stock should be made to conform to the allotment rather than vice versa. Too often in the past, Barnes maintained, allotments had been expanded arbitrarily in carrying capacity to conform to increased numbers to be grazed upon them. Barnes remained adamantly opposed to enforcing reductions on permittees while at the same time approving new applicants.[47]

In these last years of Barnes's administration, many changes were taking place within the Forest Service. The suggestion was made that the Branch of Grazing be called the Branch of Range Management, just as the Branch of Silviculture had recently become the Branch of Forest Management. More important changes occurred in the conduct of field work. During the past season of 1926 the "volume-palatability" plan, a more sophisticated method of determining range capacity, had been developed and tried in some of the western districts. It was the intention of the service to apply this method in grazing survey on national forest ranges as rapidly as practicable.[48]

In the past the problems in range reconnaissance occurred among common users, dual use, and the assumption that a forage acre was a definite standard of measurement for forage comparable to the board foot as

[46]Rachford to R. R. Hill, Forest Service, Ogden, Utah, June 4, 1928, Sec. 63, Dr. 632, RG 95, NA.
[47]Forester to Region 6, March 20, 1926, Sec. 63, Dr. 632; Barnes to Sen. Carl Hayden, November 17, 1927, Sec. 53, Dr. 71, RG 95, NA.
[48]Barnes "Memorandum for the Forester," January 6, 1927, Sec. 63, G-Supervision Meetings 1926–31, Dr. 98, RG 95, NA.

a measurement of lumber. Charles De Moisy, range administrator in the Intermountain Region, outlined these problems in a paper presented to the Society of American Foresters, Intermountain Section, at Ogden, Utah, on January 1, 1927. His presentation was a general attack on the achievements and accuracy of the early range surveys and the grazing plans that grew out of them. In the early reconnaissance efforts, a forage species was considered either 100 percent palatable or unpalatable to stock. New research showed that 10 to 25 percent of the annual production of palatable species should be left at the end of the grazing season. Defenders of the earlier reconnaissances, such as W. R. Chapline, maintained that they provided for the protection of a percentage of a species by the end of the grazing season and that De Moisy was completely off base in his criticism of grazing plans based on the early range surveys.

Range reconnaissance (the terms *reconnaissance* and *survey* were interchangable) by itself, contended De Moisy, would not show the way to proper range administration. For example, early reconnaissance failed to indicate a proper carrying capacity. The old carrying capacity figures of 0.8 and 0.3 head per month for cattle and sheep, respectively, were dropped or used guardedly as average requirements of stock. Carrying capacity was something that could only be determined by local field tests and observations over a period of time. It was now believed that much effort had been wasted in the past by employing inexperienced men to conduct range surveys. De Moisy called for more emphasis upon studying the history of an allotment in the assessment of a range condition to learn condition over a long period of time rather than the plant data from only one season.[49]

The entire range reconnaissance question was brought before a large service meeting on February 3, 1927. At that meeting it was declared: "We cannot meet our bare responsibilities as administrators of these forest resources; we cannot face the future with its demand for a more satisfactory fulfillment of our trust, unless we secure . . . data, develop plans based upon them, and make them effective." Arguments against range reconnaissance maintained that it was difficult to measure benefits derived equal to the investment in the undertaking. But arguments in favor of the reconnaissance contended it was not in the immediate returns that the value of the

---

[49] Charles De Moisy, "The Value of Range Reconnaissance in Grazing Administration," presented at meeting of Intermountain Section, Society of American Foresters, Ogden, Utah, January 1, 1927, Sec. 63, Range Surveys 1926–28, Dr. 51, RG 95, NA.

project should be measured. For example, the influence of erosion upon the productivity of the soil one hundred years from now and the effect of properly regulated grazing upon erosion was cited. A charge of two cents per acre or an amount slightly in excess of one year's grazing fees, which is the average cost of reconnaissance, does not seem an excessive price to pay for efficient plans of management," concluded the meeting.

Most importantly, the reconnaissance provided a valuable training ground for grazing officers in bringing them into contact with all range management problems. It compelled them to study plants, their values, and factors affecting their growth and demanded them to study practical methods of handling all classes of livestock on the range and to consider all the uses of forest resources related to grazing.[50] Chief of Grazing Research Chapline claimed that practically every leader of range management at that time owed an essential part of his training to grazing reconnaissance. He pointed out that there were no schools to give thorough training in range management, and until this situation corrected itself the Forest Service must train personnel in the actual work of reconnaissance.[51]

Another problem facing the Forest Service was wild horses that trespassed in the national forests. Stockmen were coming to realize that it was in their interests to get rid of worthless horses because they were using resources needed to produce high-priced beef and lamb. All forest officers carried guns and used them against the horses whenever possible. The entire Kaibab forest in Arizona was declared closed to the grazing of horses by the secretary of agriculture in order to eliminate wild horses. Unfortunately, during 1927 summer rains filled small tanks practically all over the range, enabling the horses to remain away from established water places where they were usually killed.[52]

Stability in the range stock industry could not be achieved without an adequate assessment of the resource, fees to insure efficient use, and the elimination of range competitors such as wild horses and rodent populations. To achieve these goals the research arm of the Forest Service worked

[50] Discussion of the Reconnaissance Question before the Large Service Meeting, February 3, 1927, R. R. Hill, Inspector of Grazing, Washington, D.C., Sec. 63, Range Survey 1926–28, Dr. 51, RG 95, NA.

[51] Statement by W. R. Chapline, Service Committee Meeting, February 3, 1927, Sec. 63, Range Surveys 1926–28, Dr. 51, RG 95, NA.

[52] Annual Grazing Report, 1927, Kaibab NF, December 21, 1927, Sec. 63, G-Management, Region 3, Dr. 618, RG 95, NA.

in several directions. In 1925, range research was consolidated into the service's Branch of Research under direction of Earle H. Clapp. In 1928, Congress enacted the McSweeney-McNary Forest Research Act. Although most of the original money went to fire and timber research, by 1929 Congress added $14,320 for range research. This amount, plus an additional thirty thousand dollars for soil erosion work, was a significant increase to the regular appropriation for range research. The act provided for gradual increases in all classes of forest research, including range research, each year.[53]

Another longstanding concern of the Forest Service was the problem of watershed, now popularized under the more alarming title of "soil erosion." In a widely circulated article presented at a symposium of soil erosion at the meeting of the American Society of Agronomy on November 23, 1928, Chapline outlined the fight against this problem on the rangelands of the Forest Service. Chapline noted the good work conducted at the Great Basin Experiment Station in Utah and the vital role that plant cover played in preventing erosion. But he concluded that, in general, "the range erosion research of the Forest Service has been confined largely to laying a foundation of basic and general information." The effort needed to be broadly accelerated to determine just what was the optimum stand of vegetation to resist soil erosion in the varying soil types and under the extreme climatic conditions of the West. Also to be determined was how much grazing could be allowed on each of the principal range types to assure profitable livestock production and maximum protection of the soil. Soil erosion was a question of regional and even national importance. It was a rallying point to request more funds for research from Congress during the late 1920s and especially the 1930s because of the Great Depression, drought, and Dust Bowl conditions in the West.[54]

The Hoover Years

In 1928 Herbert Hoover was elected to the presidency. The Forest Service hoped that Hoover's belief in the application of science, expert knowl-

[53] U.S. Department of Agriculture, "Forest Service to Enlarge Its Research Program," (news release), March 28, 1929.

[54] W. R. Chapline, "Erosion on Range Land," *Journal of the American Society of Agronomy* 21 (April 1929): 423–29; H. H. Bennett and W. R. Chapline, *Soil Erosion: A National Menace*, USDA Circular no. 33; W. R. Chapline, "Water Protection on Cattle Ranges,"

edge, engineer's viewpoint, and principles of business efficiency would direct the energies of government to serve the many and complex requirements of a highly organized modern world. Instead, Hoover proved disappointing. He seemed to draw back in apprehension at the "Frankenstein—just because he sees how great the field and requirements are." The president proclaimed a need to preserve individualism, initiative, and freedom of opportunity for business to carry on as a vital force in working out the economic progress and salvation of the nation. He appeared to want every agency to decentralize. This philosophy portended problems for an agency such as the Forest Service, whose function was national in scope although much of its administration appeared to be decentralized.

Hoover's views were popular. Assistant Forester Herbert A. Smith recognized that the word *bureaucracy* was being used increasingly to conjure visions of governmental goblins and to "hoodwink the crowd." He wrote, "You don't have to prove your point any longer, if you use it—just say it, and your case is won." The occasion for these bitter words about the Hoover administration was the announcement by Secretary of the Interior Lyman Wilbur that the Hoover administration favored state ownership of the unappropriated public domain and possibly of the national forests.[55]

The Forest Service was always sensitive regarding the disposition of the remaining public domain, particularly the grazing lands. Shortly after the service assumed administration of the forests, Senator Elmer J. Burkett of Nebraska introduced a bill to transfer the remaining public grazing lands to the administration of the Forest Service. Pinchot and other conservationists of the time supported the bill, but it failed passage, as did similar measures in later years. By 1928, Pinchot advised the Forest Service officials to take a more aggressive stand on the issue of the public range outside of the forest lands and to call for public regulation of these lands. Otherwise the Forest Service might suffer at the hands of the new administration, which was unsympathetic with conservation goals.[56]

Another former chief denounced the president's plan to give the public lands to the states. Colonel Graves believed that giving the lands to the states would result in virtual monopolization of the range in many places. The president's position disturbed Graves because his words implied that

---

The Producer 9 (December, 1927): 3–6; Chapline interview with author, Reno, Nevada, March, 1980.

   [55]Herbert A. Smith to Henry S. Graves, September 11, 1929, Pinchot Papers, Box 2844.

   [56]Herbert A. Smith to Henry S. Graves, December 1, 1928, Pinchot Papers, Box 2844.

the government had failed to administer the public lands effectively and therefore must give these lands to the state with the expectation that more effective conservation would take place. "This is like the argument in the old public land days," he said, "that the forests should be turned over to private individuals because the Government was incompetent to handle them properly." The reason, Graves charged, for any failure was in the incompetence of the Interior Department. His real belief, of course, was that the lands should have been turned over to the Department of Agriculture for administration through the Forest Service long ago. It was now, of course, too late for this, and the service must ride out the storm and possible threat of losing some of its lands under the Hoover administration.[57]

Pinchot feared that the administration was about to wreck the entire system of national conservation established by Theodore Roosevelt. Not surprisingly, the Hoover Commission on the Public Lands recommended the transfer of the public lands to the states, but the states refused the lands because of the cost of administration to their depression-struck economies and because the offer did not include mineral rights.[58]

The Forest Service's future under the Hoover administration looked dim and unexciting. Barnes, who was about to retire, wrote his old friend Potter that the work in the office was now tiresome, involving "a deadly round of ordinary administrative matters." He felt the old days were best, with "something doing every minute." He would not be sorry to be out of it. In looking back on some of the major questions of the decade, such as the fee issue, Barnes wagered, "I'm betting the income won't be ten cents more than it would have been had Greeley let the whole thing alone to work out as we had been doing." Barnes was especially proud of the congressional bill, for which he could claim responsibility, to purchase a small herd of Texas long-horned cattle of the Spanish breed. Both Barnes and W. A. Hatton gathered animals from Texas that were finally taken to the Wichita National Forest in Oklahoma so that future generations of Americans could observe this progenitor of the modern cattle industry.[59] But now Barnes would not be sorry to retire.

Just as the Forest Service's future, and especially its long-term pro-

[57] Henry S. Graves To Herbert A. Smith, September 9, 1929, Pinchot Papers, Box 2844.

[58] Pinchot to Herbert A. Smith, September 14, 1929, Pinchot Papers, Box 2844.

[59] Barnes to Potter, January 9, 1929, U.S. Forest Service, Range Management Office files, Arlington, Va.; Will C. Barnes, letter in *American Forests and Forest Life* 33 (March, 1927): 171.

grams of range administration, did not appear bright in 1929, neither did the predicted prosperity of the stock industry. Like agriculture in general, it had suffered throughout the twenties from a continuing decline in prices and rising costs of production. Hoover's beliefs and program had been based upon an unswerving belief and faith in the private economy and creativeness of the individual working for his own welfare in a free economy, but the failure of that economy in 1929 snuffed out Hoover's vision. The administration's drive to extend public-land resources to the states and eventually to individuals stalled. The argument was that these resources would be used creatively, but others charged this would lead to monopoly of resource use by the few. A new decade, far different from what Hoover foresaw, would challenge the collective talents of Americans and expand the services of the federal government in all areas, including resource protection.

6

Lost Opportunities in the Depression Decade

> There is perhaps no darker chapter nor greater tragedy in the history
> of land occupancy and use in the United States than the story of the
> western range.
>
> —*A Report on the Western Range*, 1936

FOREST SERVICE grazing administration faced new challenges during the nationwide depression of the 1930s. Throughout the 1920s the private economy had squeezed both stock and crop agriculture to the point that many marginal and small outfits left the enterprise. Unfortunately the private economy did not move fast enough in that direction for the general health of the industry. When the service implemented competitive-value fees and other such policies, it was, in effect, calling for a reduction in the number of users—not simply for the good of the ranges or for more efficient administration, but for the purpose of reducing the number of competitors participating in an industry overpopulated with producers. The American dream of unlimited agricultural expansion was a doomed vision in the actual operation of the private economy. In many instances the market was not returning to the producer even his cost of production of farm and range products.

Fewer producers, of course, meant an accelerated trend toward large enterprise and ultimately monopoly. Much government effort had already been expended to prevent such a result. But even large enterprises were not immune to the dangers that their own efficiency posed. The New Deal administrator and theorist Rexford Tugwell wrote as early as 1928 that efficiency in American agriculture "digs its own grave." Increased production merely brought lower prices on the market for agriculture.[1]

---

[1] Rexford G. Tugwell, "Reflections on Farm Relief," *Political Science Quarterly* 43 (December, 1928): 491–97.

If the late 1920s brought a malaise in the administration of grazing policies and a fearful attitude toward the political power of the users, the 1930s offered prospects for revitalization. As Forester Robert Y. Stuart reported in 1930, "Times of depression bring out the value of the national-forest range, with its assured stability and encouragement for the grower through efficient management to offset low prices." Other sources spoke of the stabilizing nucleus that the forest ranges provided for the livestock industry in the western range States.[2]

The 1930 *Annual Report of the Forester* revealed that the policies of distribution of grazing privileges to smaller owners had not really been carried out to any great extent. The average number of cattle per permittee in 1929 was 70, and of sheep, 1,023. In 1912 the average number of cattle per permittee was 71, just one more than in 1929, and sheep 1,421, or 398 more than in 1929. The depression from 1919 to 1922 set the sheep industry back, but there were still over 1,200 more permittees grazing sheep in the national forests in 1929 than in 1912. Many cattle raisers had changed to sheep as a method of combatting falling prices. The number of large owners in both sheep and cattle in 1929 was practically the same as in 1912, with a small decrease in the average number of stock per permit. For all permits covering over 200 cattle, the number of permits averaged 524 in 1912, as against 445 in 1929. In 1912, the average number of sheep permits covering over 2,500 head was 4,812, and for 1929, 4,575. In 1912, 93 percent of the cattle permittees grazed under 200 head each, and 87 percent of the sheep permittees grazed under 2,500 head each. In 1929 the corresponding percentages were, for cattle, unchanged; for sheep, 91 percent. In 1912, the cattle permittees with over 200 head grazed 50 percent of all the permitted cattle; in 1929, 47 percent. In 1912, the sheep permittees with over 2,500 head grazed 44 percent of all the permitted sheep; in 1929, 38 percent. From these figures the forester concluded that "while the trend has been toward a wider distribution of the grazing privilege and a decreasing proportion of range use by large owners, the change over a considerable period of years has been such as to indicate a high degree of conservatism in the procedure and stability for the industry, not violent or drastic disturbances."[3]

[2]U.S. Forest Service, *Annual Report of the Forester, 1930*, p. 36; J. W. Nelson, "National Forests and the Livestock Industry," *Western Cattle Markets and News* December 15, 1930, p. 29.

[3]Forest Service, *Annual Report of the Forester, 1930*, p. 39.

Few industries, however, could escape the economic debacle of the Depression. Many range management policies underwent reexamination and in some cases rejuvenation. Distribution briefly appealed to the social welfare thrust of the New Deal and its rhetoric about preserving the small farmer. The still-present fee issue prompted reexamination and a retreat from full implementation of the competitive rates. The Roosevelt administration would give new life to range-survey work and related soil-erosion assessments by emphasizing land planning for the future.

Land-use planning was advocated by Department of Agriculture officials like M. L. Wilson and even by the 1933 Copeland report. Begun in 1932 under Chief Forester Stuart and directed by Earle Clapp, this mammoth, 1,687-page report emerged as the New Deal's plan for foresery in the 1930s. It expressed the vigor and vitality of the early New Deal years and recognized the principle of multiple use. Tasks of rehabilitating the range and reversing soil erosion loomed large. The report urged that grazing be made compatible with the dominant uses of timber production and watershed protection that had always commanded the center stage of forestry efforts. The pressing issue of fees still faced the Forest Service as the economic outlook grew darker in 1931 and 1932 for western ranchers.[4]

The Roosevelt Administration

In 1932 the reins of government were turned over to the Democratic party and the leadership of the affable Franklin Delano Roosevelt. As presidential candidate, Roosevelt committed neither himself nor his party to fixed formulas for solving the problems of the Depression. It soon became evident, however, that the federal government would have to become an active agent in the business of bringing relief to areas hardest hit by the Depression. In areas of extreme agricultural distress, militant farm leaders had declared a "farm holiday," which meant that the farmers would not deliver their products to market until fair prices were paid. They demanded at least cost of production plus a fair profit. In some states farmers blockaded highways and dumped perishable products onto the roadside to prevent delivery to markets. The most immediate response by the Forest Service to aid stockmen was a one-half reduction in fees for 1932 and a

[4] Harold K. Steen, *The U.S. Forest Service: A History*, pp. 204–205.

deferment of payment until the end of the season rather than requiring it at the beginning.

The combination of drought and low prices brought recommendations from some of the regional offices by early February, 1932, that fees be halved. They warned that the position of the Forest Service would be untenable if this relief were not granted. The service would be seen as the villain extracting its "pound of flesh" at a time when the stock industry had been driven to its knees by hard times. "It is more than a matter of mathematics. It is one of intensely important human relations," wrote one regional forester. Most foresters did not suggest that the basic fees or computation be altered, only that they be temporarily cancelled to meet the emergency.[5]

In 1932 the Department of Agriculture announced the hoped-for one-half reduction in fees. The basic change in the schedule tied fee prices to fluctuation in livestock prices. The average national forest grazing fees, of 14.5 cents per head per month for cattle and 4.5 cents per head per month for sheep, were to be used as the basic fees. Each year, the basic fees would be subject to adjustment in accord with fluctuations in livestock prices. The adjusted fees each year would have the same ratio to the basic fees that the average price received by producers in the eleven western states during the immediately preceding year had to the corresponding average price during the period 1921–30, inclusive, in the case of cattle, and during the period 1920–32, inclusive, in the case of sheep. For cattle in 1933 the new ruling meant a fee 37.6 percent lower than the appraisal rates agreed upon in 1927. For sheep in 1933 the average fee was 54 percent lower than would have been charged under the old appraisal rates. The chief forester was also authorized to make adjustments necessary to establish equitable fees between allotments, forests, regions, or states.

The study admitted that, "No usable means of determining directly the value of forage in terms of livestock market prices had been devised." It was still maintained that the best and most direct index of the value of forage on national forests was the price which stockmen paid for forage on comparable privately owned lands. Rental values of private lands reflected price levels received for the commodities produced on the lands but lagged behind the changes in livestock prices. By correlating the grazing fees as determined from the forage values on leased private lands with the average prices received for livestock over a representative period of years, a basis was provided for determining a working relationship between current fees and current livestock prices.

The recognition of the principle of "the ability to pay" was a major departure from the previous view that if the producer could not pay, he should not remain in business. Perhaps this was the most pronounced social-welfare gesture of the New Deal toward the range users in the forests. The plan would be applied broadly, and the fees could not be subject to problems of individuals or localities.[6]

Although Rachford had long been a champion of fair-market value in setting fee rates, he rejected suggestions that charges for ranges be placed on a competitive basis, especially in these times of economic hardship. The effect of this practice would be to substitute local stockmen with dependent property for other owners who "because they [were] better fixed financially or [had] more credit [could] outbid the present permittees." These new owners might be absentee landlords with great resources located long distances from the forests. If local stockmen were excluded from the forest range, their property would depreciate in value and in some cases be abandoned as virtually unsalable. It was the permitted access to forest ranges that gave value to small range properties which were held primarily to meet the commensurate property qualifications.[7] The Depression era's concern with "ability to pay" was more in keeping with the earlier social policies of the service.

The Depression, thus, gave the Forest Service agencies opportunities to expand upon their original missions. One task pursued more aggressively was land use planning or, as the New Dealers preferred to say, "land utilization." With the creation of the Soil Erosion Service in the Department of the Interior in 1930, a foundation was laid for land-classification projects that eventually sought to restrict the use of land for certain types of agricultural enterprise. The work of the Soil Erosion Service, which was transferred to the Department of Agriculture in 1935, aided the Forest Service in its land classification work and supported its efforts to close lands to grazing because of the threat of soil erosion.[8]

[6] "The Forest Grazing Fee Case," *National Wool Grower* 21 (October, 1931): 6–7; Forest Service, *Annual Report of the Forester, 1933.*

[7] C. E. Rachford to R. B. Beckman, Denton, Montana, May 5, 1933, Sec. 63, Dr. 37, RG 95, NA.

[8] John M. Gau and Leon O. Wolcott, *Public Administration and the United States Department of Agriculture*, pp. 135–37

In 1934, Congressman Edward T. Taylor of Colorado introduced a bill to extend grazing regulations to the public lands under a Division of Grazing in the Department of the Interior. Despite its experience, the Forest Service was not the designated heir to these lands for a number of reasons: (1) the stock industry's resentment of the service and its policies; (2) the desire to have the new agency more under the control of stockmen; (3) the desire of the Interior Department for greater authority; and (4) the continuing lack of any explicitly stated lawful authority for the Forest Service to administer range resources. Although the last reason could have been easily remedied by Congress, the Department of Agriculture agreed that chances for the bill's passage depended upon keeping the Forest Service removed from the administration of the lands.[9]

Some administrative features from the Forest Service were included in the Taylor bill, but far more decision-making power rested with local advisory boards in the grazing districts. The Department of the Interior established these grazing districts and issued the permits for their use. Preference was extended to established stockmen, land owners, settlers, and owners of waters. Mindful of the past hazards encountered by the Forest Service and eager to win the good favor of stockmen, the Department of the Interior determined not to base grazing fees on their economic value. They would be based on cost of administration. Administration was supposed to be decentralized, not concentrated in Washington, as many believed was the case with the Forest Service.

Under the Taylor Grazing Act, advisory boards had more authority, and membership was elected by permittees. The Grazing Service was to draw its personnel not from the universities, but from men with range experience. According to an amendment in 1936, officials had to have been residents for at least a year of the public land states in which they were employed. Forest Service grazing men had traditionally taken pride in their professional training, although they often received ridicule for being mere college boys.[10] Now stockmen filled the ranks of the new Grazing Service.[11] The Forest Service had little contact with the men in the Department

[9]Paul W. Gates and Robert W. Swenson, *The History of Public Land Law Development,* p. 611; "A New Deal for the Public Domain," *Pacific Rural Press,* 127 (April 17, 1934): 319; Richard Polenberg, *Reorganizing Roosevelt's Government: The Controversy over Executive Reorganization, 1936–1939,* p. 101.

[10]Gates and Swenson, *History of Public Land Law Development,* p. 614.

[11]Wesley Calef, *Private Grazing and Public Lands: Studies of the Local Management of the Taylor Act,* p. 56.

of the Interior who were developing plans to administer the Grazing Division.

In 1924 the Forest Service had yielded to the demands of users for long-term permits in the interest of stability in the grazing community. When Chief Forester Silcox refused to renew these ten-year permits in 1934, users protested, fearing radical changes in grazing policies. The Forest Service was accused of contributing to greater chaos in an industry already disrupted by drought and depression. Many felt this refusal portended a more vigorous distribution policy against the older and larger users, perhaps even eventual elimination of grazing from the national forests.

A conference of large stockmen in Washington, D.C., in early March, 1936, pressed for three concessions from the Forest Service: (1) extension of the ten-year permits; (2) protection from reduction, especially for distribution purposes; and (3) demand for vested property rights in the allotments. "Behind this movement, of course," reported Rachford, "was the strategy of playing the Interior Department against the Forest Service." [12]

The Forest Service responded quickly. It contended that the long-term permit prevented the rapid adjustment of grazing numbers needed to meet conditions created by drought.[23] Silcox also reminded the stockmen that the number of small operators outside the forest equaled the present number of persons and firms having permits. Therefore, large operators must be called upon to relinquish some of the privileges they enjoyed. In addition, the Forest Service was working with state planning boards to determine the role of the national forests in the interest of community and national welfare. All of these considerations required flexibility in forest administration that made inadvisable an extension of the ten-year permits. Therefore, at the beginning of 1935 Silcox proposed that the years 1935 to 1939 be considered as a readjustment period and that permits be issued only for 1935.[13]

In February, 1936, the chief forester outlined a more conciliatory policy. The ten-year permits would be issued, despite previous indications to the contrary. Reductions, however, could be made up to 30 percent, or 15 percent in any one year, for the period from 1935 to 1940. After 1940, re-

[12]C. E. Rachford, Memorandum to Hammatt, March 6, 1936, Sec. 63, Dr. 98, RG 95, NA.

[13]F. E. Silcox, "Forest Grazing Policies for the Future," *National Wool Grower* 25 (February, 1935): 23.

ductions for protection could be made in term permits as the circumstances justified. Provisions were also made for reductions for distribution, but a reduction for distribution could not exceed 5 percent in any one year. Clearly the Forest Service made a concession in granting ten-year permits through 1945, but it built in provisions for protective and distributive reductions. Distribution, however, had the last priority. Silcox said he could not freeze grazing privileges to present permittees or to specific range property forever, but he could fix the privileges on "a fairly permanent basis for a specified period of reasonable duration." [14]

Additional rulings were made regarding the size of future permits. A lower limit fixed the number of livestock up to which grazing preferences could be consolidated through the purchase of a permittee's livestock or ranch property, or both, and below which no adjustment would be made for distribution except in case of transfer. The upper limit allowed a degree of consolidation in the interest of economy and efficiency of operation. Ideally it was placed at or near the upper level of operating efficiency. Finally a special limit could be applied to an individual preference which was above the locally fixed upper limit and which, in the judgment of the regional forester, would be protected against adjustments for distribution.[15]

Stockmen correctly saw the new policy as a victory. It offered protection from arbitrary reduction. The program set for each permit a minimum number (not below an "economic size") and a maximum number. In no case could the stockmen be cut below the minimum and in good years the maximum would be allowed. The greatest victory, of course, was the provision that these limits could not be changed for ten years.[16]

The extension of the ten-year permits caused dismay in conservationist circles. To many it appeared that Silcox had given way to pressures from the livestock industry, because in 1935 he had talked seriously of offering only five-year permits. On the other hand, it may have been a shrewd administrative move to enter into long-term administrative agreements with stockmen as a means of improving the Forest Service's image among users at a time when a new competitor in grazing administration entered onto the western range scene. An extremely restrictive policy involving

[14] F. E. Silcox, "Grazing Policies for Ten Years," *National Wool Grower*, 26 (March, 1936): 6.

[15] W. L. Dutton, "Introductory Statement Opening Discussion of the Distribution Topic at the Ogden Policy Conference," May 22, 1944, Sec. 63, Dr. 60, RG 95, NA.

[16] Clel Georgetta, *Golden Fleece*, p. 185.

temporary yearly permits, and reductions for protection and distribution might provoke a reaction against the service that would only fuel Secretary of the Interior Harold L. Ickes's drive to transfer at least the Forest Service ranges to the Department of the Interior. Clearly the large stock organizations gave every indication of supporting a bill to transfer the entire Forest Service to a new Department of Conservation. The concessions made by the service in 1936 to the stock industry appear to be made in response to this threat. Until World War II the industry used the transfer issue to keep the Forest Service grazing policies in line with its point of view.[17]

Those involved in professional range management generally believed that the Taylor Grazing Act raised more questions than it answered. Associate Forester Earle Clapp declared shortly after its passage that the range question would again be an important issue in the next Congress. Perhaps this was one reason why Clapp threw himself so earnestly into supervising the production of *A Report on the Western Range* (to be known as the "*Green Book*"), a compilation of thirty-five studies by range experts in the Forest Service and the Department of Agriculture. In the major general finding of the report, he declared: "There is perhaps no darker chapter nor greater tragedy in the history of land occupancy and use in the United States than the story of the western range."[18]

In *The Western Range* Clapp emphasized the need for further legislation to place the public domain under effective management. The essential measures he saw needed were (1) equitable distribution of grazing privileges, (2) reductions to bring down the numbers of stock on the range (which he declared was overstocked by 43 percent), (3) consolidation of the range administration—both in the national forests and in the unreserved portions of the public domain—under one federal department, (4) avoidance of any move by users to establish prescriptive or property rights to the range, and (5) revision of the grazing act "in the public interest" to prevent a conflict between federal and state authority.

One of Clapp's strongest assertions was an estimate that fifty years of

[17]Silcox, "Forest Grazing Policies for the Future," *National Wool Grower* 25 (February, 1935): 47; Patrick C. West, *Natural Resource Bureaucracy and Rural Poverty: A Study in the Political Sociology of Natural Resources*, pp. 80–83.

[18]U.S. Congress, Senate, *A Report on the Western Range: A Great but Neglected Natural Resource*, 74th Cong., 2d sess., 1936, S. Doc. 199, p. 3; Elwood R. Maunder, *Dr. Richard E. McArdle: An Interview with the Former Chief, U.S. Forest Service, 1952–1962*, pp. 205–209.

careful range management would be necessary to build the range up to the point where it would safely carry the livestock then being grazed. Clapp implied that the proper place in which to conduct range studies and land classification work was not in Interior, but in the Department of Agriculture, which he believed had more experience and a superior record in the use and conservation of land. The report said that the Department of Agriculture should be called upon to classify the rangelands not only for suitability for private ownership, but also for the size of the units required for economic success.[19]

These statements represent a heightened proprietorial attitude on the part of the Forest Service. The agency's accumulated experience as a public land administrator and the crisis of the depression and drought enhanced the paternal role of many government agencies, making such a role more acceptable to Congress and the general public. The administrative actions became more bold than they had been in the previous decade, in which bureaucratic power was the frequent object of public resentment and ridicule.

From the field came criticism of the new grazing administration of the public domain. A growing number of stockmen believed the Forest Service more dependable and its policies open and clear-cut. They believed that "It knows its mind and that it moves and does things." There was a growing feeling among stockmen that the new Grazing Bureau had offered only unredeemed promises "and cock-sure statements that in due time prove to be pretty much hollow shells and delays."[20] Rumors circulated that Grazing Bureau administration would fall by default to the Forest Service.

In the meantime, *The Western Range* received much criticism. In the year following its publication critics termed it a propaganda document excessively praising Forest Service range administration and an example of the "sour grapes" attitude resulting from being passed over in the assignment of public range administration.[21]

Subsequent depreciations of the report were attempts by later writers to convey the impression that (1) the Forest Service spent a great deal of energy self-righteously criticizing the work of other land agencies in the

[19]U.S. Congress, Senate, *The Western Range*, pp. 3, 55.
[20]Evan W. Kelley to Earle H. Clapp, May 15, 1936, Sec. 63, Office of the Chief, Dr. 26, RG 95, NA.
[21]Gates and Swenson, *History of Public Land Law Development*, p. 615.

government, and (2) although the service had been an early advocate of land management, its accomplishments in range management were probably overrated. The secretary of the American National Livestock Association, F. E. Mollin, attacked *The Western Range* as a "self-serving compilation of falsehoods" with one goal in mind: extension of the Forest Service bureaucracy over the public range. He contended that the condition of the ranges stemmed from the drought, and no amount of Forest Service ameliorative administration could restore the range without the healing gift of rains, a frequent but thoroughly discredited claim of stockmen.[22] The highly respected William R. Chapline, one of the architects of the study, denied bias in it and saw it focusing primarily on private rangelands.

Clarence L. Forsling, who became chief of Forest Service research in 1937 and headed the Grazing Service from 1944 to 1946, acknowledged that one of the purposes of the report, other than showing the condition of the western range, was to point out the inadequacies of the Taylor Grazing Act as an instrument of administration. Time, he believed, had sustained that judgment. Nevertheless, some embarrassment over the report occurred within the Forest Service. Walt L. Dutton, who spent much of his career in the national forests of the Pacific Northwest Region as a range specialist and forest supervisor before he became head of the Range Management Division in Washington, D.C., charged that the report was full of inaccuracies. The evidence was manipulated, he said, to show a greater contrast between national forest ranges and the unreserved and unregulated public domain than was actually the case. There was no question, Dutton conceded, that the public domain stood in disrepair, but he emphasized that national forest ranges were certainly no shining example of successful protective administration, either.[23]

The Western Range remained a controversial document; it illustrated the growing vigor of the Department of Agriculture during a tumultuous decade of proliferating social and economic assistance programs. Secretary Wallace said the report was inspired by a desire and need to rehabilitate western agriculture and conserve natural resources. Solving the range problem, asserted Wallace, would make an important contribution to so-

---

[22] F. E. Mollin, *If and When It Rains: The Stockman's View of the Range Question.*

[23] Clarence L. Forsling to Frank J. Harmon, July 30, 1975, and Walt F. Dutton to Frank J. Harmon, August 30, 1975, History Section, U.S. Forest Service, Washington, D.C., Office (hereafter cited as FS, WO).

cial, economic, and human welfare. The entire problem, he said, demanded public action for its solution since public neglect had in the past been partially responsible for its creation.

Whatever the strengths of *The Western Range*, it only increased tensions between the Departments of Agriculture and the Interior. Shortly after his appointment, Ickes hoped to bring the national forests back into Interior. Until World War II, he tried to convince Congress and the president to establish a Department of Conservation that would take over many of the functions of the Department of Agriculture.[24] Ickes maintained that natural resource administration should be concentrated in one department. *The Western Range* may have been a necessary defensive tactic on the part of Agriculture to keep the national forest ranges under its control, free from the growing power of Ickes. The Forest Service's range policies not only had to hold many traditional user-group "enemies" at bay, but also had to be on guard against an "enemy" from within the ranks of the Washington bureaucracy. These combined forces served to sap the energy of the Forest Service and even diminished the aggressiveness of its enforcement of range regulations. This abatement was somewhat surprising in a decade that saw such growth of federal government power and influence.

Some conservationists and retired Forest Service personnel maintained that the effectiveness of national forest grazing policies declined in the years of administrative controversy following the publication of *The Western Range*. One survey showed that the fear of the Grazing Service and the Interior Department influenced the Forest Service to go slow in stopping destructive grazing on the ranges in the 1930s. One request for admission of a new grazier was met with an answer by the regional forester that there was no room for new permittees "unless his neighbors provide[d] it by voluntarily reducing their herds."

Apparently voluntary reduction was the only type of distribution that some foresters intended to suggest despite an official policy of "distribution reductions." One forest supervisor even believed it dangerous to make a public announcement of such a policy.[25] Still, the director of the

---

[24]Gates and Swenson, *History of Public Land Law Development*, p. 615; Harold L. Ickes, *The Secret Diary of Harold L. Ickes*, vol. III, p. 21; Allen J. Soffar, "Differing Views on the Gospel of Efficiency: Conservation Controversies between Agriculture and Interior, 1898–1938" (Ph.D. diss., Texas Tech University, 1974), pp. 392–94.

[25]Memorandum to Mr. Granger, May 31, 1939, from Supervisor, Coconino NF, Re-

Division of Range Management from 1936 to 1953, Walt L. Dutton, re-called that the chief foresters under whom he served—Silcox, Clapp, and Watts—supported programs of wider distribution. In the end, however, their policy failed because of resistance from livestock organizations, per-mittees, Forest Service field personnel, and even the secretary of agricul-ture. In 1951, Secretary of Agriculture Charles F. Brannan ordered Chief Forester Lyle Watts to remove the distribution requirement from Forest Service grazing policies.[26]

In 1936, the Forest Service began a "Distribution Policy Survey" of its regions. The survey covered the general economic situation, the range situation, the basis for the distribution policies and need for wider distri-bution. The position of the government was to allow citizens, by their in-dustry and managerial skills, to increase their holdings beyond subsistence levels. This distribution of grazing privileges, should allow a unit to in-crease to its maximum efficiency level, while warning that "beyond that point it should not yield to the device of citizens to monopolize the use of public resources."[27]

The Distribution Policy Survey revealed that seven percent of the cattle permittees who held permits for more than 200 head controlled 44 percent of the permitted cattle. Their average permit was for 425 head. The 38 percent of sheep permittees who held permits for more than 1,000 head controlled 79 percent of the permitted sheep, and their average per-mit was for 2,231 head. Only 4 percent of the sheep permittees held per-mits for numbers in excess of 4,000 head, but their average permit was for 6,647 head and they controlled 22 percent of the permitted sheep. Clearly, a small group was being allowed to obtain more than a proportionate share of range use. While this did not appear to be consistent with the accepted social policy, it was evident that applied distribution was destructive to lo-cal economic welfare and was being rejected by local forest officials.

An economic analysis determined that two hundred head of cattle or one thousand sheep "as the sole source of income" could provide only a reasonably satisfactory family income. In some cases, the reductions made

---

gion 3, Sec. 63, Dr. 643; Evan W. Kelley to Sen. Burton K. Wheeler, May 31, 1939, Sec. 63, Dr. 579, RG 95, NA.

[26] Walt F. Dutton to Frank J. Harmon, August 30, 1975, History Section, FS, WO.

[27] Distribution Policy Survey (November 30, 1936), Acc. No. 59A1532, Box 64, Wash-ington National Records Center, Suitland, Md. (hereafter cited as WNRC).

in the larger permits to admit new applicants caused livestock numbers per operation to fall below the number required to support a family. The result was a destabilization of local communities. The conclusions of the study were decidedly against further distribution except when transfer of permits occurred. Any surplus range which became available was to be used first for range protection; second, to increase the permits of small qualified users; and third, to admit new applicants.[28]

Higher on the agenda of the chief forester was the question of integrated land-use planning. Silcox denied that the Forest Service intended to eliminate grazing from the national forests. The Forest Service, although it consulted experts, believed its decisions should also be made with input from local communities on a democratic basis. Silcox was convinced that the Depression presented Americans with an opportunity to establish a government bureaucracy closely related to the needs of the people. Citizens should join in planning boards and local advisory boards to develop an integrated land-use policy. Silcox believed the Forest Service could easily move in these directions, considering its past traditions of decentralization and social commitment.

It was suggested that the national forests might play a role in a back-to-the-land movement fostered by some New Dealers. The movement reflected the spirit of the old Forest Homestead Act, the bane of many forest grazing administrators in the past. If the Agricultural Adjustment Administration wished to buy land next to national forests on which irrigated agriculture could be practiced, settlers could raise vegetables, graze stock, and be provided jobs in the forests. The Bankhead-Jones Farm Tenant Act of 1937 extended low-interest loans to tenant farmers for the purchase of farm livestock, farm equipment, and supplies. American public forestry again acknowledged its role in promoting the welfare of agricultural settlers and herdsmen. Those who first conceptualized public forestry in the United States believed it vital to insure the welfare of nearby dependent communities. The Depression offered the opportunity to revive aspects of this social mission, although at times it conflicted not only with strict forestry but also with economic efficiency and the minimum protection of the range resource itself.[29]

[28] Ibid.
[29] Quarterly Informal Report, Rocky Mountain Region, April, 1935, Range Management Division, FS, WO.

The Roosevelt administration did move to experiment with placing dispossessed farmers, workers, and families on submarginal lands, or small viable homesteads. The National Industrial Recovery Act of 1933 included appropriations for purchasing farmland for subsistence homesteads. At the direction of the president, the Department of the Interior created a Division of Subsistence Homesteads whose first action was to acquire land to resettle impoverished people. The Department of Agriculture was also involved in the program, as were a number of national forests. Eventually the plan called for the settlers to purchase the lands, but few of these lands ever became private, because both settlers and government lost interest in the program as prosperity returned. Many of the lands fell into the hands of state and local agencies. By 1954 most of the remaining lands were designated "Land Utilization Projects" and turned over to the Forest Service administration. Many in the West became national grasslands, also placed under Forest Service jurisdiction in 1960. Other federal agencies, such as the Bureau of Land Management and the Agricultural Research Service, obtained a portion of these lands.

Other New Deal agricultural programs paid farmers not to plant crops such as wheat, corn, and cotton in order to reduce surpluses and improve market prices. In many areas of the South, farmers turned to livestock production when farm crops were curtailed. The national forest lands there were affected by the shift, and the numbers of grazing permits increased compared to those issued in the 1920s. When asked what the national forest grazing program was contributing to "the advancement of the Negro race," Chief of Range Management Dutton replied, "Very little." He was reasonably sure that there were no blacks among western permittees, and their use of the national forests in the South was minor. Although southern whites who had permits might occasionally employ blacks in a livestock operation, the white permittee was "not much better off, economically, than the Negro, and [was] seldom in a position to employ any help." [30]

As established stockmen felt the sting of drought and depression, they too wished for more security on their ranges. The longterm permits and rules against extreme reductions for either protection or distribution were

---

[30] Joseph Kircher to Chief, January 25, 1940, Sec. 63, Dr. 634, RG 95, NA; U.S. Department of Agriculture, Economic Research Service, *The Land Utilization Program, 1934 to 1964: Origin, Development and Present Status*, Agricultural Economic Report no. 85; Memo from W. L. Dutton, "Negro and Forage Resources of the Forest," March 29, 1940, Sec. 63, Dr. 590, RG 95, NA.

important guarantees. In addition, users could look for opportunities in range improvement under some of the public make-work programs of the Roosevelt administration. These emergency programs offered opportunities to speed range improvements that would have otherwise taken much longer under normal appropriations from Congress. The young men of the Civilian Conservation Corps, which established camps in nearly all of the National Forests, built range fences and stock-watering places, and artificially revegetated many acres of range. Workers under the National Industrial Recovery Administration also undertook these projects, and also improved stock trails, opened new ones, and manually removed poisonous plants from the ranges. In cooperation with the USDA Biological Survey, hordes of range rodents, particularly prairie dogs, were poisoned on thousands of acres.

Other moves on the part of government agencies assured the livestock industry a long-term interest in the forest ranges. But the Forest Service always took precautions to prevent users from obtaining a prescriptive right to their allotments by compensating them for material improvements in the ranges through cooperative contracts. The service authorized reduction of fees to compensate a permittee for range improvements he installed at his own expense. In any event the service made it clear that there would be no conveyance of property rights to the permittee, and that ownership of the improvement would revert to the government. For example, posts could be cut free of charge from national forest lands by the permittee, with the Forest Service offering wire staples to help in construction, but the fence and the lands it covered remained in government ownership.

One of the government experiments of the Depression was the Farm Credit Administration, which backed low-interest loans to ranchers. Banks were encouraged (though not by the Forest Service) to recognize the national forest permits as collateral for the loans. This broke with past practices in which government agencies refused to acknowledge property rights or ascribed value in assignment of permits. Forest officials believed that the loans could pave the way for large third-party (that is, bank) takeovers of forest allotments should the loans default.[31]

Diversified use weighed heavily upon the determination of grazing capacity by the late 1930s. There was renewed emphasis on the variety of

[31] Memo ca. 1937, Sec. 63, Dr. 592; W. L. Dutton to John R. Camp, March 12, 1938, Sec. 63, RG 95, NA.

resources and values to be considered in the forest before its range-carrying capacity could be determined. Diversity of uses for watershed, wildlife, timber, and recreation could all in one way or another reduce the allowed grazing capacity. One regional forester in the West admitted that in distributing the use, the pie had to be cut into small pieces, and frequently the result was not satisfactory. Other officials frankly invited stockmen to cooperate with the Forest Service in determining carrying capacity of their ranges. But as always, there would be instances when the service and users could not come to an agreement. In these cases the final determination would rest with the service, based upon range surveys and actual use records. In making this determination, southwestern Regional Forester Frank Pooler, at Albuquerque, promised that the service would keep abreast of all new methods in the assessment of the ranges under its jurisdiction. Among these methods was aerial survey, which ever since the 1930s appeared to be an essential and desirable part of any overall range evaluation. One comment from the field in 1934 said that for accuracy and speed, no method could compare with aerial photography. This comment was probably overly optimistic, because aerial survey could never be relied upon entirely for the determination of carrying capacity.[32]

Management Plans in the 1930s

Range-survey data were essential to the formulation of range management plans. Many times it was impossible to explain to stockmen the necessity for the expensive reconnaissance work. An explanation usually produced more difficulty, for compared to timber cruising, range measurements appeared to be mere guesswork. The timber cruiser could measure his work and read his "stick" to substantiate his estimates. The range reconnaissance man had only his paper estimates, checked by the chief of the party and others in the crew to insure uniformity. The entire work had to be uniform, because if the range management office proved that the final carrying-capacity estimate was low, then all estimates would be low and they would be boosted equally.

[32] R. H. Rutledge, "Farm Pastures and the Summer Range Problem," *National Wool Grower* 27 (April, 1937): 29; C. W. Pooler, "Policies of the Forest Service Explained," *American Cattle Producer* 16 (August, 1934): 16; "Photo Surveys," July 21, 1939, Sec. 63, Dr. 590; Lee M. Frost to R. R. Hill, Inspector of Grazing, March 25, 1934, Sec. 63, Dr. 98, RG 95, NA.

The range survey provided critical information on the "forage-acre factor" for the writing of a range-management plan. A forage-acre was an ideal surface acre having a 10/10 "palatable vegetation" density and a 100 percent palatability, the highest possible rating. In short, the forage-acre was a unit of measurement applied to the density and palatibility of grasses, grasslike plants, and other herbaceous plants and available or grazeable browse contained in each vegetative type. A palatibility table provided by the regional office gave the palatability for individual plants and for all classes of stock. By multiplying the percentage of each individual by the palatability number the surveyors determined percentages of palatability for individuals, which, when added, gave the volume palatability of the type. This volume palatability multiplied by the density (estimated to hundredths, that is, 0.30, 0.35, and so on) yielded the aforementioned "forage-acre factor" more commonly known as FAF. For example, a sheep utilized 0.3 forage-acres per month, and a cow 0.8 forage-acres per month. On this basis the actual animal-unit-month (AUM) in any given type, unit, or forest could be figured, and when the length of season was determined, the number of stock which any area would support for the grazing season could be determined.

This method had been pioneered by the Forest Service twenty years earlier in determining AUMs. Clarke A. Anderson of the Holy Cross National Forest offered an up-dated explanation. Of more immediate interest than the explanation itself was his belief in the accuracy of the measurement. Throughout it he used the phrases, "It has been definitely proven. . . . It is possible to accurately estimate the percent. . . . A palatability table is accurate in all respects. . . . The number of stock which any area will support for the grazing season is easily determined." Little wonder that stockmen sometimes withdrew in disbelief at such glib acceptance of the accuracy of field measurements.[33]

After the compilation of range survey data, the building of range-management plans began. An essential part of a range-management plan was an illustrated and labeled map. By 1939, The Office of Range Management ordered regional foresters to include the following information in their range management plans: allotment boundaries in colored india ink; management camps; salt grounds and distribution units; surface and forage acres in each; name of allotment and number of each smaller unit (or name if desirable); class, season, and number; rotation scheme, if any; band days per camp unit; and dates if desirable. Also were included the numbers of surface and forage acres and AUMs or number of stock for special-use pastures, listed separately for fenced and unfenced tracts of private land. Ordinarily, since land status was a permanent map feature, the boundaries of special uses and fenced and unfenced private lands, were to be shown in colored ink and their capacities entered. Existing and proposed range improvements were to be shown, and where water was scarce, it was to be traced in blue. Temporary water was designated with dates when available. Other special information was to be shown when it related to local management. Since the Forest Service had been attempting to gather this type of information on its allotments for over twenty-five years, it had much experience to offer to the land-use and land-classification movement in the 1930s. The entire history of an allotment could be effectively shown through a study of these plans.[34]

The Forest Service had pioneered range surveys, beginning in 1911. Now there appeared a need for a uniform survey method that other agencies could use. Discrepancies in range-survey results among Forest Service, Grazing Service, Soil Conservation Service, and AAA range examiners tended to discredit the entire range-survey program. In April, 1937, an interagency range conference in Salt Lake City, Utah, agreed to work for standard instructions for range surveys. The conference recommended that all agencies planning and encouraging proper use of grazing lands take steps to place federal government programs on a unified basis to coordinate results. Another interagency conference was held to determine stricter range-survey guidelines, which included a standardized list of eighteen vegetation types that were used by federal agencies performing range surveys.[35]

Recreational demands on the national forests, although reduced, did not disappear in this decade of economic stress. The *Yearbook of Agriculture* of 1933 referred to the conflict between grazing interests and recreational groups, noting that no other practice presented such possibilities for

[34] Memo from W. L. Dutton to Regional Foresters, May 10, 1939, Sec. 63, Dr. 579, RG 95, NA.

[35] "Range Surveys," March 11, 1939, and Dutton to S. R. Barnes, in charge of survey coordination, USDA Office of Land Use Coordination, December 5, 1939, Sec. 63, RG 95, NA.

conflict with grazing as the use of ranges by game animals.[36] The passage of the Wildlife Restoration Act (Pittman-Robertson Act) in 1937 by Congress, imposing excise taxes on guns and ammunition for the restoration of native wildlife, caused some uneasiness in the stock industry. The temporary interruption of American prosperity during the Depression had relieved much sportsman pressure upon game populations in many areas, but this new act promised a much more aggressive defense of range game by the federal government.

By the end of the 1930s big game herds increased on the national forests to nearly 1.6 million head, an estimated 140 percent increase since 1924. Although the Depression reduced recreational hunting, permitting game populations to explode, the increase had not been expected. The hard times could have prompted greater harvesting of game both in and out of hunting seasons, in poaching forays. Undoubtedly some poaching did occur, but obviously not to any appreciable extent. The numbers pointed to an impending crisis as game animals challenged domestic animals' use of the forage resources. In addition, the coming of World War II curbed leisure time, access to ammunition, and gasoline. Recreation partisans approved of the large increases in game and demanded that the Forest Service make provisions for the protection and perpetuation of these numbers by restricting the numbers of domestic stock allowed to compete for the forest ranges.[37]

Earlier in the decade, largely in response to the popular appeal of national parks, the Forest Service had begun creating primitive and wilderness areas in some national forests. Some critics feared that those areas might eventually reduce or exclude domestic stock grazing. However, livestock grazing was permitted to continue in those primitive and wilderness areas where it was an established practice. And when Congress passed the Wilderness Act in 1964, livestock interests succeeded in having included the protection of established grazing in national forests.

The efforts of its partisans notwithstanding, recreation was subordinated in the 1930s to the more practical problem of putting people to work in constructive employment instead of healthy play. Moves to prevent higher recreation uses of the forest such as summer homes pleased livestock interests. The Washington office recognized that the elimination or restriction of domestic-stock grazing, in favor of wildlife and recreation

[36] U.S. Department of Agriculture, *Yearbook of Agriculture, 1933*, p. 215.
[37] O. A. Fitzgerald, "Feud on the Ranges," *Country Gentleman* 108 (April, 1938): 15.

often increased the fire danger. Heavier vegetation would result from curtailed grazing, especially if not compensated by increased grazing by wild animals and increased fire protection by rangers.

Stock spokesmen, including federal grazing officers, also opposed those who saw the forest only as a source of timber. To recognize timber as the only legitimate product of forests would overlook or submerge the broader aspects of "land-use planning," declared Walt Dutton, the Forest Service's range-management chief.[38]

By the mid-1930s forest supervisors used the term *multiple use* regularly to describe their management philosophy, especially when they had to justify one resource or use at the expense of another. In such cases the Forest Service established "priority of use," in some cases giving logging a priority over a livestock operation.[39] While forest management attempted to adjust to new demands on the forest, the training of field officers in grazing administration apparently changed little from that of twenty years earlier. Notebooks from range schools conducted in the mid-1930s reveal that the topics were similar to those of the earliest days of administration. The course of instruction in 1935 included:

1. Range plant identification with emphasis upon plants poisonous to cattle and sheep.
2. Grazing applications with sub-topics of commensurability, how determined and how applied
3. Counting of stock when entering the forest or in feedlots when departing or leading on to trains
4. Grazing plans
5. Salt plan
6. Work with stock associations
7. Grazing trespass
8. Range inspection
9. Reseeding the ranges[40]

[38] FS, RM, WO, C. E. Rachford to Kneipp, June 2, 1933, Range Management Division, FS, WO; Memorandum for Mr. Ganger from W. L. Dutton, October 26, 1936, Sec. 63, Dr. 98, RG 95, NA.

[39] R. W. Hussy, Forest Supervisor, Coconino NF, Region 3, to Cecil H. Miller, November 22, 1937, Sec. 63, RG 95, Federal Records Center of the National Archives, Laguna Niguel, Calif.

[40] Notebook, Ranger School 1935, Region 2, "Grazing Administration," pp. 98–139, Sec. 63, RG 95, Federal Records Center, Denver, Colo.

Range research in the Forest Service continued to emphasize four broad phases: range forage, range management, artificial revegetation, and watershed protection. In 1928 the McSweeney-McNary Forest Research Act had made possible five regional forest and range experiment stations, equipped to conduct research in all aspects of rangeland use and development. The sixth station, in the Rocky Mountain Region, opened July 1, 1935. With the establishment of these stations, responsibility for range and range-watershed research was extended to all range lands, public and private, within each regional boundary. There were other stations in the Lake States, Central, Northeastern, and Southern regions, as well as Alaska, but these stations at first conducted only limited range studies. Larger programs began in 1939 in the northern Ozarks, in 1940 in eastern North Carolina and southern Georgia, and in 1944 in Louisiana.

Forage investigations had identified over three thousand species and had yielded data on their ecological and economic nature. A general handbook of "key" range plants appeared in 1938 from the Forest Service research staff through the aid of emergency funds for travel expenses for the authors and assistants. It enabled field administrative staffers to identify plants readily and have concise information about them. Emergency funds were similarly used to prepare a range bibliography and other emergency publications, including one relating to flood control on Utah watersheds.

Range-management studies sought to develop methods of grazing more consistent with the conservation and use of other land resources. These practices included the following:

1. Deferred and rotational grazing until after seed dispersal on a different portion of the range each year
2. Later opening dates for ranges more in harmony with readiness of plants for grazing
3. A fairly good basis for determining the approximate grazing capacities of mountain range types
4. Improved methods for grazing sheep and goats, such as open and quiet herding, and bedding down in new places each night
5. Obtaining better distribution of cattle on the range through well-placed watering places and better salting methods
6. Eradication of tall larkspur

Studies deemphasized the theoretical aspects of the relation of plant succession to range management; the drought of the 1930s demanded immediate answers, not long-range theoretical solutions.

Artificial revegetation and watershed protection were the remaining fields of investigation. The objective in artificial revegetation was to develop methods and species for seeding or transplanting on rangelands where natural revegetation was failing. One of the most important experiments in revegetation was conducted by Leon Hurtt, in charge of range research at the Northern Rocky Mountain Station, Missoula. Hurtt hired about twenty-five farmers and ranchers, recommended by county agents, to conduct reseeding tests in eastern Montana. He also bought the entire crested-wheatgrass seed crop that year, as well as small amounts of other grass seeds. Each cooperator fenced about a ten-acre test area. For crested wheatgrass, he followed the procedure recommended by the North Dakota Agricultural Experiment Station at Mandan, which was to prepare a good seed bed and to cover the seed about one-half inch deep. Then Hurtt seeded other plots in furrows two and four inches deep, and varied the rates of seeding from five to twelve pounds per acre. All tests of the five-pound-per-acre seeding and four-inch furrows came through the 1931 and 1934 droughts without loss of stand, while the shallow seeding and heavier amounts could not live through the drought periods. Later, the USDA Soil Conservation Service successfully seeded millions of depleted range acres in the Great Plains from North Dakota to southern Colorado using these research results. Emergency money was also used for fences, housing, and office facilities, not only at new research locations but also at many other facilities.[41]

For watershed protection, the Department of Agriculture conducted a coordinated program of erosion-streamflow research. The Forest Service studied watershed conservation on forest and rangelands, while the Soil Conservation Service studied erosion problems on agricultural lands. Watershed-protection research of the Forest Service on rangelands sought to determine how vegetation cover controlled erosion and streamflow and the extent to which the cover could be utilized without damaging watershed values. These studies included the following areas:

1. The relation of different types and conditions of vegetation to soil, run-off, percolation, use of moisture by vegetation, and delivery of usable water for irrigation, power, and domestic use.

[41] W. R. Chapline, "Range Research in the United States" (1938), Coll. 8, Box 5, Fd. 10, Work Projects Administration History of Grazing Papers, Special Collections Library, Utah State University, Logan; Ronald C. Tobey, *Saving the Prairies: The Life Cycle of the Founding School of American Plant Ecology, 1895–1955*, pp. 110, 143.

2. Erosion control primarily through vegetation
3. The cost of control work that can be justified on rangelands on an economic basis[42]

By the end of the decade, Chapline could say that work in range-forage investigations overshadowed dendrology research in the Forest Service. In 1936 so much effort was devoted to the development of the *Range Handbook* that routine plant work and identification fell behind schedule.

While the Forest Service was defending its grazing policies to both conservationists and forage users, rumors persisted inside the government of an impending transfer of the Forest Service to the Department of the Interior. The ambitious Secretary of Interior Ickes prevailed upon Roosevelt to support the transfer in order to consolidate conservation activities in one governmental agency. At that point, toward the close of the decade, many users preferred that the Forest Service stay in Agriculture, which they felt had shown its dedication to conservation through use. Even F. E. Mollin, secretary of the American Livestock Association and longtime critic of national forest grazing policies, opposed the transfer. He applauded the Forest Service's "new policy" of restricting reductions, especially for distribution to new applicants. Vernon Metcalf, secretary of the Nevada Land and Livestock Association, emphasized that competition between the Forest Service and the Grazing Service resulted in more consideration for users' needs: "Should either get into the saddle exclusively, the range users' needs, it is feared, soon would not be given so much consideration." In effect Metcalf called for maintaining the status quo until further competition between the two agencies could determine which promised to give the user a fairer deal in its rules and policies. Others expressed more confidence in the stable administration of the Forest Service.[43]

Senator Key Pittman of Nevada assured his constituents that he opposed any transfer of the Forest Service to the Department of the Interior. On the presidential level, Roosevelt encountered heavy opposition to his and Ickes's transfer proposal from the Forest Service lobby in Congress. Reluctantly the president had to retreat on the issue. He eventually sent Pittman a letter giving assurances that there was no intention to transfer the

[42]Chapline to History Section, May 24, 1982, FS, WO.
[43]Vernon Metcalf to Pittman, March 30, 1940; B. H. Robinson, Eastern Nevada Sheep Growers Association, to Pittman, January 19, 1940, Key Pittman Papers, Box 71, Library of Congress, Washington, D.C.

Forest Service to the Interior Department. The letter addressed the senator by first name, showing how closely Pittman worked with the administration. The letter read as follows:

March 21, 1939

Dear Key:

In regard to the Forestry Bureau, I have no hesitation in telling you that I have no thought of transferring them to the Interior Department. I am meeting with a good deal of success in getting the public lands and forestry people to work together in such a way as to prevent duplication of work and render better service to the cattlemen. I think that working along this line for some time to come will produce results without any drastic change in organization.

Always sincerely yours,
[signed]

P.S. This [letter], of course, should not be used in any way until the Reorganization Bill is finally disposed of in both Houses and has been acted on by me.[44]

Apparently livestock users were now satisfied with the ten-year permits and the commitments to reduced redistribution. A transfer to Interior under a proposed Department of Conservation would upset a status quo and create uncertainty about the future of grazing in the forests. Senator Pittman, as a Democrat friendly to the administration, took pride in bringing the assurances of continued Forest Service grazing stability directly from the president himself. From 1936 to 1939, however, a bitter public struggle raged between Interior Secretary Ickes and Agriculture Secretary Wallace for the Forest Service. The principal administrators of the service fiercely resisted the transfer and mobilized a powerful Forest Service lobby against it. Much to the chagrin of Ickes, and even Roosevelt, the transfer never took place for lack of enough support in Congress. Ickes believed that Roosevelt let him down on this issue.[45]

The Depression presented many opportunities for the Forest Service to carry out traditional social goals based upon the principals of resource use and protection. The democracy and volunteerism built into many of the New Deal agencies that sought local approval and advice was familiar to

[44] Roosevelt to Pittman, March 21, 1939, Pittman Papers, Box 15, Roosevelt File.

[45] *Nevada State Journal* (Reno), May 10, 1939; Polenberg, *Reorganizing Roosevelt's Government*, pp. 100–22; Maunder, *Dr. Richard E. McArdle*, pp. 100–101; Frank E. Smith, *The Politics of Conservation*, p. 267; Soffar, "Differing Views of the Gospel of Efficiency," pp. 393–94.

the service, even though many users of grazing land accused the service of an arrogant and elitist attitude. No doubt such charges stemmed from the service's emphasis upon the use of trained experts and their tendency to reduce problems into detailed studies. Such procedures characterized modern government agencies, which had to demonstrate thoroughness, balance, efficiency, and effectiveness in writing to superior officers and Congress. These studies also revealed that under Chief Silcox the Forest Service leadership was in step with the philosophical ideals of prominent administration appointees.

On the surface it would have seemed that the Depression decade offered the kind of opportunity for which the Forest Service had prepared itself ever since the days of its founders. Many of its previous policies had been rebuffed, but now users felt so betrayed by the private economy that they accepted more readily the attempts of public officials to guide economic development and plan for future use. Unfortunately, the experience and potential of Forest Service grazing administration was not completely realized in the decade, primarily because of the introduction of another grazing agency engaged in parallel work. This competitor seemed to cause the service to become defensive and more conciliatory to narrow user interests. Users testified to this shift, as did wildlife associations who accused the service of catering to stock organizations. Clearly the opportunities offered by the Depression for an agency such as the Forest Service that specialized in the assessment, protection, and planned use of resources were not as great as might have been had the administration of all public grazing lands been extended into the Forest Service's experienced hands. On the other hand, some argue that conservation would have been better served in the long run had the Forest Service lands been consolidated with the Department of the Interior's lands in a new Department of Conservation.

7

New Resolves in the 1940s

I wanted the Forest Service to get on top of its range problem,
whether that meant reduced stocking or something else.
—Earle H. Clapp

As the Depression came to a close, many Forest Service administrators became disheartened and highly critical of range-management policies. They
complained of the deterioration of ranges since the 1920s, and the concessions made to users to help them in hard times. Now another emergency,
World War II, again drew efforts away from constructive programs for
range rehabilitation. A sense of frustration with the control that national
events exerted over serious range management appeared in departmental
memoranda. The intemperate public investigations and attacks on public
range conservation by Nevada's energetic Senator McCarran, although
aimed mainly at the Grazing Service, kept range managers in the Forest
Service apprehensive. Once again the Forest Service's conduct was under
scrutiny by an unfriendly western congressional committee supporting
short-term user interests over the national interests of range conservation
and restoration. Few events in recent years seemed to encourage progressive range management. Attacks from Congress and the Department of the
Interior and distracting emergency programs prompted some to say de-
spairingly that thirty-five years of range management in the national forests
had failed.

The official publications of the Department of Agriculture for 1940,
on the other hand, claimed that the national forest ranges improved 29 percent in productivity during these years of management because of sound
range management and conservation procedures. However, others, both inside and outside the department, charged that increased stock numbers on
the ranges occurred at the expense of range resources in some forests.
In the meantime, the McCarran committee kept alive rivalries between the

Grazing Service and the Forest Service while finding fault with both their performances.

Senator Patrick McCarran of Nevada was a powerful force in national grazing politics until his death in 1954. In the summer of 1940 he introduced Senate Resolution 241, which authorized a complete investigation of public lands administration. McCarran said he would particularly examine work done under the Taylor Grazing Act. The numerous committee hearings, held in nine western states in the next three years, often were in McCarran's home state. The length of the investigation and the highly outspoken roles played in the hearings by western senators gave the committee a political life of its own. In return the committee itself drew much criticism. Some charged that it existed to promote McCarran's and other senators' reelection campaigns and that it spent enormous amounts of tax monies for nothing more than these political ends. Also, there was clear evidence that McCarran and his committee staff worked closely with the livestock industry in setting up the hearings and getting its support to renew its operating budget each year. The committee effectively demonstrated the political power of the stockmen and succeeded in convincing most range administrators of the need to be even more generous than usual in their dealings with stockmen. Many administrators were so intimidated that they fully accepted the views and demands of the industry.[1]

Although the McCarran committee's main target was the Grazing Service, the Forest Service braced itself for the upcoming hearings. It feared that McCarran's forums would take testimony only from the large stockmen and representatives of the national stock organizations. Some Forest Service officials instructed regional offices to encourage small-owner permittees and members of local associations to testify. Supervisors and rangers were urged to explain to these men the purposes of the hearings through information and education programs, always proceeding, however, "within the bounds of propriety." The early hearings in Elko, Nevada, produced little hostility from witnesses to either the Forest Service or the Grazing Service. Those advisory board members in the Grazing Districts who offered comments could not cite one instance when their decisions were reversed by officials. Ranchers expressed satisfaction with the Grazing Ser-

---

[1]Committee work files, Patrick McCarran Papers, Nevada State Historical society, Reno.

vice and agreed it brought a welcomed stability to the open-range stock industry.[2]

The testimony was a far cry from the harsh criticism coming from the pen of F. E. Mollin, secretary of the American National Live Stock Association. He said the national forest advisory boards were powerless, and he frequently charged the Forest Service with arbitrary actions that made the existence of these boards meaningless. As a result, he declared, stockmen showed reluctance to present their problems. In addition, Mollin said, because the Forest Service had for so long adhered to a policy of distribution, it was quite natural that stockmen would not even wish to serve on the boards, whose main function, he insisted, was to approve the taking of forest grazing rights away from neighbors to give them to strangers.[3]

As the McCarran committee traveled throughout the West, it began to criticize the Forest Service. In Arizona, McCarran seized on accusations that the Forest Service allowed its employees to hold grazing permits in Apache National Forest. He told stockmen attending the subcommittee hearing, "We are going to find out how many cases there are of this kind." He then demanded Forest Service records for examination, asking, "What is going to happen to the citizens trying to make a living on the grazing areas if the Forest Service is going to be run for [its] employees?" McCarran's tirade appeared in the Tucson newspapers. The disclosure that a Forest Service employee held a grazing permit, while other residents near the forest were unable to obtain permits, caused raised eyebrows. When contacted in Albuquerque, Regional Forester Frank Pooler said a mistake had been made and the Forest Service would rectify it as soon as possible. Pooler explained that there was a shortage of experienced men to work with the Civilian Conservation Corps when its program began in the national forests. The man holding the grazing permit was employed because of his competence and ability to handle these workers. Regardless of the correctness of that decision at the time, it was apparent that local officials were embarrassed. McCarran, of course, was pleased and did nothing to ease the embarrassment.[4]

[2] E. W. Loveridge, Memorandum, August 20, 1940, Sec. 63, Dr. 590, RG 95, NA; *Elko Free Press* (Nevada), June 27–28, 1941.

[3] F. E. Mollin to Dutton, January 4, 1940, Sec. 63, Dr. 585, RG 95, NA.

[4] "Forest Worker Has Permit to Graze Claim," Tucson newspaper clipping, December 2, 1941, Sec. 63, Dr. 539, RG 95, NA.

The committee's temporary focus on the Forest Service gave the Grazing Service a brief respite. But throughout the hearings an atmosphere of one-upmanship prevailed between the two grazing administrations. On a less public level the competition between the two administrations continued in local disputes. The supervisor of the Gunnison National Forest, M. J. Webber, wrote in confidence to the Region 2 Office in Denver that the Grazing Service encouraged stockmen to take action against Forest Service policies "with the idea of stirring up dissension and thereby strengthening their own position." Webber said the Grazing Service was deferring needed range-management practices in order to win the approval of stockmen and avoid further criticism by the politicians. He asked how much longer the Forest Service was going to appease the Grazing Service and urged either a more aggressive attitude or an executive order requiring the Grazing Service to stay within its own jurisdiction.[5]

Higher officials in the Forest Service grazing administration still regretted the "mistake" by Congress in continuing public-domain grazing control in the Interior Department. As things now stood, national forest grazing administration faced threats from hostile congressional committees and a rival service. Some critics particularly complained that the Forest Service advisory boards were not as powerful as those of the Grazing Service. In 1940, Acting Chief Christopher Granger acknowledged that these boards on most national forests were loosely appointed or elected and had been inactive for years. He urged the regions to revitalize the forest-boards movement. This in turn would promote the organization of a local stock organization behind each board.[6]

When McCarran wound up his hearings in late 1943, he had succeeded in casting suspicion upon the good will of the federal grazing administration and gained some publicity and support for a move to offer the grazing lands to state ownership. Some witnesses made the point that they would prefer to lease lands from the state than deal with the federal government. While the final report of the committee did not make this demand, it did conclude that its efforts had tangible impact upon the administration of the public lands by both the Grazing Service and the Forest Service. Reports from users to the committee members were unanimous in concluding

[5]M. J. Webber to Region 2 Office, February 12, 1941, Sec. 63, Dr. 589, RG 95, NA.
[6]W. L. Dutton to M. S. Eisenhower, Land Use Coordinator, Acc. No. 59A1532, Box 585, Washington National Records Center, Suitland, Md.; C. M. Granger to Regional Foresters, February 5, 1940, Sec. 63, Dr. 585, RG 95, NA.

that there had been a "striking improvement in the attitude and actions of administration officials." Grazing officials, reported the committee, appeared much more willing to find solutions to problems and showed a more ready spirit of cooperation than before the hearings.[7]

Forest Service Policies During the Second World War

The war emergency of 1942 interrupted the deliberations of McCarran's committee. Hearings resumed in 1943 amidst wartime demands that American agriculture once again produce at full throttle to feed allies around the world. Government agencies on all levels sought now to avoid many of the mistakes made during World War I. The 1942 annual report of Chief of the Forest Service Earle Clapp asserted that during the previous war, "unrestricted expansion" of cattle and sheep in the West on both private and public lands (permitted on national forests by then Acting Chief Albert Potter and Grazing Chief Will Barnes) had "failed to give the expected increase in meat and wool." Instead, he said, "it caused serious range depletion, erosion, financial loss, and social misfortune." Clapp emphasized that "sustained production during this war must be achieved without a repetition of the mistakes of World War I."

In the months just prior to the attack on Pearl Harbor, Clapp noted that the numbers of livestock in the West were at "near an all-time high and still increasing." He did not wish to see a repetition of the ill-advised expansion and collapse that occurred during World War I. If the same course were followed now by an administration gripped by a wartime resolve to meet food needs, the western range (inside and outside the national forests) would face the complete denudation of its resources. Clapp warned that the West would no longer be able to supply one-third of the nation's beef, one-half of the mutton, and three-fourths of the wool if the United States entered the war. These proportions were an exaggeration. At no time, before, during, or since World War II have the western ranges produced such volumes, but often administrators and politicans vastly inflated the contributions of the western ranges to American meat production. Regional foresters saw the necessity of impressing upon all farmers and stockmen that

[7]U.S. Congress, Senate, Committee on Public Lands and Surveys, *Administration and Use of Public Lands: Partial Report of the Committee on Public Lands and Surveys, Pursuant to Senate Resolution 241*, 78th Cong., 1943, S. Rep. 404, pp. 80–81.

placing more animals on the ranges was not the answer to high production goals.

Forest grazing officials effectively used the argument that a sudden increase in livestock would not increase production, but only damage the ranges to the point that they would be completely unproductive. So rash a move might ultimately be detrimental to the entire defense and war effort. Apparently these arguments prevailed. Lyle Watts, who succeeded Clapp as chief forester in January, 1943, also "held the line" on extravagant requests for increased allotments either from producers or the Department of War Production.[8]

With the question of increased production settled early in the war, the Forest Service was asked to commit range researchers to the production of the desert shrub guayule as a much-needed rubber substitute. Questions bombarded the Office of Range Research in the Forest Service about the value of rabbitbrush of the genus *Chrysothamnus* as a source of rubber. Preliminary tests, conducted in Washington, D.C., were forwarded to the Guayule Emergency Rubber Project in Salinas, California. On more traditional questions the research office claimed that its findings helped convince stockmen that conservative utilization of forage was the key to greater production of meat, leather, and wool. Its experiments with artificial reseeding placed the Forest Service in a good position to respond to armed services requests for detailed planting instructions for camouflage, dust control, and fire-hazard reduction on Army and Navy bases at home and abroad.[9]

In several areas of the western states where the War Department expanded military bases and test facilities into the public domain, the Forest Service expressed dissatisfaction with monetary compensation for the grazing privileges of ranchers made by the War Department's Real Estate Section. Such outright payments based upon current community land values, said the Forest Service, would lead the government in the direction of recognizing these privileges as private property rights on the public lands. The U.S. Attorney General's Office, however, gave assurances that there was no basis for such claims.

Resistance to wartime demands for increased grazing led to the recog-

[8] Clapp to M. L. Wilson, October 13, 1941, and Memo from Frank C. W. Pooler, December 10, 1941, Sec. 63, Dr. 590, RG 95, NA.

[9] Clarence L. Forsling to W. G. McGinnies, April 14, 1942, Sec. 134, RG 95, NA; U.S. Forest Service, *Report of the Forester, 1942*, pp. 20–21; *1943*, p. 19; *1944*, p. 15.

nition that the ranges were truly unprepared for any additional stocking. The most serious criticism of conditions came from Regional Forester Clarence N. Woods. On December 4, 1942, emboldened by his imminent retirement, Woods sent a long, nagging, intemperate letter to the chief forester describing what he believed was the sorry state of the ranges in his region (Region 4). Much of the blame he placed on the former administration of Rutledge and insufficient oversight by the Washington office. Earle Clapp routed it to the grazing officials and used it to underline his own drive to reassert a more effective grazing program in the Forest Service. The letter, quite understandably, caused a stir among the Washington grazing administrators.

Woods contended that thirty-five years of management had failed to improve range conditions. He gave six general reasons (1) not enough rangers and administrative guards, (2) forest officers not spending enough time on range management, (3) forest officers not practically and technically qualified for range management, (4) failure to adequately impose reductions, regulate length of seasons, or supervise the handling of livestock, (5) incorrect grazing policies and regulations, and (6) lack of support from the regional and Washington offices. Woods believed that during any ten- or fifteen-year period within the years of Forest Service administration, stocking could have been brought to capacity with only mild protests from permitees. Reluctance to enforce restrictions occurred, he said, because some felt good public relations were more important. But Woods believed that the best public relations possible was good management of the resources of the forests.

Woods also claimed that Region 4 went too far in its redistribution programs and that the reductions that did occur made way for the admission of new applicants instead of protecting the range, so allotment lines were constantly redrawn and no permittee felt secure in the lands he grazed. This policy promoted neglect of the allotments and failure to perform improvement work. He concluded that the redistribution program did more harm to the established users than the benefit to the new applicants. "We carried this policy too far and continued it too long," he declared, adding that, when making reductions, officials made blanket percentage reductions instead of reductions on each allotment according to its conditions. In addition, Woods declared, there was no attempt earlier to fix individual responsibility for the condition of an allotment. When this policy was changed in the direction of holding the individual permittees responsible for the condition of their allotments, he pointed out, permittees were persuaded as seldom before to move their numbers down to carrying capacity.

Even the advisory boards and some local livestock associations recognized advantages of reducing to range-carrying capacity for the production of larger animals. Many understood that more animals did not mean more marketable pounds of beef or mutton. The number-one job facing forest officials in Region 4, wrote Woods, was to make adjustments that prevented further damage to forage and watersheds, thus providing a rehabilitated range. These goals could only be achieved with the full support of the Washington office. Woods was also disturbed by the common practice of making the larger owners absorb all protective cuts. More often they were better range managers than the smaller owners, he said, observing that small owners were often sloppy and indifferent to recommendations on how best to handle their stock to avoid range damage. After all, if damage did cause forest officials to demand reduction, Woods declared, the small owners would understand that not they, but the larger owners would be the ones to receive reductions.

Woods complained that higher administrative levels in the Forest Service did not always support the local rangers' management efforts. The basic reason for this lack of support, he contended, was a lack of understanding in Washington of the local situation, or more often a misinterpretation of information. Curiously, he made no charge that the officers in Washington shaped their policies and reactions to local events on the basis of political pressures. No doubt his criticism of the heavy emphasis that the regional and Washington offices habitually placed upon the necessity to keep up good public relations covered this deficiency. Woods sent his letter not only to the chief forester but to all six regional offices as well.[10]

Grazing Chief Walt Dutton relayed the letter to Chapline and C. L. Forsling, who both replied with insightful comments endorsing many points in the Woods letter. Forsling said he witnessed the breakdown of range management in Region 4 after it had been raised to a vigorous level in the 1920s. (Forsling had been director of the Great Basin Range Experiment Station at Ephraim, Utah, during the decade.) In part, the attention given range management in the central (Utah) portion of Region 4, he explained, was a reaction to the disastrous floods that had plagued central

[10]C. N. Woods Memoir, December 19, 1942, History Section, FS, WO.

Utah towns since the turn of the century because of overgrazing in the mountains. In the northern part of the region, central Idaho forests largely ignored grazing problems. "The R.O. was asleep at the switch," said Forsling. The supervisors, who were mostly concerned with timber and fire prevention, convinced the regional office that no grazing problems existed; therefore, it was not until 1927 or 1928 that the region realized it had a range problem in the north. But generally during the 1920s the region had a keen appreciation of range matters and carried on programs that gave first priority to the range situation. As Forsling put it: "Rangers and Supervisors lived and slept grazing. The men on the ground took grazing correspondence courses. Training meetings were held every two or three years. Technicians from the Regional Office . . . spent time with the Rangers and Supervisors and their guidance was eagerly sought. Rangers put in study plots to learn more about what was happening and what needed to be done."

Unfortunately, related Forsling, the office soon issued a study of time use that alleged that rangers spent too much time on range management. In the face of this criticism, rangers began to cut corners on range administration and even perform it in absentia. On the heels of this retreat in range management came the CCC program that further drained the time of local officials from their traditional work patterns. These developments, combined with Regional Forester Rutledge's philosophy of sacrificing the resource, if deemed necessary, to maintain the goodwill of the livestock industry, all served to curtail effective range management in the region. Forsling echoed Woods's opinions that Rutledge's grazing administration was totally oriented toward public relations.

The Forest Service had, of course, backed away from reductions for protection that were needed in time of drought because it did not want to add to the economic burdens of the users. Forsling's solution was to return to the range-management methods of the first eight years of the 1920s. He further asserted that the depleted range conditions in Region 4 demanded more training of personnel and more applied knowledge.

W. R. Chapline also spoke of the achievements of range management in Region 4 during the 1920s and said it should not be interpreted from Woods's remarks that poor conditions had prevailed for thirty-five consecutive years. By 1921 the 15 percent increase permitted during the war had been eliminated in Region 4, he noted, and range-manangement officers gave every indication that they intended to carry out protective policies. Later, however, the field personnel were not held accountable for the conditions they permitted to develop. Inadequate policies and the low priority given range management accounted for the failure to apply much of the knowledge accumulated about proper methods to manage ranges, he wrote.

Both researchers made the point that where forest supervisors were informed about range management, important progress in building up the ranges could be made. Chapline emphasized that forest officers must stay abreast of the available technical information on range management. It was realized that management procedures in fire or timber problems were almost always of greater interest to rangers and supervisors. Therefore technical knowledge of grazing management would have to be given particular emphasis and the lower echelons held responsible.

Only with a vigorous administrative policy could the Forest Service expect the field officers to put into effect plans and policies that have shown proved results. Always eager to emphasize the accomplishments of research, Chapline ventured the opinion that the recent completion of many studies in the field made Forest Service officials more conservative in such matters as estimation of carrying capacity than they had been twenty years earlier. Only since the mid-1930s, he believed, had an adequate range-research organization existed. Now, in 1942, researchers worked with administrators in the forests of Utah to overcome some of the unsatisfactory conditions that Woods outlined.

Finally Chapline voiced a frequent complaint of those who pioneered efforts in range management. He urged the same type of sustained effort in range management as that which was accorded the prevention and fighting of fires. If the same effort were put into range-management programs as into fire programs, he said, the range situation in the Forest Service lands could quickly be brought under control. Unfortunately the two were not seen by the public as comparable. Fire was a universally recognized demon, but protection of common forage was a much less exciting enterprise.[11]

The call for closer administrative supervision was sometimes difficult in an organization that prided itself on decentralization. In an earlier response to the Senate's investigation of grazing lands, an internal study of Forest Service grazing administration noted that field officers must do much of their work apart and alone. Barriers of distance cut them off from

---

[11]C. L. Forsling Memo, December 12, 1942; W. R. Chapline to W. L. Dutton, December 17, 1942; W. L. Dutton Memo, December 12, 1942, Acc. No. 59A1532, Box 64, WNRC.

close supervision. Also, because of the diversity of the forests, the duties of the supervisors and rangers could not be standardized and directed like those of employees in a factory. Filing reports according to forms found in an instruction book to an official hundreds of thousands of miles away did not guarantee the accomplishment of policies. Too often it meant detailed, neat reports, but little in the way of achievement.

The forest ranger himself bore a heavy responsibility in performing duties faithfully and making correct judgments on the conditions of the allotments under his administration. Because he and his family lived in the communities affected by his decisions, he personally felt reactions and protests against reductions. Without strong organizational support behind him, his entire way of life in the community was jeopardized if he made judgments more in keeping with the protection of the resource and ignored the impact upon friends and neighbors. Under these conditions, placing the weight of effective resource protection on the local ranger was not always the wisest course. In many ways, however, it was dictated by the effort to orient administration to the local level in Forest Service organization. Although the chief forester in Washington acknowledged ultimate responsibility for the protection of the resource, he had to admit his dependence on the local rangers. Developments on the local scene thus sometimes escaped correction from Washington either from unawareness or from a desire not to insist that the supervisors offend local users.[12]

In the spring of 1942, Acting Chief Clapp addressed all regional foresters on the grazing question. Clapp's assessment was that past and present progress in obtaining needed adjustment in problem areas was not satisfactory: "There must be a more effective drive to obtain proper management of National Forest ranges generally, including reduction in use where such reduction is needed because of overstocking. The war demands on our resources gives added emphasis to this." The renewed interest in the range problem came at a time when other government agencies pressured the Forest Service to open its ranges to more stock. As one means of defending itself against these pressures, the service emphasized the deteriorated condition of its ranges, although this admission did not reflect well upon its past accomplishments. The service argued that its retreat had been caused

[12] E. D. Sandvig, "Report on the Administration and Use of the National Forest in Response to Senate Resolution 241," 1941, Sec. 63, Dr. 541, RG 95, NA.; Herbert Kaufman, *The Forest Ranger: A Study in Administrative Behavior*, pp. 62–63, 190–91.

by a decade of social and political policy whose goals were primarily to salvage the economic fortunes of stockmen and serve the purposes of the make-work programs of the CCC.[13]

In early January, 1943, Roosevelt appointed Lyle F. Watts, regional chief at Portland, as chief of the Forest Service. Clapp stayed on as associate chief. Immediately Watts faced the problem of stock reduction. Much of the interest in some regions to bring the ranges down to capacity after the policies of concession during the 1930s grew out of Clapp's assurances that Washington was once again interested in serious scientific range management. But the new interest in effective range management remained largely that. Dutton, chief of the Range Management Division, informed Watts in early 1943 that net decrease in stocking in 1942 was less than 1 percent. The decrease was the smallest since the peak of stocking in 1918 with two exceptions in 1929 and 1934. These years showed a 1 percent increase over the previous years. The average annual reduction over the past twenty-four years was 2½ percent.

Dutton could also point out that total net figures for forests and regions were not a reliable reflection of the problem. Non-use, unused range, inaccessible range, and understocked areas all reduced the reported net overstocking. Simply because a forest did not show a net total understocking was no indication that it did not contain critical problem areas for which there were no solutions in sight or planned. He concluded that there were many allotments "where the conditions are a disgrace to the Forest Service and livestock industry, and where we are not making any progress at all." The reasons these conditions were allowed to develop were extremely important because, "they continue to have a powerful influence on our failure to meet the issue." [14]

In a study entitled "Postwar Plans of the Forest Service for Seventeen Western States," the "Range Highlights" section called for reductions on the ranges in all states. It argued that the rancher would not be adversely affected because larger animals kept the general income up. The concept of subsidies for range improvements was supported. The leadership of the Forest Service started suggesting that the administration of the national-

[13] Clapp to Regional Foresters, April 29, 1942, Earl D. Sandvig Papers, Box 246, Natural Resource Collection, Denver Public Library.
[14] Earle H. Clapp to C. M. Granger, January 15, 1943, Acc. No. 59A1532, Box 64, Fd. G-Supervision, WNRC; W. L. Dutton to Lyle F. Watts, February 22, 1943, Sec. 63, Dr. 598, RG 95, NA.

forest range resource must be brought up to the standard set in timber management. E. W. Loveridge in the Washington Office charged that, "Because the Grazing Service has pampered the grazing permittees—and for other reasons—we have failed to put into effect a comparable procedure in range management." In any event, he said, the Service would soon be in a position to change its ways in range management with the beginning of a new ten-year term permit period. Dutton understood that the job of obtaining range adjustments did not lend itself to the same brand of publicity that was effective in fire-control work. He also agreed that specialized range problems did not need to be aired in the public arena, "except as a last resort after failure to deal with the individuals or groups affected." [15]

Dutton also noted certain contradictions in the reporting on range matters. While Region 4, for example, announced the goals of getting down to capacity by 1946, it continued to report an increasing overall capacity by 1943. Dutton believed that the region's appraisals were too generous. The regional office would have to exercise a more critical appraisal of range conditions. If this duty had been performed faithfully, Dutton said, he would have more confidence in the reports from the individual forests. It was his feeling that further study of range conditions on the ground would influence the regional office to question estimates from its forests. If this were done, he believed, it would be found that the size of the adjustment job was much greater than now reported by the region.

In other regions reporting a surplus of carrying capacity, Dutton found the foresters reluctant to indicate less than satisfactory conditions because the regional office would then insist upon the type of actions "that would result in a local mess." On the other hand in another region, forest supervisors were merely waiting for the "green light" from the regional office before they felt confident enough to take corrective actions. Washington largely relied on the judgment of regional foresters on how far and how fast adjustment could be made "without jeopardizing the success of the whole program." Dutton emphasized that the Washington office gave every opportunity for the regions to solve their own problems, but occasionally did question whether a region correctly assessed its problems and the speed of recovery. [16]

[15] NA, RG 95, "Range Highlights" April, 1944, Sec. 63, Dr. 592; E. W. Loveridge to Lyle F. Watts March 17, 1944, and Dutton to John Spencer, R-2, April 7, 1944, Sec. 63, Dr. 592, RG 95, NA.
[16] W. L. Dutton to Ben Rice, March 16, 1944, Acc. No. 59A1532, Box 64, WNRC.

After Dutton's careful but firm criticism of Region 4, the regional office admitted that it had many protection problems to work out with its stockmen. The Ogden office placed the concerns of moving downward to grazing capacity and protecting watershed as upper most in its planning. It admitted that it gave little attention to other questions such as who used the range and how much they pay for it. Many, of course, saw that the range problem directly related to the fee question. But to address this issue and at the same time attempt to reduce usage would be totally out of the question. The Forest Service still held to its policy of charging only "nominal fees" for protection and improvement.[17]

In 1944, the suggestion was made that grazing allotments be administered under a contract system similar to timber management contracts. A memo responding to this suggestion was written by Earl D. Sandvig, an assistant forester in Region 1. The allotment system as it existed already was, in a sense, a contractual agreement. Unfortunately, range managers did not always know the amount of resource they had available while timber managers fairly well knew the quantity of goods to sell within agreed limits. More control could be exercised over men cutting timber than over animals cropping grass. It was extremely difficult for the government to make a contract on the basis of such an unstable and unpredictable product as forage resource. But if the number of livestock based on a close estimation of the resource coupled with agreement on management details could be worked out each year, contracts could probably be issued. Sandvig asserted, "If mastery of this management problem had existed in the past, few ranges would now be in substandard condition. That the Service has not attained such mastery is attested by the conditions existing on many ranges today." This memo went to Regions 2, 3, 4, 5, and 6 as well as the Washington office.

Sandvig believed, however, that the Forest Service possessed the tools for successful range management without resorting to a formal contract system. He pointed to the authority that the service held over resource administration and demanded that that authority be coupled with the application of rigid standards. The underlying cause of range deterioration was not the Forest Service's system of administration, Sandvig insisted, but its unwillingness to carry out its own policies. There had been a lack of conviction for more than a decade in range management, contended Sandvig,

[17] U.S. Department of Agriculture, *Yearbook of Agriculture, 1940*, p. 454.

which could not be solved by the mere drawing of a contract nor by the appeasement of stockmen. Appeasement for the sake of political and organizational peace would not win the respect of stockmen which must be obtained if the ranges were to reach a point of restoration, he warned.

Sandvig's memo continued in this vein. He emphasized a proper philosophy was necessary at the top. From there its dissemination down the line must occur with the replacement of any weak links who would not embrace both ideas and action. The regional forester and the chief of range management must be of strong character to support the technical men in the field. The technical effort must be headed by a person who directed the application of practices on the range, kept abreast of developments on the ground, and constantly advised and distributed information. The men in the field must be properly schooled in their business, amenable to suggestion, and tactful with users. These actions must offer results—an improved range and ultimately fatter, more valuable stock. To put such a program into practice, Sandvig believed, it would take both faith in the philosophy and hard actions based upon these principles. To do this, range managers in the Forest Service must offer advice based upon tangible proof to support it and refuse to be influenced by the tactics employed by the Grazing Service that might persuade foresters to follow conciliatory policies to win favorable applause from users. Sandvig concluded that, "We still hold the reins of leadership, even though less firmly than before. Let's regain undisputed pre-eminence in range management by analyzing our own deficiencies and then taking action to get out in front and stay there." [18]

The Ogden Conference and Its Aftermath

In late May and early June, 1944, a conference on range management was held at Ogden, Utah. Stockmen at the conference were Henry Boice of Arizona, past president of the American National Livestock Association; Rosco C. Rich of Idaho, chairman of the Advisory Board of the American Livestock Association; William B. Wright of Nevada, past president of the National Wool Growers' Association and first vice-president of the American National Livestock Association; and John Reed of Wyoming, president of the Wyoming Woolgrowers' Association. The conference addressed all range management issues and controversies, intending to inspire the re-

[18] E. D. Sandvig to Regions 2, 3, 4, 5, 6, May 16, 1944, Sec. 63, Dr. 600, RG 95, NA.

gions to implement more vigorous range policies in the immediate postwar years.

One of the most objectionable phrases coined by the Forest Service from the point of view of livestock men holding permits was "reduction for distribution." Regional foresters were authorized to make reductions on problem ranges where damage was extensive. But in each case they were cautioned that evidence must justify the move because the proof of damage must rest with the Forest Service. Above all, the actions should not cause protests in the state or national livestock associations.[19] In the Southwest there was widespread resentment against distribution adjustments. One advisory board protested the proposed appointment of an assistant supervisor because he had been associated with a study that suggested wider distribution of grazing privileges. It did not matter that the individual was working under routine instructions. The protest was strong enough to force the regional forester to withdraw the appointment. But other government agencies criticized the Forest Service for its failure to push distribution policies and its "coddling" of the larger users. In response the service urged that a uniform policy be worked out among the Bureau of Agicultural Economics, the Farm Security Administration, the Soil Conservation Service, and the Forest Service. The Farm Credit Administration and the Forest Service particularly needed close cooperation to avoid extension of credit beyond the safe grazing capacity of the mortgaged lands.[20]

At the regional level the Forest Service clearly expressed little enthusiasm for distribution. Dutton, who as chief of range management assumed a key role at the Ogden Conference, pointed out that a distribution survey conducted in 1936 showed no possibility of developing a distribution system to provide even a majority of ranchers in adjacent areas with national-forest range. If all qualified individuals obtained permits, they would be so widely distributed that no one would benefit. Equal distribution ignored the size of varying ranch units and was both economically and socially detrimental. Experience and various studies led regional foresters to declare themselves against the policy. Too often distribution damaged the permittee whose stock was reduced without benefitting the new applicants

[19] "Policy on Forced Protection Reductions During the War," Sec. 63, Dr. 598, RG 95, NA.
[20] W. L. Dutton to C. M. Granger, January 11, 1941, Sec. 63, Dr. 600; Dutton to R. F. Hammatt, December 10, 1941, Sec. 63, Dr. 600, RG 95, NA.

appreciably. It ignored the hallowed policy of the "greatest good to the greatest number" and undermined range-management practices.[21]

At the conference, representatives of the American National Live-stock Association warned against new distribution policies from the Forest Service that would threaten the cooperation of users. Permittees generally felt they had enjoyed greater stability during the past ten-year permit period than in any other time in the history of the Forest Service. Of course, the end of the ten-year period was now approaching and was the occasion for uneasiness among users. Chief Watts assured user representatives that they would be consulted and informed of any policy changes. He noted that there were still overgrazed allotments, and the Forest Service was under obligation to protect the lands from deterioration. Watts stressed that the policy of distribution was still alive. The door was not closed to new applicants who could present "highly meritorious cases." The so-called "up-the-creek" operators had to be given a fair hearing and opportunities to use the forest ranges.

Another problem considered at the conference was the blending of the welfare of wildlife with domestic stock grazing. The Forest Service felt increasing pressures to allow for the use of forage by wildlife in the determination of range-carrying capacities. Wildlife management, however, was complicated because of divided jurisdiction between the federal government and the states, who were jealous of their powers over game laws. Finally, Watts spoke on the transferring of grazing privileges for money among permittees.

The four issues of reduction, distribution, game management, and the transfer of permits prompted extensive replies and discussion from the livestock men. Boice warned that in some areas the ranges would not support both cattle and the growing numbers of big-game animals. He feared that the Forest Service would find it easier to reduce livestock than to remove big game, especially if vocal sportsmen's groups objected. Efforts should be made to promote mutual understanding between stockmen and sportsmen's conservation groups, he suggested. On the issue of buying and selling preferences, Boice asserted that the practice had always existed and forest officials knew full well that it occurred. It was not a case of sell-

[21] W. L. Dutton to Ogden Policy Conference, May 22–June 3, 1944, Sec. 63, Dr. 600; C. N. Woods to C. E. Farve, n.d., Sec. 63, Region 4, Dr. 604, RG 95, NA.

ing government range, he explained, but a case of selling something that somebody else wanted; the issue caused greater concern now only because of the extremely high prices paid in the past year. The livestock men recommended that the Forest Service continue to ignore the private payments made in the exchange of grazing permits. They also felt that increased grazing fees would have no impact on this practice. Fees were still related to market prices for livestock; both livestock interests and the Forest Service considered the fees nominal.

Dutton ventured the opinion that one of the reasons for the continued resistance to reductions was that ranchers had made large investments held in grazing privileges and could not allow that investment to evaporate in the name of range protection. Reductions often were more acceptable if the individual allotment holder could be promised the future benefit of conservation measures, he noted. Much greater cooperation was forthcoming from permittees when they were given direct responsibility of the condition of their individual allotments. Common use of the range by cattle and sheep made such programs difficult and the stockmen suggested that moves to eliminate common use would be moves in the right direction. Stockmen should also be given promises that their allotments would be increased if the condition of the range improved.

In spite of all the objections, Chief Forester Watts said that the service wished to keep the door open for distributions, although he saw "no epidemic" of new distribution in the future. The stockmen wanted protection in their right to use the allotments on a permanent basis and pass them on to the next generation. Rich of Idaho stated, "If 'the man up the creek' has been there a long time he has missed his change to get a preference. If he is a newcomer, it is too late for him to cut in."

Most stockmen agreed that the Forest Service should give wider publicity to the availability of nonuse permits. The practice of issuing nonuse permits dated back to the drought and depression of the previous decade. In the early 1930's either permittees did not possess the stock, or the range was too dry to support stock. In response, the service issued nonuse permits that guaranteed the user the right to the allotment later. Nonuse could help determine the carrying capacity of a given range where there were differences of opinion between the supervisor and permittee. The permits also helped in relieving certain ranges of stock when improvements such as water development and fencing needed to be constructed. The Oregon sheepmen had taken good advantage of the policy in 1943, when seventy thousand sheep were under nonuse because of a wartime shortage of labor. With the labor difficulties during the war, many ranchers felt under pressure to keep their numbers of stock up for allotments and were not aware that they could obtain nonuse reductions without having to fear that reductions would be permanent.

It was the general opinion at the conference that a permittee preferred to deal directly with forest officers about problems with allotments. Advisory boards gave too much public attention to problems that could be best worked out between the individual and the forest officer. Only if an agreement could not be reached should the advisory board advise on the settlement of the matter. Boice believed that the permittees would like to have advisory boards make recommendations on allotment boundaries, season of use, matters affecting preferences, distribution, grazing privileges, nonuse, and carrying capacity. These would be general policy recommendations not dealing with individual cases. Stockmen present accepted the view, according to Forest Service records, that the Forest Service must make the final decision in all administrative matters.[22] These questions were of vital concern to stockmen as the ten-year permits came up for renewal. Assistant Forester Granger took the opportunity to announce that renewals would occur except in cases where adjustments were deemed necessary. The announcement struck a note of satisfaction with stock representatives as the conference ended.

In the days and months after the Ogden Conference, several important letters came to the chief forester's office from the regions expressing fear that relations between the Forest Service and users were too harmonious. Even the Range Management office in Washington was not completely certain that the chief forester's office would welcome the proposals for stricter policies in range management. This uncertainty grew out of a longstanding suspicion among range managers that the Forest Service leadership often subordinated range issues to the more important questions of timber management. If problems in range threatened the overall goals of the service in timber policies, too often compromises and retreats occurred to preserve the larger goals.

But trouble was brewing among the Forest Service range managers. Their letters sounded an alarm over the deteriorated condition of the

[22] Report of Conference with Representatives of the Livestock Industry at the Third Ogden Grazing Meeting, May 26–June 4, 1944, as recorded by Edward P. Cliff, Sec. 63, Dr. 600, RG 95, NA.

ranges. The war, the emergency programs of the Depression, and the laxity of control under the ten-year permits were some of the reasons cited for the deterioration of range conditions since the mid-1920s. Aggressive measures to correct some of the mistakes of the recent past would require unyielding determination to prevail against the protests of the users, who would fight back with arguments and direct political pressure through western congressmen.

Allen Peck, a regional forester, suggested that reductions could be achieved with no loss of good will if stockmen were offered compensation for the cancellation of grazing permits. Under the Triple-A range program, the government paid stockmen to reduce their stock on private lands. What the government did for private lands could also be done in the interests of conserving resources on public lands. If adequate funds were made available for this purpose, forest ranges could be rejuvenated and the angry voices of stockmen quieted. Peck believed support could be found for this proposal in the light of the government attitude in the Depression to aid citizens in their difficult economic plights. He noted that the elimination of a stockman's grazing privilege was a virtual confiscation of property. Often the stockman had indirectly purchased it either through his ownership of commensurate property or the purchase of stock that carried with it a grazing privilege. Finally, payment to the stockman would be less expensive than attempting to maintain the stock number through reseeding, range improvements, and structural devices that amounted to subsidies. To move toward reductions without offering a plan of compensation appeared foolish.[23]

All of the western regions by 1944 talked freely of the shortcomings in range management both in achievements and in the administration of the preference system itself. It was held that the government should not be a party in any way to extending preferences to buyers of property that have permits associated with it. Deficiencies in the present regulations allowed violations of the intent of the regulations, promoting crooked manipulations by some permittees and "to [the] abandonment of intellectual honesty by some officers who basically are fine, upright characters."[24]

Many of the letters that flowed to the chief forester from the regions in summer and fall of 1944 were prompted by the points of discussion at the

[23] W. L. Dutton to R. F. Hammatt, December 24, 1941, Sec. 63, Dr. 590; Allen S. Peck, Annual Report, 1939, Sec. 63, Region 2, Dr. 590, RG 95, NA.

[24] Evan W. Kelley to W. L. Dutton, August 11, 1944, Sec. 63, Region 1, Dr. 598, RG 95, NA.

Sheep grazing under special-use permit in Muddy Meadow, with Mount Adams (12,307 feet) in the background. Gifford Pinchot National Forest, Washington, July 28, 1949. (*Courtesy, Forest Service*)

Cattle grazing under special-use permit on Tatoosh Mountain Range, Gifford Pinchot National Forest, Washington, August 14, 1949. The district ranger and a permittee are making an inspection of range conditions on the grazing allotment. (*Courtesy, Forest Service*)

Sheep grazing on Campo Bonito allotment, Rio Grande National Forest, Colorado, June 27, 1950. (*Courtesy, Forest Service*)

Cattle grazing on crested wheatgrass on Glorieta Mesa, Santa Fe National Forest, New Mexico, August 25, 1949. (*Courtesy, Forest Service*)

Tractor pulling two brushland plows hooked in tandem, removing sagebrush from land to be reseeded to crested wheatgrass, part of the program to rebuild seven thousand acres of overgrazed rangeland on Mesa Viejas on the Canjilon Ranger District, Carson National Forest, New Mexico, March 25, 1951. (*Courtesy, Forest Service*)

Cattle grazing under special-use permit on reseeded rangeland on the Carson National Forest, New Mexico. This area, part of the North Agus Reseeding Project on the Tres Piedras Ranger District, was reseeded with crested wheatgrass in 1949. No grazing was allowed until the plants had become fully established and the area was ready to be grazed. (*Courtesy, Forest Service*)

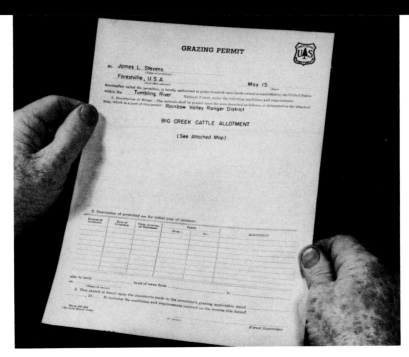

Official Forest Service grazing permit, 1954. Local rangers and farmers may graze a specified number of their livestock on national forest rangeland adjacent to their lands, if they are issued such a permit, upon payment of a nominal fee, on a specified allotment. Permits are subject to renewal. (*Courtesy, Forest Service*)

Forest Service Ranger LaVerne Schultz of Bears Ears District goes over a map of Douglas Creek sheep allotment and discusses details of grazing permit agreement with the range foreman on Routt National Forest, Colorado, as a sheep herder looks on. July 8, 1965. (*Courtesy, Forest Service*)

Ogden conference in late May. But the Ogden conference was not the only arena where grazing policies and administration were discussed in 1944. *American Forests* magazine ran the provocative article "Emergency in Grass." The article focused upon the good conditions in the Tonto National Forest in Arizona but made broad, mostly unfavorable generalizations about all the forest ranges. The article described the conditions of the ranges as depleted from fifty years of overuse and in need of a ten-year restoration period. It asserted that most national forests and other land-management officials had "a do-nothing policy toward restoring the range," with one exception. In Arizona, F. Lee Kirby, supervisor of the 2,411,000-acre Tonto National Forest, was called the nation's "number-one" crusader for grass restoration. Kirby was described as a man who had proved that ranges could be maintained in good condition without stifling the cattleman in the process. It said the entire land management bureaucracy could learn much from what had been accomplished on the Tonto forest in Arizona. That the Forest Service was not in control of its grazing situation was becoming public knowledge, unfortunately with all the attendant exaggerations and errors.[25]

After the Ogden conference, correspondence from the regions indicated that the new ten-year period would emphasize reductions and rebuilding of the range. For those eager to implement the new policy directions, policy makers and even research offered little guidance. Regional Forester Kelley from Missoula believed the program for the fall range-management conference appeared to be filled with only talk of policies and principles. Since he had heard so much recently of how the service had failed in range management, he did not see that the proposed program held any promise of transforming failures into achievements. As it stood the program for the fall conference seemed to start out in the air and stay there, said Kelley. Good range management should begin with the soil. Oddly, there was little talk about soil at the Ogden conference. "The time [has] come," said Kelley, "to point range management into the ground." Too much emphasis, he felt, had been placed on utilization of forage and measuring its disappearance with slide rules.[26]

A closer reading of the regional forester's suggestions revealed a basic complaint that forestry schools neglected training in the basics of soil sci-

---

[25] Oren Arnold, "Emergency in Grass," *American Forests*, 50 (June, 1944): 280–83.
[26] Evan W. Kelley to Walt L. Dutton, July 7, 1944, Sandvig Papers, Box 206.

ence and ecology. Too much emphasis was placed on utilization and management techniques by schools whose only goal seemed to be to offer job credentials. If the present and future employees in range management did not have a basic education in the hard sciences related to the management of the resources, they would be all too inclined to cooperate with users who were also primarily interested in utilization. Future range managers needed the know-how to protect resources through an understanding of the entire cycle of forage growth and developement. Otherwise rangers ignored fundamentals and glaring truths about the depletion of the resource and chose to adopt policies that attempted to "manage more grass" into the allotments.

Criticism of the Forest Service's range management continued through the end of the year. At a Denver conference on range management, a range examiner outlined some of the chief weaknesses in past grazing plans. The older plans and many of the newer ones indicated superficial analysis of all the elements affecting the use of allotments. The plans too often appeared in the form of a written exercise aimed at meeting the administrative requirements of a grazing work plan. Range inspectors rarely studied a forest's grazing allotment plan before going out on the ranges. Of course, the most detailed plans were useless in the face of a totally unacceptable case of overstocking. In these instances the rangers' efforts would be best spent in obtaining drastic reductions.[27]

By the early 1940s the regional forester for Region 8 concluded that sheep, swine, and cattle grazing was detrimental to the production of longleaf pine and hardwoods. The Chattahoochee study in northern Georgia, for which two years' worth of data were available, showed three times as many reproduction stems on fenced, ungrazed plots as on the unfenced plots. Also, the reproduction most palatable to cattle included the most important timber species: poplar, white ash, dogwood, white oak, and basswood. Unfortunately, the accessible cattle range and the best timber growing sites were the same, making the damage more extensive.

The grazed and ungrazed plots in the hardwood bottoms of the Texas national forests showed results similar to those found in the Appalachians. In eastern Texas, stockmen wintered great herds of cattle in the hardwood bottoms. Certain species, such as white ash, were headed for complete elimination there. The regional forester concluded that there was no imme-

[27] Stanton Wallace, "Individual Allotment Plans," Sec. 63, Region 3, Dr. 574, RG 95, NA.

diate solution for the grazing problems in his region, which he apparently judged only in relation to timber protection. He could predict only slow progress primarily because of the social problems in the region. Many small communities throughout the region were desperately hanging on to their worn-out holdings and using the forests to help them survive. Most of these situations were doomed, but in the meantime, complained the forester, "county agents, in their zest to hold their jobs and in order to have something to sell, have finally made an organized front in the raising of livestock to solve the people's problems." The regional forester was skeptical about the results and critical of the continued social need to keep southern forests open to livestock grazing.[28]

Over the next few years the Range Management Office in Washington detected the timber bias in the southern region. To Dutton, the region clearly was not interested in the contributions of grazing to family livelihood, and made no effort to show how it would be prepared to sacrifice timber, recreation, and wildlife values to meet family needs. Reports from the region definitely gave the impression that family welfare of the residents within and immediately adjacent to the forests was subordinated to the goals of intensive timber management. Good range management also implied a sense of social mission which the southern region appeared to lack.

In a sharply critical letter from Assistant Chief Granger, the southern region was told to give more attention to its grazing resources. Studies began in 1940 in south Georgia and eastern North Carolina, through the initiative of the Division of Range Research, showing that prescribed burning could benefit both stock raising and pine-tree regeneration. These studies indicated that with proper range management some southern ranges could become major beef producers. New studies by the Southern and Appalachian Forest Experiment stations indicated that livestock grazing had a more important role in the management of southern forests, particularly in the Coastal Plain, than had previously been recognized. Granger said studies were favorable to the possibilities of large commercial grazing enterprises on the coastal plain. The region should have a flexible attitude toward this development because it may be "determined that on a long-range basis the resulting social and economic benefits exceed the damage to the forest growing stock from such use."

[28] Joseph C. Kircher to the Chief, January, 1941, Sec. 63, Region 8, Dr. 634, RG 95, NA.

The low grazing fees suggested by the region also met with objection in Washington. No doubt the low fees were influenced by the frequency of subsistence grazing operations in the region and by the low rates in effect on western national forests. "There is a strong feeling among western grazing men, and this office concurs," wrote Granger, "that our grazing fees are much too low." Many agreed that administrative difficulties in range management were partly traceable to low grazing fees. It was no secret that the Forest Service was considering an entirely new grazing-fee structure. Granger agreed that the social and economic conditions were vastly different in the South. Purely subsistence-type settlers who were receiving other forms of government assistance could be subsidized through free or nominal grazing fees. But he questioned this policy in areas where commercial grazing could be practiced. In those areas it would be better policy to establish grazing fees which represent the commercial value of the forage.

Finally, Granger urged southern forests to avoid a blanket policy of allowing all settlers to run ten head of exempt stock. Instead, where grazing was conducted on a family-subsistence basis, free grazing should be limited to the numbers of stock actually required to meet domestic requirements. Written permits should be issued for the exempt stock as well as for those under paid permits where grazing was conducted on a commercial basis. Washington agreed that under present conditions formal permits would not be issued to the large number of subsistence settlers who have only a few head of exempt stock. Still, the policy would eventually move to the issuance of written permits to all who pasture livestock on the national forests. "To do so," concluded Granger, "should gradually create more respect for regulation of use of the forests and result in more adequate control of livestock grazing." [29]

Throughout the ranks of range managers in the Forest Service, 1944 had been a year of growing discontent with past accomplishments and policies. That the service could acknowledge failure was a testimony to its determination to become a more effective guaradian of forest resources in the future.

[29]C. M. Granger to J. C. Kircher, December 2, 1944, Acc. No. 59A1532, Box 64, WNRC.

8

New Directions—Old Themes

> We should be morally right and we should be scientifically correct,
> but neither is the controlling factor in getting the job done. The
> controlling factor is public opinion.
> —*Instructions to Range Administration Trainees*, 1956

To many, the newly prescribed course for range management came as a jolt. Those who expressed the most surprise at plans for reduction were western congressmen and senators. Many of them had just succeeded in undermining the Grazing Service, if not almost dismantling it, through biased committee hearings and legislative budget cuts. The Forest Service's new forthrightness (even aggressiveness) made it appear to be walking into the lion's den. Many users had been lulled by the Forest Service's past attempts to accommodate and adjust to user needs. Clearly the new policies invited challenges in the form of renewed investigations and punitive legislation.

Even as congressional reaction became a certainty, the regions took steps to implement reductions that Acting Chief Forester Clapp had urged earlier in the decade. Now they were being methodically and dutifully implemented by the new chief, Lyle Watts. Of course, the need for reductions varied from region to region and forest to forest. Recommended steps included contacting the ranchers personally and informing them of deteriorated conditions, in some cases riding the ranges in their company. This approach emphasized that protection of the range was a cooperative undertaking in the interests of the rancher and the Forest Service.

Probably the region that experienced the least difficulty in this new period of range regulation was Region 1. Reductions had continued there throughout the Depression under the leadership of the tough regional forester Colonel Evan W. Kelley despite Chief Forester Silcox's "go-easy" policies that placed the economic welfare of stockmen first in times of economic crisis. The ranges in Region 1 were in such good condition that it was actually in a position to announce increases in permitted stock at a time when the other regions moved toward reductions. The Denver, Albuquerque, and Ogden regions, for example, were fraught with problems. These regions fell within the arid zones of North America, with little rain and inordinately long grazing seasons because of the mild climate. Natural defenses of the forage resources were not as great as in the northern areas with their longer winters and greater annual moisture supplies.

In April of 1945, Region 5 circulated a *Report on Range Allotment Analysis*. The study attempted to pinpoint deteriorating or deteriorated ranges in the region. It commented on conditions on each of its 764 allotments and suggested possibilities for future sustained use in competition with other users of the forests. It identified problem areas and suggested remedies and strategies for their implementation. Tactful sample letters were included for use in situations where reductions would be necessary. The report provided guidelines for action, and ultimately had much to do with clearing the high Sierra of harmful livestock grazing.

Not all of Region 5 responded so calmly to the reduction policies. Residents of Modoc County (northeastern California) condemned the Forest Service for its new policies and, in 1949, set off a series of controversies called the "Modoc Grazing Wars." Ranchers, merchants, and other landowners united against the service, charging that it was denying their right to a living. Local citizens refused to cooperate in firefighting and posted "no trespassing" signs on private lands against service personnel and hunters arriving from the cities. The citizens contended that the Forest Service was "ruining" the main industry of the county.

In the fall of 1945, Regional Forester Stuart B. Show had confidently told the Washington office, "You can rightly expect aggressive action to put needed changes into effect." At the same time, Show recommended more supervision of the forests and more regionwide centralization. Snow said he believed in full decentralization, but in the case of range management he thought the service and the regions had gone too far. The new, tighter grazing policy meant that some local autonomy must end. Also he feared that other regions would not move as swiftly and as determinedly. He did not wish his office to appear too conspicuous in the field of restrictive-grazing regulations lest his region be caught out on a limb. Show acknowledged that some of the service's range policy was impractical, lacking direction and consistency. He ventured that preoccupation with persistently quarrelsome relations from the vocal factions of the range livestock industry had absorbed too much time and that too little attention had been paid to the position of range in the total scheme of Forest Service duties. Show was a careful administrator who recognized that abrupt changes could threaten the stability of programs.[1]

In 1946, professionals in range science and even in forestry began to talk of forming a professional society of range managers. A survey was conducted to determine interest in the formation of a new society for the promotion of range management and its resource ideals. More than five hundred individuals in government, universities, and the private sector expressed interest. The organizers hoped the new organization would seek a consensus on range-management objectives and professional standards. The first meeting of the Society for Range Management was held in Salt Lake City in January, 1948. The members elected officers, adopted a constitution, and established the *Journal of Range Management*, inviting the submission of scholarly research in range science and management. The meetings, conducted on an annual basis, would not only conduct the business of the organization, but also provide a forum for the delivery and criticism of scholarly papers. The society soon boasted more than five hundred members.[2]

Over the next two years, the Forest Service received advice from its own experts on stock reduction as well as criticism from users and their political spokesmen. Some regional foresters complained, "We just do not have reliable records of conditions measured periodically from which trends can be determined." The Washington Office was urged to select a method. Field officers differed widely on how to judge range deterioration, on what remedies were adequate, and how far and how fast the program should be pushed. Some even suggested a moratorium until a more favorable time or until a more thorough application of range improvements. The field men had many specific questions about the new policy and behind all their questions was an underlying reluctance to incur serious disputes with the users.

[1] S. B. Show to Chief and Assistant Chiefs, October 22, 1945, Sec. 63, Box 561; "Report on Range Allotment Analysis—Region 5, 1945, Sec. 63, Box 561; C. M. Recter to Regional Forester, September 1, 1949, Sec. 63, Inspection, R-5, 1949, RG 95, NA; *Modoc County Times*, August 25, 1949.

[2] Joseph Pechanec, "Our Range Society," *Journal of Range Management* 1 (October, 1948): 1–2.

In the bargaining process, if indeed the reductions were subject to negotiations, it was asked, "Should more reductions be sought than were thought necessary?" In other words, should room be left for compromise? If so, the goal of the rangers was to make the best deal they could with the permittees. Some suggested that moderate reductions be made. Others asked whether their information and education work should be done for a year or two before moving on the reduction program. Still others insisted that it would be better for the service to buy the preference from the stockmen. Finally came the hesitant question, "What will the chief's office and the secretary do when 'the heat is turned on' and the going gets tough?" All of these questions reflected a degree of confusion in the field about Washington's determination and sincerity in this new course of range reform.

Range Inspector F. Lee Kirby urged an appropriate statement of policy from Washington at this time "to put the field men straight on what is expected of them and to unify their efforts and approach." After all of the high-sounding words out of Washington, and the extensive conferences on the range problem, it was surprising that Kirby's report still showed local officials to be uncertain about the signals coming out of Washington and whether they would be backed in tough reduction programs. Kirby, however, knew from personal experience that the crusade for range reform could lead to abrupt transfers within the service. His early, well-recognized work on the Tonto forest in Arizona had been cut short by his removal as supervisor and reassignment as range examiner. Kirby's words surely grew out of his own experience.[3]

Region 4 attempted to move boldly on the grazing issue in 1945. Regional Forester William B. Rice scheduled meetings at the end of the year with all Utah supervisors to discuss their progress and report range conditions. Rice was most concerned with the Manti forest in the dry southeast. Historically it had the weakest grazing program, and its ranges were in the worst condition. For twenty years (under supervisor Joseph W. Humphrey) virtually nothing had been done in the Manti in the way of range management and adjustments. "To be frank and not for the record," Rice wrote, "the permittees did just about as they pleased." Humphrey had been succeeded in 1941 by Allen C. Folster, whom Rice also did not consider to be a strong or aggressive controller of grazing. The new supervisor, Robert H.

[3] Lee Kirby to W. L. Dutton, March 18, 1974, Sec. 63, Box 574, RG 95, NA; P. V. Woodhead to WO July 2, 1947, Acc. No. 59A1532, WNRC.

Park, now had the unenviable task of putting the Manti's grazing affairs in order. It was feared that the permittees would protest the sudden shift in policy. Rice was concerned that Washington would then accuse the region of acting too hastily and without due notice to the stockmen.

In his campaign to bring reductions to Region 4, Rice also appealed to the leadership of the Mormon Church. His letter to Ezra Taft Benson (later secretary of agriculture) stressed the region's deplorable range and watershed conditions and the need to build up and protect the resources for future generations. Elder Benson replied that he was convinced that the church could help greatly in calling the attention of "our people" to the problems. Later in the year Benson, in an address entitled "All of America is Zion," declared that Mormons should utilize the information developed by the Forest Service, the agricultural colleges, and leading ranchers to restore the ranges and increase the number of livestock to be carried.[4]

While field men complained about the vague commitments from Washington, Chief Watts expressed irritation that field officers failed to follow some of the most rudimentary principles in dealing with the public. Watts said this was especially apparent in the cases of grazing appeals and complaints relating to stock reductions to protect the range. The cases referred to his office for action and review revealed "in too many instances, a disturbing lack of common sense handling in the field." Specific instructions regarding advance notice and discussions with permittees too often were disregarded. Watts deplored sudden newspaper publicity announcing proposed drastic cuts and a failure to work with individuals, small groups, and local associations for an amicable solution of differences. Close cooperation, he said, with livestock associations was not only desirable but also mandatory.

Local forest officials, on the other hand, saw these complaints from the chief office as evidence that the Washington men wanted as little trouble as possible from the regions on the grazing issue. Watts must have anticipated this reaction because he closed his letter to the regional offices with reassurances that he understood the seriousness of the range situation and that appeals would be expected even with the most careful management in the regions. He said that his request for compliance with "the co-

[4]W. B. Rice to W. L. Dutton, December 14, 1945; Rice to Ezra T. Benson, March 8, 1945; Benson, address to semi-annual conference in the Tabernacle, October 7, 1945, Sec. 63, Dr. 592, RG 95, NA.

operative method of approach" in no way lessened his support for regional actions to obtain proper stocking of the ranges.[5]

Some of the greatest difficulties in adjustment came in the Region 2. Even the regional office urged some forest supervisors to take it slowly at the outset. In particular if one forest announced heavy cuts, an adjacent forest that might also serve the same users was advised to refrain from cuts until the stockmen could absorb the losses on the first forest. Such was the case with the Medicine Bow National Forest in Wyoming and the Routt National Forest in Colorado. Assistant regional forester for Region 2, Earl D. Sandvig, told the supervisor of the Routt forest that since the Medicine Bow forest had already announced a reduction program that would affect many permittees of both the Routt and Medicine Bow forests, it would not be "good strategy to press too strongly for the reductions you need on the Routt at this time." Sandvig reminded the supervisor of the fury that an earlier attempt at reduction had caused in the forest. Still, he conceded, it might be well to place the reduction program before permittees this fall and tell them that the goals would have to be achieved in three to five years.

All of Sandvig's advice came too late to avoid controversy on the Routt. Supervisor Charles E. Fox had already informed permittees in the Routt forest: "For one reason or another our ranges in general are overstocked and on many not only have inferior species become established, but active erosion is occurring." He warned that some ranges would have to be closed entirely to begin the work of restoration, and he concluded: "A few years of nonuse will not do the trick; neither will a reduction of a few hundred head here and there. The situation calls for rather drastic action, and as land managers responsible to the people of the United States, there is no alternate course open to us. We must ask that substantial reductions be made, beginning with the 1946 season."[6]

This letter was sent without prior notice, personal contact, or riding of the range with the permittees. Those permittees who met with the supervisor on the ranges in question said his mind was closed to their arguments. All of these complaints were taken to the advisory board and sent on to Denver. Resolutions from the advisory board challenged the supervisor's

[5] Lyle F. Watts to Regions 1–6, February 11, 1946, Sec. 63, Dr. 575, RG 95, NA.

[6] E. D. Sandvig to Routt, December 13, 1945; C. E. Fox to Permittees, Routt National Forest, October 11, 1945, Sec. 63, Dr. 592, RG 95, NA.

"estimates of grazing capacities" and most of all his method of approach, which they felt was "dictatorial and unreasonable to put it mildly." Protests from the Routt graziers had already reached congressmen. Immediately the Washington office wanted to know what was causing all of the bad feeling. The explanation was conveyed to Chief Christopher M. Granger on December 3, 1945.

The reply from Region 2 was apologetic for not holding a tighter rein on Fox's moves and promised that the requests from the Routt and North Park advisory boards would be granted. These requests were merely that no reductions be made in 1946, that the regional office reexamine grazing capacity and discuss estimates with users, and that any reductions made necessary by the 1946 findings be phased in over a three-year period. Admittedly, accepting or granting these requests undercut the supervisor, but there did not seem to be any other option in the light of the supervisor's arbitrary actions.

In addition, Regional Forester John W. Spencer said the region was moving to head off protests against the reduction of thirty-one thousand head of sheep from the Carbon County Woolgrowers Association that Fox had ordered. The situation was "potential dynamite," far more serious than the North Park controversies. Spencer hoped all of this could be quieted down, because he noted that the Colorado legislature on November 23, 1945, had called for a congressional investigation into the Forest Service's grazing permit reductions. The memorial closely followed the wording of one recently passed by the Arizona legislature which also was sensitive to reduction programs. Spencer hoped that he and Sandvig could work fast enough to reach a workable understanding with the livestock industry of Colorado and Wyoming before the congressional committees took up the cause.[7]

As the McCarran committee's intermittent work and yearly appropriations came to an end in late 1945, other western congressmen stood ready to launch their own investigations. During hearings of the McCarran committee at Salt Lake City in September of 1945, Walt Dutton, the chief of the Division of Range Management, hinted that the Forest Service was planning some important reductions in the postwar period. His words

[7] John W. Spencer to Chief, Forest Service, December 10, 1945, Sec. 63, Dr. 592, RG 95, NA; Colorado General Assembly, Senate, *Senate Journal of the 35th General Assembly of the State of Colorado*, November 23, 1945.

alerted Congressman Frank A. Barrett of Wyoming to the possible difficulties that the shift in Forest Service policy posed for his stockmen constituents. McCarran had already demonstrated the power of a committee; the Grazing Service was now weak and hesitating in its tasks of grazing regulation on the public domain. The Forest Service appeared to be moving in a direction where it could be taught a similar lesson. Congressman Barrett hoped he could be its chief instructor through the establishment of a new congressional committee. Under House Resolution 93 in the Eightieth Congress, Barrett's committee gained authorization to investigate public land administration. Like preceding investigations, the Barrett committee began in Washington, D.C. (in early 1947) and traveled a predictable course, first to Montana and Wyoming, then to Colorado and Utah, over to California and Nevada, and back to Arizona, where the call for a new congressional investigating committee had originated.

Spencer's prediction of a hostile congressional investigation became a reality. The new undertaking was the third attempt since the mid-1920s to investigate and pressure agencies administering the public lands. The Stanfield committee of the 1920s, the McCarran committee of the early 1940s, and Congressman Barrett of Wyoming all "rode the range" to seek out federal "wrongdoing." William Voigt, Jr., in his book *Public Grazing Lands* (1976) saw the work of this congressional committee as the second major attempt to initiate a "land grab" by western states. While Congressman Barrett eventually stopped short of offering a congressional bill to give all public grazing lands to the states, his committee's work concentrated on trying to expose injustice in the Forest Service's reduction program. Voigt summarized the committee's intent as "the humiliation and domination of the Forest Service." [8]

The grazing situation in the West soon commanded the attention of the national press. An editorial in *American Forests* in February, 1947, took issue with the resolution passed a month earlier at the fiftieth annual convention of the American Livestock Association in Phoenix, Arizona. The resolution called for an investigation of the national forests and for legislation to transfer the grazing lands from the forests into private hands or to the Department of the Interior for leasing out or sale. The editorial pointed out that grazing fees established by the Department of the Interior

---

[8] William Voigt, Jr., *Public Grazing Lands: Use and Misuse by Industry and Government*, pp. 83, 97; Bernard DeVoto, *The Easy Chair*, p. 249.

were only about one-seventh of those prevailing on national forests. When the House Committee on Public Lands in 1946 raised the question of increasing the fees to a more equitable level, stockmen protested vigorously. According to the editorial, the proposed increase was blocked by breaking the back of the Grazing Service through drastic appropriation cuts. The editorial saw "an overall plan of strategy" not only to destroy the grazing districts of the public domain, but also to break up the National Forests.[9]

The most influential outcry against stockmen and their political representatives came from articles by Bernard DeVoto, editor of the widely-read *Harper's* magazine. Although DeVoto was editor of an eastern magazine, he had been raised in Salt Lake City. He repeatedly used the words *land grab* to describe the motives of stockmen and their vociferous leaders such as F. E. Mollin, secretary of the American Livestock Association. Congressman Frank Barrett presented an especially good target for DeVoto's journalistic salvos. Barrett had a record of opposing public land reserves in his home state, especially President Roosevelt's attempt to create a Jackson Hole National Monument. DeVoto pursued the theme of "The West Against Itself" in an important article in January, 1947, and continued his critical coverage of the Barrett committee's progress in his monthly column "The Easy Chair."

DeVoto's attacks on the stock industry and their political allies were wide-ranging and sometimes unfair. Yet readers understood the message that stockmen wished to plunder the nation's resources under the banners of states' rights and private enterprise. DeVoto insisted that western stockmen viewed themselves as the great defenders of free enterprise against the "communism" of government interference. Yet they constantly called for government tariff protection from Argentina and government improvement of the rangelands for their benefit. Even small users of the ranges had "destroyed" the forage resource. In Utah the Mormon desire to hold the family together resulted in dividing and subdividing the family lands. The pressure to support an increasing ranch population resulted in overgrazed ranges and impaired watersheds.

The Barrett committee was one of those groups that sought a "land grab," according to DeVoto. The lands would be transferred to the states, and then the states would be free to let them fall into private ownership. The ultimate objective, DeVoto said, was to convert to private owner-

[9] "Lest Congress Forget," *American Forests* 53 (February, 1947): 55.

ship all public lands in the western states, which would mean the end of conservation and watershed protection. DeVoto referred to the Barrett committee's investigations as "Congressman Barrett's Circus" and quoted the *Denver Post*'s description of "Stockman Barrett's Wild West Show." Other reasons behind Barrett's performances, according to DeVoto, were to reduce appropriations for the Forest Service, thus forcing it into a subservient position similar to that of the Grazing Service. Finally, DeVoto attacked Barrett's bill for the admission of Alaska as a state. The bill proposed to turn over to the new state all public lands within its boundaries. This proposal would set a dangerous precedent by opening the way for other western states to demand the public lands.[10]

The columns of other journals and newspapers took aim at the "land grabbers." Conservation writers wielded their pens against the latest threat from "avaricious" westerners. The widely read *Collier's* magazine and sportsmen's publications such as *Sports Afield, Field & Stream, Outdoor Life*, and *Outdoor America* attacked the tactics of stock organizations and the ultimate goals of the Barrett committee. The *Salt Lake City Tribune* also chimed in against the "land grab."

The editorial section of the *Denver Post* featured a guest editorial by the Denver freelance outdoor sport and conservationist writer, Arthur H. Carhart, who had been the Forest Service's first landscape architect: "Stockmen's Proposal Called Monopolistic: Plan Seen as Menace to U.S. Parks and Forests." Admittedly some of the rhetoric was extreme and unfair, but the conservationists made their point to sportsmen and preservationists alike. After World War II the growing cities of the West were sensitive about moves to give away millions of acres of recreational lands to graziers. William Voigt, Jr., of the Izaak Walton League's office in Denver; Hoyt Wilson, editor of the *Denver Post*; and Carhart spearheaded the journalistic effort against the Barrett committee in the Rocky Mountain press.[11]

One of the hopes of the stock organizations and politicians such as Congressman Barrett was that the postwar period would witness a dramatic reaction against "New Dealism" and the agencies that administered natural resources. But the Forest Service had a longer history than the New Deal,

[10] DeVoto, *The Easy Chair*, pp. 231–55; *Harper's* 194 (June, 1947): 543–45; 194 (January, 1947): 46; 198 (January, 1948): 30.

[11] Voigt, *Public Grazing Lands*, pp. 191–95; *Denver Post*, February 9, 1947; Lester Velie, "They Kicked Us Off Our Land," *Collier's* 120 (July 26, 1947): 20–21 and 120 (August 9, 1947): 72–73.

and its roots of support went deeper into the soil of American reform than the crisis of the recent depression. The protests against the Forest Service questioned only the need for reductions. Stockmen contended that protection of the resource should not be the criteria for the reduction, but rather ranching economics. Stock interests also questioned the ability of the Forest Service agencies to judge the need for reductions upon the basis of their observation and study. They wanted the proposed reductions delayed at least a year and perhaps several years to await further analysis. In the meantime the service and other public land management agencies should proceed with range-improvement programs such as reseeding, clearing brush, and the construction of watering facilities.

The stock industry sought a recognition of the legal rights of the permittee to his allotments. It contended that users needed quasi-property rights to these grazing areas to insure stability. For many ranch properties the seasonal ranges provided in the Forest Service lands formed an integral part of their operations. Without the forest ranges their lands in the valleys would be substantially less valuable and produce less stock despite their large investments in irrigation and haylands. The recognition of a property right in these ranges would go a long way toward providing better stability of tenure to the rancher. In addition, a property claim to the lands would give the allotment holder access to the courts in any disputes with the Forest Service. A major complaint of permitees was that they had no other recourse under the present system than to appeal to the administrative agency in case of disputes. They complained that in range matters the Forest Service was the legislature, the executive, and the judicial body all in one. Forest Service leadership had consistently opposed any concessions in the direction of recognizing property rights in use of allotments. This question had arisen earlier in controversies over allowing permittees to construct their own range improvements without a cooperative agreement or the participation of the service. If such arrangements were allowed, the allotment holders would be in a position to claim they had improved the property to such an extent that they now had a vested right in it.

The Forest Service stood firm against most proposals to weaken its longtime authority over the administration of grazing lands. To subject every range management decision to possible challenges in local or even federal courts would create an impossible situation in the administration of the lands. The Forest Service did approve, however, the creation of mandatory advisory boards to which stockmen could appeal their disputes, but from that level of appeal the dispute had to enter the normal channels of appeal to the region, to the chief, and finally to the secretary of agriculture.[12] Considering the wide range of demands being made, the Forest Service conceded very little. The advisory boards were merely to be given the power to review local forest decisions and make recommendations to Forest Service personnel in an advisory capacity. It was true that the Barrett committee suggested that "appeal boards" have final authority in disputed cases, but as the secretary of agriculture pointed out, the department only supported the position that the boards have an advisory responsibility.

As the Barrett committee wound up its tour of western communities and cities in the late months of 1947, it sent to Secretary of Agriculture Anderson a group of recommendations, among which was a three-year moratorium on further reductions. The secretary said that he was "convinced the overgrazed conditions on many national forest ranges [were] too serious from the standpoint of both watershed and forage to brook the delay." He noted that although the committee had traveled throughout the West, it did not take his recommendation to go out onto the ranges to see the examples of serious overgrazing, needs for reseeding, range improvements, and better management by the permittees." The committee made the charge that the reduction program threatened the nation's and the world's beef supplies with higher prices. The secretary dismissed this charge, saying that if all the ranges on the national forests were closed to grazing, less than 1 percent of the nation's total animal-months' feed requirements would be involved. For the purposes of his argument he omitted the important complementary role played by these ranges for recovery of nonforest ranges on a yearly basis. Forest grazing was the key to a successful system of "transhumance" ranching worked out in the valleys and mountains of the West. Using forest ranges in the summer freed outlying ranges from use that would otherwise deplete them.

The proposal for more cooperation between stockmen and the Forest Service for the improvement of ranges was accepted by the secretary. The committee's proposal that "all conditions required of a permittee or imposed upon him, or agreements or promises made to him by forest officers in connection with his grazing permit be in writing and their validity recognized by any successors to such officials," was merely termed good admin-

---

[12] Mont H. Saunderson, *Western Land and Water Use*, pp. 197–209; *Record Stockman: The Weekly Livestock Newspaper* (Denver, Colo.), March 7, 1946.

istration. The final suggestion from the committee asked for an amendment to the 1897 Forest Administration Act to provide specifically for grazing as a basic use of national forest lands. This recognition of grazing, said Secretary Anderson, would give rise to the designation of other specific uses. Stockmen should recognize, he continued, that such a definition of uses might ultimately work harm to their interests.[13]

By the spring of 1948, Chief Forester Watts acknowledged that the service had endured "a pretty tough fight" over the grazing issues. He asserted that the service was "not afraid of that fight," but he conceded that the "fight would have been so much easier if we were a bit more skillful in handling our public relations. Part of our fight is right there." Probably to improve public relations, Watts announced that the service accepted a one-year delay in its reduction program. This announcement was hailed by stock organizations, but those interested in the protection of watershed in the West were greatly disappointed and distressed. For example, one city council member from Grand Junction, Colorado, berated the secretary of agriculture for delaying reductions until the fall of 1949. "To continue to graze cattle on these raw, eroding slopes now," he argued, "is just plain ridiculous and the people of Grand Junction are up in arms about it." Without attacking the interests of the cowmen, he said it would be just as fair to close them out of the ranges now while the price of cattle was still high. He drew the conclusion that the interests of the twenty-five thousand people of Grand Junction were being slighted for the interests of eighteen stockmen who used the ranges in question.[14]

While battling the stock organizations, the Forest Service sometimes neglected to emphasize that stock grazing on the forests always had to be coordinated with watershed and forest protection as well as the needs of the local population. In one exchange with Congressman Barrett, Chief Forester Watts pointed out the large numbers of people besides stockmen who were vitally interested in the manner in which the national forest range resources were managed. In the forests outside the West, most of the land was acquired under the Weeks Law of 1911, which prohibited homesteading. In Tennessee the service's main concern was the protection of timber and watershed values. Grazing by domestic livestock there was either ex-

[13] "The Secretary Stands Firm!" *American Forests* 54 (February, 1948): 61.
[14] Regional Foresters' and Directors' Meeting, ca. April, 1948, Sec. 63, Dr. 562; A. G. Martin to Secretary of Agriculture Clinton P. Anderson, March 24, 1948, Sec. 63, Dr. 636, RG 95, NA; Harold K. Steen, *The U.S. Forest Service: A History*, p. 273.

tremely restricted or prohibited in order to protect the other values of greater importance from a public standpoint.[15]

On the Monongahela National Forest in West Virginia (Region 7), officials protested that the low grazing fees encouraged overgrazing in the forest. The low fees aroused some antagonism among private landowners, who charged unfair competition because of low rates charged by the national forest. The regional forester also protested the rates to Washington: "In view of our regional policy against building up a grazing business, the present schedule of fees places us in an awkward position of offering cut rates on business which we do not care to attract." The region proposed three types of land classifications for its grazing fees in order to raise them to comparable market value. But this issue was much farther down the road for the Washington office and could not be addressed even on one eastern forest. In addition, the eastern forests, where little grazing occurred, protested the requirement that they submit a grazing map for each forest to Washington.[16]

In the fall of 1949 the Anderson-Mansfield Act to provide for range reseeding on an estimated four million acres of national-forest range lands became law. The Forest Service reaffirmed its policy that ranchers could receive a reduction in grazing fees in return for improvements they made on their allotments. The service also agreed to hold hearings at the request of the permittees on matters affecting grazing permits. It agreed to adopt the following statement of policy:

As a general policy the Forest Service will undertake to provide a stenographic transcript of any hearing on any range administrative matter, when requested in writing by a grazing permittee and when in the judgement of the regional forester the matter is of sufficient importance to justify the cost. The location of such hearings will have to be determined by the circumstances in each case and will be influenced by availability of recording equipment or qualified stenographers, accessibility of witnesses, space accommodations, and other pertinent conditions. Legal council representing permittees will be recognized .[17]

Despite these gestures toward the stock industry, the Forest Service still insisted on reducing numbers on the ranges. It also asserted its con-

[15] Watts to Frank A. Barrett, March 25, 1946; Watts to Estes Kefauver, March 23, 1948, Sec. 63, Dr. 561, RG 95, NA.

[16] R. M. Evans to Chief, March 6, 1947, Sec. 63; Mary E. Price to Dutton, November 21, 1945, Sec. 63, Dr. 534, RG 95, NA.

[17] "Reductions in Grazing Fees for Improvements," ca. 1949, Acc. No. 59A1532, Box 59, WNRC; Walt L. Dutton, "Range Management Report," June 6, 1949, Sec. 63, Dr. 646, RG 95, NA.

tinuing right to determine range capacity and to impose reduction.[18] By 1949, the Forest Service and the stock industry appeared to be locked in a more determined struggle. An old "war horse" for the stockmen, Vernon Metcalf, of Nevada, told the Idaho Wool Growers Association that the Forest Service was the "worst possible landlord in the United States." He far preferred the Grazing Service because he was convinced that it offered stockmen more stability, collected lower grazing fees, provided transfer of grazing privileges by law instead of by edict of local administrators, and gave users more voice in range use than did the Forest Service. For him, even the recent recommendations of the Hoover commission that all grazing lands be placed under one agency in a move to consolidate the Bureau of Land Management and the Forest Service was not an adequate solution. There was no guarantee that the Bureau of Land Management would be the agency to receive control of the grazing lands.[19]

In Region 2, during the summer of 1949, feelings continued to grow bitter between stock organizations and the Forest Service. In northern Colorado, Roosevelt National Forest officials announced the elimination of grazing from certain portions of the forest and a reduction in the length of season in other areas. In late May the *Denver Post* announced that the Forest Service had decided to eliminate all livestock grazing along the front range of the Colorado Rockies from a point near Boulder to the Colorado-Wyoming line. By August the paper reported that ranchers were up in arms against the service. The president of the Larimer County Stockgrowers Association attacked its dictatorial methods and promised a fight. He said Forest Service officials were mistaken to believe that they "can cut the ranchers' throats and have them smile about it." It was apparent in his eyes that the Forest Service was not motivated by watershed protection or soil conservation. He claimed it wanted to cater to new users of the forests such as tourists and sportsmen and to enlarge its bureaucratic empire by attempting to make a playground out of the West.[20] A rebellion was beginning in Region 2 that would ultimately test the conviction of the service to carry out a far-reaching reduction program over the next decades.

In the meantime, the hoped-for relief legislation from the onslaughts of Forest Service reductions was not supported by Congress. Congressman

[18] Watts to Congressman W. K. Granger, June 16, 1949, Sec. 63, Dr. 644, RG 95, NA.
[19] Edward P. Cliff, "Vernon Metcalf's Uncomplimentary Remarks," 1949, Sec. 63, Dr. 636, RG 95, NA.
[20] Clipping file, *Denver Post*, May 29, July 5, August 9, 1949, Sec. 63, Dr. 636, RG 95, NA.

Walker K. Granger of Utah sponsored a bill "to facilitate and simplify the work of the Forest Service." Edward J. Thye of Minnesota sponsored the bill in the Senate. As a result of the act, grazing was for the first time legislatively recognized by name as one of the major legitimate uses of forest resources. The act gave lawful recognition to ten-year grazing permits and made local advisory boards an appeals body against administrative decisions. The decisions of the boards, however, could be appealed to higher administrative authority within the service to the secretary of agriculture. Under this system of internal appeals the Forest Service still retained its right to combine legislative, executive, and judiciary functions in the implementation of its policies. Thus the Granger-Thye Act was no great victory for stockmen.[21]

The continuing controversies in Region 2 now moved toward an unexpected showdown. Criticism of local forest supervisors, particularly of Clarence K. Collins, supervisor of the Uncompahgre National Forest in southwestern Colorado, continued unabated. The complaints oftentimes went directly to Washington, bypassing the regional office and supervisor John Spencer, who had fallen into disfavor with industry representatives several years earlier over the reduction programs.[22] To make matters more confusing in the region, Lynn H. Douglas, a former assistant regional forester in the Denver office, who had retired in January, 1948, publicly criticized Forest Service range administration in speeches before local stock associations.

Douglas began his attacks on the Forest Service during the presidential campaign of 1948. In letters to Republican candidate Thomas E. Dewey, he explained that he took early retirement from the service because he could no long stand the "new dealish" influence that dominated a "formerly fine and efficient agency." He said the past years had seen the Democrats build paper organizations devoted mostly to the function of planning instead of doing. The leading administrators in the conservation agencies, he charged, could not be depended upon to spend appropriations wisely: "They have either grown up under 'spend and spend; tax and tax; elect and elect' influence or have become contaminated." By late 1949, Douglas was still speaking to local stock organizations and obtaining newspaper coverage. His chief theme was that the Forest Service was a large organization

[21] Steen, *U.S. Forest Service*, p. 274.
[22] F. E. Mollin to W. L. Dutton, January 18, 1949, Sec. 63, Dr. 637, RG 95, NA.

that had used its appropriations to grow bigger and that placed its own interests before the public's interest.[23]

With all of the controversy swirling about the grazing question on the Colorado forests, the National Forest Advisory Board was called upon to investigate the problem in the Roosevelt National Forest. The advisory board was made up of three consultants appointed by the secretary of agriculture to advise him on questions concerning the administration of the national forests. Its report appeared on January 25, 1950. It designated for the forest a priority of uses which gave first consideration to watershed protection, followed by recreation, livestock grazing, and forest production. The list of priorities generally supported the Forest Service's reduction programs. Also in 1950 at the request of a joint committee of the American National Livestock Association and the National Wool Growers' Association, the National Forest Advisory Board reviewed aspects of national forest range-management policy. After hearings in Denver, the board recommended that the service continue its policy of making reductions at the time when permits were transferred from one party to another. It called for certain clarifications requiring notification of reductions to the prospective buyer. It also encouraged the Forest Service and other department of agriculture agencies to help grazing permittees improve the productiveness of their private lands to relieve their dependence on federal lands.

Finally the board took notice of the tremendous amount of publicity that the range reductions had caused in the press. Many of the articles in the national and local press had led many stockmen to believe that the Forest Service was moving toward a total elimination of grazing. This charge was repeatedly denied by the Forest Service, but nevertheless the impression remained from the impact of some of the articles emanating from the conservationist authors such as DeVoto and Carhart. The service was advised to give more publicity through educational programs to its goals of protecting watershed and other range values that overall contributed to a permanent and stable livestock industry.

The board believed that the root of the serious controversy between the Forest Service and stockmen in Region 2 grew from the publicity by "over-zealous writers in the public press attacking stockmen." These writers characterized stockmen as abusers of the natural range resources and "robber cattle barons." On the other hand, spokesmen for stock organiza-

[23] Clipping file, *Denver Post*, October 26, 1949, Sec. 63, Dr. 636, RG 95, NA.

tions attacked Forest Service personnel in the press as "dumb bureau-crats." The entire situation fomented suspicion and stubborness on both sides. No doubt the rapid turnover in service personnel, inexperience, and lack of diplomacy because of an insufficient public relations program con-tributed, but the involvement of a strident press caused bitterness on both sides.[24]

All of the notoriety and publicity began to take its toll upon the inter-nal structure of the Forest Service both in Washington and in the Rocky Mountain region. One of the principal advocates of a hard line in the pro-tection of range resources in the region was Earl D. Sandvig, in charge of the Division of Wildlife and Range Management for the Rocky Mountain Region since 1944.

Sandvig's transfer to Denver came at just the time the service moved to upgrade its protection of the range resources. His background suited him well for this undertaking. Five years later Sandvig had the reputation among stockmen in the region for being hard-nosed when it came to the question of protecting the ranges. He believed large stock reductions were in the interests of the stockmen themselves and not detrimental to their in-terests, because the reductions protected the resources by which they lived. These arguments, however, were not always effective with stockmen who saw their allotments being cut back year after year. By 1950, Sandvig's work in grazing-reduction programs earned him several uncomplimentary epithets, such as the "scourge of the Rockies," among the stockmen.

On the other hand, what did the appointment of Edward Cliff as successor to supervisor John Spencer mean for the region's grazing policies or the service's long-range policies? Cliff had long been close to Chief Watts since Cliff's student days at Utah State Agricultural College, where Watts was once a professor. The connection made Cliff a virtual emissary of the Washington office to Denver. Many saw his moves as indicative of the sentiments and wishes in Washington as the region worked to solve its grazing crisis. Sandivg, Cliff remembers, resented his appointment. In any event the two men did not see eye to eye on approaches to the grazing prob-lem. Cliff was already known for his interests in working out compromises with the users of the range. Some called him the "friend of the small

[24]U.S. Forest Service, *Annual Report of the Forester, 1951*, p. 58; National Forest Board of Review, "The Grazing Situation on the Roosevelt National Forest, State of Colo-rado," Acc. No. 59A132, Box 59, WNRC.

rancher." Sandvig feared that such compromises meant complete retreat for reduction programs in the region. He resented Cliff's eagerness to please the people in Washington and establish good public relations at, what he believed, was the expense of the resources.[25]

An early indication that Sandvig's hard-line policies were in trouble was a memo from Assistant Forester C. M. Granger to Regional Forester Cliff on August 29, 1951. The memorandum was essentially a bill of good health for the ranges of Region 2. In some forests there were critical areas, but Granger was careful to write: "I have no illusion that anything can be suggested which will eliminate the need for seasonal and numbers adjustments, but something might well be worked out which would reduce that need. In any event it is the best way to proceed from the standpoint of public relations."

What is known as the "blowup in Region 2" came shortly after the appearance of the Granger memorandum in the fall of 1951. In November, Sandvig received notice that he was to be transferred from the region. The reason for the transfer, though never stated officially, was that Sandvig could not refrain from leaking information about the need for further reductions to the *Denver Post*. In one article he charged that grazing fees were little more than a giveaway and in another he said little range progress had occurred in the region since 1937.[26] These comments only served to further rile stockmen in the region and defeat his efforts to build back their confidence in the Forest Service. Although Sandvig was unhappy over the order, he was able to be transferred to the regional office of his choice in Portland, Oregon. Cliff viewed Sandvig as insubordinate, with little sympathy for the economic problems and investments of the ranchers. Sandvig saw Cliff as an appeaser who made decisions from a political, rather than an ecological, point of view.

The transfer immediately captured headlines in the *Denver Post*. The *Post*, which had long been sympathetic to Sandvig's stand against the large stock interests, said many western-slope stockmen were coming to Sandvig's defense, revolting against "a powerful radical stockmen minority who said they'd get Sandvig." Arthur Carhart wrote directly to Watts, protesting the transfer and asking for reconsideration. Carhart said that those conserva-

[25] Edward P. Cliff, interview with author, Washington, D.C., April, 1980; Earl Sandvig, interview with author, Portland, Ore., August, 1980.

[26] Collection, Granger to Cliff, August 29, 1951, Natural Resource Collection, Denver Public Library; Sandvig interview, August, 1980; *Denver Post* (February 23, 26, 1951).

tionist groups that had backed the chief in his campaign for sound forest management were surprised, hurt, and angered. The stockman clique would view the transfer as a victory in having Sandvig "off their backs." According to Carhart, Sandvig had become a symbol in the Denver area of an honest public servant working to protect the properties entrusted to him. Carhart said that he and others could not escape the feeling that "the stockmen politicos have badgered and bullyragged you into retreat, leaving us very much out on a limb."[27]

The appointment of Cliff as regional forester did indeed seem to be a signal of retreat. Cliff was eager to clear up the controversy in the region and restore a semblance of amicability—some would say, at any price. His correspondence revealed a determination to rid the region of grazing administrators who had antagonized stockmen. Cliff wanted to start with a clean slate and build back the good public relations that had been absent in the region for so long. At the same time, he and the Washington office maintained that Forest Service policies on grazing remained unchanged. The service issued subsequent statements to the Denver press to that effect.[28]

Both Washington and Cliff were upset at the manner in which range problems had been handled in Region 2. Range Inspector Avon Denham reported he found a lack of "team play" between the Division of Range Management in Region 2 and the Washington office range-management inspectors. In other western regions, suggestions from the Washington inspectors on reseeding methods, management, and adjustments appeared to be welcomed and used if applicable. "This is not true of the Range Management Division in Region 2," Denham wrote. "Practically all suggestions are challenged." Region 2 range managers objected to alternatives of range improvements and better management techniques that were being suggested as alternatives to reductions. Cliff, too, reported to Washington that some grazing men were basically antagonistic toward the stockmen. Roy Williams, supervisor of the Bighorn National Forest in Wyoming, should, Cliff felt, be moved out of that position, which brought him in direct contact with ranchers. Cliff wanted him moved before the beginning of

---

[27]Clipping file, *Denver Post*, November 30, 1951; Arthur H. Carhart to Lyle Watts, November 30, 1951, Sec. 63, Dr. 658, RG 95, NA.

[28] "The Record" recorded by Edward C. Crafts, December 3, 1951, Sec. 63, Dr. 658, RG 95, NA.

another field season or "before additional incidents occurred which might upset the improved relationships which have been brought about." [29]

By late November, 1951, many of those in Region 2 who had become involved in rows with stockmen in past years felt their days were numbered. Williams detected quite early Cliff's antagonism toward him and Sandivg. Before the announcement of Sandvig's transfer, he wrote Sandvig, "I think Cliff is after you as he is me in order to score with the politicians in Washington." Soon important transfers did indeed take place within the region. Cliff would argue that the basic Forest Service policies were not changing, but that an attempt had to be made in the region to correct the climate of antagonism between the users and the Forest Service before future progress could be made in protecting the resource. [30]

In 1948, the research arm of the Forest Service quietly initiated a study to obtain a method of demonstrating the condition and direction or trend in which the vegetation of a range was moving. The investigative task fell to Ranger Conservationist Kenneth W. Parker. His study utilized the contributions of over fifty people inside and outside the Forest Service to develop a method for determining range trends. The goal of the study was to establish a standard method of measurement that could be easily demonstrated to stockmen. The question of range condition was always a point of controversy between the service and stockmen when the service called for reductions. Stockmen maintained that they were the best judges of range condition because their livelihood depended upon it. They resented officials on the federal payroll making what they regarded as snap judgments on the condition of the range. Therefore, the service called upon science and its research arm to provide an objective methodology that would inspire the confidence of the stock industry.

By 1951, Chief Forester Watts announced the completion of a three-year study for measuring trend in range condition. The method was presented at a meeting in Denver on August 11, 1951, when Kenneth W. Parker presented the results of his study, entitled, "A Method for Measuring Trend in Range Condition on National Forest Ranges." It was hoped the system would be reasonably simple, rapid, and accurate in determining the condi-

---

[29] Avon Denham to C. M. Granger and W. L. Dutton, November 9, 1950; Cliff to Granger, August 30, 1951, Sec. 63, Dr. 658, RG 95, NA.

[30] Roy Williams to Sandvig, November 29, 1951, Earl D. Sandvig Papers, Natural Resource Collection, Box 246, Denver Public Library; Cliff interview, April, 1980.

tion of the range. It was recommended for perennial grasslands, mountain meadow, open-timber lands, and sagebrush-grass types found in national-forest ranges in the West. The methods were the following:

1. Measurement and observation of the essential features of vegetation and soil as recorded on permanently established transect lines and plots located on the usable parts of the range. Measurement is made by means of a small ring or loop at one hundred points along each transect line.
2. Classification of these data as to condition of vegetation and soil stability and estimation of current trend in condition.
3. General and close photographs from permanently located photo points. Application of the three-step method on an allotment basis requires mapping of the usable range areas by broad vegetatives types and by condition situations within these types as a prelude to sampling. Trend is determined by comparison of records made at periodic intervals.

In 1952 the *Annual Report of the Forester* announced that the three-step method had been adopted for general use on western national forest ranges. Within the regions and the forests where it was implemented the method became known as the Parker Three-Step method. The method involved establishing permanently marked transects and the collection of samples along these transects from which could be measured forage, type, and species. Comparisons of data taken over a period of several years obtained in the three steps could yield an understanding of the range condition and trend. Experiments showed that different individuals measuring the same transect obtained nearly identical results. This approach was particularly valuable in the view of the stockmen because it minimized chances for error and biased interpretation. If the measurement was taken in cooperation with the permittee and the statistical data shared, a climate and spirit of cooperation would be generated between the service and the stockmen as never before existed. The Forest Service made it clear that the new method could not determine carrying capacity, but it could determine trends in utilization.[31]

The hope that scientific analysis as expressed in the three-step method could solve the problems between ranchers and range managers in evaluating the range was short-lived. The hope probably sprang more from wishful

[31] Forest Service, *Annual Report, 1951,* and *1952,* p. 63 and pp. 24–25, respectively; J. M. Jones, "Measuring Range Trends," *National Wool Grower* 41 (September, 1951): 41.

thinking than from the past history of relationships on this issue with the stock industry. Representatives of stock organizations were soon charging that carrying capacity was determined by the "unrealistic hoop method." They described the method as throwing down a hoop in a designated area and counting the forage contained within it. "On the basis of such inconclusive, impractical and theoretical information, drastic reductions in grazing allotment have been made," they complained. "To base decisions on scientific facts alone has seldom proven entirely satisfactory in any field of agriculture." The organizations now asserted that range managers should emphasize instead the history of the allotment, local conditions, and experience of the ranchers in utilizing the range.[32]

The stock industry even testified before a Senate investigating committee that the method developed by the Forest Service had shown inaccuracies "except when correlated with actual stock-carrying performance." Their source was a text entitled *Range Surveying and Management Planning* by Laurence A. Stoddart and Arthur D. Smith. Stoddart had long been associated with the Department of Range Management at Texas A&M College, and Smith with Utah State Agricultural College. Both schools had pioneered range studies as a serious discipline—especially Texas A&M, as evidenced by the research efforts of E. J. Dyksterhuis.

The most significant passage seized upon by the representatives of the stock industry concerned the determination of grazing capacity: "Perhaps the best method of determining proper stocking is a study of the history of the stocking over a period of years, together with a very careful study of its effect upon the range. This requires training and knowledge of plants, but it is nothing that the observant stockman cannot master."[33]

The Forest Service responded promptly to such criticism. A detailed letter from Chief Forester Richard E. McArdle (included in a Senate subcommittee's report on the public domain lands in January, 1960) addressed allegations that range-analysis procedures used by the Forest Service were

---

[32]U.S. Congress, Senate, Subcommittee on Public Lands of the Committee on Interior and Insular Affairs, *Hearings on Grazing on Public Domain Lands*, 86th Cong. 2d sess., 1960, part 1, vol. 3, pp. 1–7.

[33]Laurence A. Stoddart and Arthur D. Smith, *Range Surveying and Management Planning*, p. 223, as quoted in p. 9, note 32, of Stoddart and Smith, *Range Management*, which identified two methods of determining grazing capacity, the ocular reconnaissance and the plot method, and concluded: "It is evident that little reliance can be placed upon grazing capacities arrived at by either survey method" (p. 175).

impractical and unreliable. The service pointed out that the range-survey procedures had been developed from fifty years of research and practical range experience by the agency and its personnel. The service emphatically believed that its range-analysis method was sound, was adequately applied, and offered a realistic evaluation of range and watershed conditions on a national forest land. Range analysis, it maintained, was designed to determine all of the following:

1. The portion of each grazing allotment that can be used by domestic livestock in harmony with other national-forest values on a longtime basis
2. The condition and trend of the vegetation and the stability of the soil on the allotment
3. Areas on the allotment that are amenable to development through artificial means
4. The most practical system of management that will result in efficient use of the forage by domestic animals in harmony with other national forest values
5. The grazing capacity of that portion of the allotment that can be used by domestic animals over a long period of time under an attainable system of management

Range analysis was further divided into the following five areas of investigation:

1. Range suitability. What parts of the range were suitable for domestic livestock? For the intermountain region this was defined as "forage-producing land which can be grazed on a sustained yield basis under an attainable management system without damage to the basic soil resource of the area itself, or of adjacent areas." This task called for the classification of land that the earlier overlay maps attempted to illustrate. This involved topography, soil type, vegetation type, distance from water, and poisonous plants.
2. Range condition and trend. This tries to answer questions about plant health and soil stability. Is the range condition trending upward or deteriorating downward, or is it static with no apparent change? The condition of the vegetation was compared to "a situation that would exist under pristine or near-pristine conditions," or what the ecologist terms a "climax" plant cover as determined by climate and soil.

3. Grazing capacity. The goal of this feature of range analysis seeks to achieve "indicated grazing capacity." Ideally this is the amount of use in animal unit days or months obtained at the time proper use is achieved. This also will determine the degree of use, time in the season, and the frequency of use. Soil and plant condition analysis play the important role in these questions.
4. Range improvement. Range analysis should always point out areas on the range that can be improved by both artificial and natural means. This could involve reseeding, the application of herbicides, water development, stock trails, fences, and burning.
5. Management plans and application. All of the previous steps formed the basis for the development of a management plan. Such a plan was formed in cooperation with the permittee or permittees and the Forest Service. The plan described specific details of the management including objectives of the plan, maps and other basic data collected during the analysis. Rate of stocking, seasons of use, responsibilities for range improvements, schedules for examining forage condition were all written up in the management plan.[34]

A cursory reading of these steps and plans reveals a striking similarity to the goals and questions addressed by the Forest Service in the development of its range survey (reconnaissance work) prior to World War I. The service was not playing casually with history when it said that it had been at work on these procedures for at least fifty years. One avenue that helped to blunt criticism in the 1950s after the drive to reduce allotments was cooperative range-improvement programs. These policies expressed a commitment to expanding the resource in order to avert the need for future reductions. As one observer saw it, "the midcentry liberal policy was not to disturb entrenched interests, but to attempt amelioration by increasing the size of the resource."[35]

The presidential elections in 1952 raised the prospect of the first major change in national administrations in twenty years. A major portion of the campaign rhetoric centered upon the role of government in American life. The out-of-power Republicans, of course, cried for less government and

[34]U.S. Senate, *Hearings on Grazing*, Pt. 2, Appendix, pp. 114–17.
[35]Voigt, *Public Grazing Lands*, p. 150; Clayton R. Koppes, review of Voigt's *Public Grazing Lands*, in *Journal of Forest History* 21 (October, 1977): 225.

more private initiative to utilize and produce the wealth of the country. The unwieldly and overly burdensome bureaucracy that the Democrats had built was the principal target of the Republicans. The Forest Service had responded by initiating more flexible policies, based upon "public relations" and cooperative methods to develop greater range resources.

The fall elections of 1952 brought the Republican candidate Dwight D. Eisenhower to the White House and a Republican majority in Congress. The Republican party platform said, "We favor restoration of the traditional Republican lands policy. . . ." DeVoto asked just what this policy was. Was it the policy of Theodore Roosevelt, who laid the basic foundations for a conservation policy and created the Forest Service? Or was it in the tradition of those western Republican congressmen who opposed Roosevelt's and Pinchot's policies? These Republicans had fought practically every conservation measure, standing for free and unregulated exploitation of the resources of the lands. DeVoto believed that the new Republican platform stood squarely opposed to Theodore Roosevelt's conservationism. About the public lands the new platform said: "In the management of public lands and forests we pledge the elimination of arbitrary bureaucratic practices. To this end we favor legislation to define the rights and privileges of grazers and other co-operators and users, to provide the protection of independent judicial review against administrative invasions of those rights and privileges, and to protect the public against corrupt or monopolistic exploitation and bureaucratic favoritism." The words, DeVoto believed, were aimed primarily against the Forest Service. He declared that the people who would benefit from these moves represented only about 10 percent of the western cattle business and 30 percent of the western sheep business.[36]

In the new session of Congress, Republican Congressman Wesley D'Ewart of Montana quickly introduced a Unifrom Federal Grazing Bill. The bill confirmed all of DeVoto's suspicions and alarmed conservationists throughout the country. The D'Ewart bill proposed to apply uniform grazing rights to all federal range lands, guaranteeing continuation of the grazing privilege for permittees, the right of transfer, and a uniform fee. Most importantly, the D'Ewart bill, which Congressman Barrett from Wyoming joined in sponsoring, sought to subject administrative decisions to local

[36] DeVoto, "The Easy Chair: An Old Steal Refurbished," *Harper's*, October, 1952, pp. 65–68.

court review or appeal. Such a move, although innocently described as offering the stockman "his day in court," would transform the grazing permit from a "privilege" to a legal right. *Audubon* magazine, *American Forests*, and even newspapers in the West charged that this bill would give permittees vested rights in their grazing privileges.

By the following year the bill was reintroduced as the Hope-Aiken bill. Although greatly modified, it still did not pass Congress. By that time the opposition in Congress and the western press was simply too great. The Democrats mercilessly reiterated that the resource legislation of the Eisenhower years was a pure giveaway program. The Democrats protested most strongly the passage in 1953 of the Off-shore Oil Lands Act, which assured the states the right to control offshore oil, denying federal control over that resource.[37] The principal opposition in the western press stemmed from the fear that certain portions of the public lands would be devoted for all time to the grazing interests, excluding other resource users. The small farmer, the irrigation developer, urban needs for watershed resources, and sportsmen all represented additional demands for a varied resource use. Any legislation giving stockmen exclusive rights to the lands was always resisted by westerners outside the stock industry.

The Forest Service did in fact react to political and general industry-user pressure in the decade. Moves on the part of Forest Service range managers to emphasize range improvements and sustain and increase capacity reflect efforts to retain a range-protection program and at the same time win support of users. The government as landowner was the key to providing improvements in the following areas: fences, stock driveways, rodent control, poisonous and noxious plant control, revegetation of grass and shrubs, water developments, corrals and loading facilities, and brush control. Range research played an important role, but no improvements would be made without the government's willingness to pay for them. A partial answer was to develop cooperative agreements with users so that they might shoulder some of the expenses of these programs.[38]

[37] John H. Baker, "Stockman's Bill in Congress," *Audubon Magazine* 55 (May–June, 1953): 108; "Stockmen's Bill Challenged," *American Forests* 59 (June, 1953): 6; DeVoto, "The Easy Chair: Heading for the Last Roundup," *Harper's*, July, 1953, pp. 49–52; "The Pattern of Grazing Legislation," *American Forests* 60 (June, 1954): 32–33; A. H. Carhart, "Grazing on National Forests," *American Forests* 60 (December, 1954): 3–4; Elmo Richardson, *Dams, Parks and Politics: Resource Development and Preservation in the Truman-Eisenhower Era*, pp. 102–103; Steen, *U.S. Forest Service*, pp. 275–77.

[38] Forest Service, *Annual Report, 1953*, pp. 46–47.

While the stock industry worried about its future on public lands with the wider acceptance of multiple-use concepts, the Forest Service encouraged its range managers to become public-relations experts. Its ranger-training sessions on range administration emphasized the crucial role of public opinion in successful range management. A program could not extend beyond the ranger's skill to promote it with the resource user. Trainees were told that neither moral nor scientific correctness of a program was the determining factor in its implementation. The key to going forward with programs would be public acceptance: "Let's keep in mind that in conducting business for Government, we should be morally right and we should be scientifically correct, but neither is the controlling factor in getting the job done. The controlling factor is public opinion. Therefore our first job in putting over a program, or getting a job done, is to sell it to the people it affects and interests." The Forest Service warned new range trainees of the current situation facing them: "Basically, we have not yet sold good management to our range users and to that segment of the public that actively influences our programs." This need for acceptance was the central challenge facing the service's range administrators by the end of the decade and would remain so for each new generation of managers.[39]

The Forest Service acquired almost four million acres of rangeland in 1954 as a result of the transfer of the Land Utilization Projects to its administration from the Soil Conservation Service. Some of the lands became national forests, while others fell under the new classification of national grasslands. In eastern Montana the lands were so interspersed with Bureau of Land Management lands that the Forest Service soon recommended that the bureau assume their management. Likewise other Land Utilization Projects lands in California, Texas, and Utah were transferred to the Department of the Interior for grazing supervision or for wildlife refuges of the Fish and Wildlife Service. Stockmen were troubled by the rumors that many of the best grazing lands would be turned over to agencies to be used for purposes other than grazing. They protested to the Secretary of Agriculture, who repeated that range use would continue under Forest Service management. By 1960 the secretary had designated 3,822,000 acres of the Land Utilization Projects as national grasslands under the administration of the Forest Service.

[39] 1956 Rangers' Training Camp, "Range Administrators," May 7, 1956, Box 3, 13/2/1:3, RG 95, Federal Records Center of the National Archives, Denver, Colo.

All of these lands had originally been obtained under the New Deal AAA program to purchase submarginal farm lands in the depth of the Depression. In 1934, M. L. Wilson, AAA administrator, had invited several eastern Montanans to Washington to receive advice on how the farm and ranch situation could be helped in their part of the state. The group had recommended the so-called "Malta Plan" or government purchase of privately held marginal lands. Wilson himself had been a farm economist during the 1920s at Montana State College and already believed that many farmers on these marginal lands must leave.[40] Just as the government had purchased drought-stricken cattle and surplus commodities, it began a land-purchase program of these marginal lands by the Resettlement Administration under the AAA. In part the effort was an attempt to correct a mistake caused by government land policies earlier in the century. Thousands of farm families had been encouraged to move out onto the Great Plains after 1900 through liberalized homestead laws. The Kinkaid Act for western Nebraska in 1904 and the Enlarged Homestead Act of 1909 offered from 320 to 640 acres of free land to settlers willing to accept the challenge of plains agriculture. As a result, more free land was homesteaded in the twentieth century than in the nineteenth, but much of it was marginal and never should have been brought under the plow. The Great Plains dust storms of the thirties became stark testimony to the error in land policy and incorrect utilization.

Purchases occurred in Montana, the Dakotas, Wyoming, and other Great Plains states; in the Dust Bowl areas to the south, and in areas where problems occurred in timber-denuded areas of the Northeast and Northwest. In 1937, Title III of the Bankhead-Jones Farm Tenant Act extended the purchase program that saw millions of acres of deteriorated lands acquired by the government. In the first four years of its existence, the Land Utilization Program was administered by five different federal agencies until it was transferred to the Soil Conservation Service (SCS) in 1938. Almost a million acres were reseeded with crested wheatgrass imported from Russia. The SCS initiated watershed and erosion protection projects on the lands and also extended grazing privileges to interested stockmen.[41] For the

[40] "Evolution of the National Grasslands," Range Management Office, U.S. Forest Service, Arlington, Va.; William D. Rowley, *M. L. Wilson and the Campaign for the Domestic Allotment*, p. 50.

[41] U.S. Department of Agriculture, Economic Research Service, *The Land Utilization Program, 1934 to 1964: Origin, Development and Present Satus*, Agricultural Economic Re-

TABLE 7. States with National Grasslands.

State	Acreage
North Dakota	1,105,000
South Dakota	864,000
Colorado	612,000
Kansas	107,000
Nebraska	94,000
Oklahoma	47,000
Texas	117,000
New Mexico	134,000
Idaho	48,000
Oregon	103,000
Wyoming	573,000
Montana	1,900,000

SOURCE: U.S. Department of Agriculture, Economic Research Service, *The Land Utilization Program, 1934 to 1964: Origin, Development and Present Status*, Agricultural Economic Report no. 84, pp. 33, 76–77.

most part these lands, which were eventually transferred to the Forest Service and in the case of Montana to the Bureau of Land Management, concentrated in twelve states, shown in Table 7.

When the Forest Service acquired the lands from the SCS, it also accepted their patterns of grazing administration. It chose not to disturb long-established practices and demonstrated a flexibility rare in bureaucratic agencies. SCS policy had tried to involve the lands of private users in the shaping of the utilization and grazing practices on the lands. This involvement was accomplished by making agreements with local associations of grazing users. The agreements were sanctioned by state law for ten-year periods. Permits were issued to the associations, which in turn distributed grazing privileges among members according to overall grazing limits. Traditionally the Forest Service confined its range-management concerns to the land within the national forests and issued permits directly

port no. 85, pp. 31–32; "National Grasslands Established," *Journal of Forestry* 58 (August, 1960): 679; Keith A. Argow, "Our National Grasslands: Dustland to Grassland," *American Forests* 68 (January, 1962): 10–12; David Beatle, "Visit to a National Grasslands," *National Parks Magazine* 38 (October, 1964): 19–13.

to individuals. It was often argued that Forest Service range management practices should act as a catalyst for good management on surrounding private lands, but the service had no authority to require adherence to good management practices on nearby private lands.

Under the SCS, the grazing associations reviewed applications from local livestock owners who were willing to include their private lands in the program. The association allocated permits, collected fees, established upper limits, protected land from trespass and fire, and performed the day-to-day task of range management. The policies and procedures for this work were contained in section 44732 of the SCS's instruction manual (1945). According to the manual, permittees using Title III Lands were "expected to apply sound conservation practices on their own lands, and refusal or failure to do so [could] result in denial of a permit." This section of the manual went on to say: "By placing responsibility for a large part of the details of management in local organizations, it is possible to obtain better and more complete integration of the use of Title III lands with private and other public lands. Accordingly it is the policy of the Service to place responsibility for the management of Title III lands, wherever practical in local organizations of users." [42]

When the lands transferred, these policies were not readily accepted by the Forest Service range managers. Personal arguments and bureaucratic maneuverings followed. The Forest Service was not practiced at including large areas of private land into its range-management studies and programs. Some in the Forest Service argued that fifty years of their range management practices should not be swept away in favor of practices that had occurred on these Land Utilization Projects. They suggested all the land be converted to national forest and be subjected to usual Forest Service regulations and procedures. Such activities as issuing permits, collecting fees, controlling trespass and fires should not be delegated to associations. Finally, they maintained that the Forest Service had no authority or responsibility to shape livestock grazing policies on private lands.

Some project managers such as Lloyd Good and Clarence Dyson, who had worked for the SCS in North and South Dakota, were now transferred to the Forest Service. They were convinced that the management policies

[42] U.S. Soil and Conservation Service, "Policies and Procedures Governing the Use of Title III Lands" (1945), typescript, Range Management Office, U.S. Forest Service, Suitland, Md.

under the SCS were the correct ones for those lands, and they fought for their continuation. They argued with some truth that Title III lands were in better condition than most national forest ranges and that associated private lands were in good condition as a result of these policies. The changes suggested by the Forest Service would only weaken the good work that had been accomplished. With the support of some Forest Service personnel, Region 1 decided to continue the existing programs. Other regions decided to incorporate some of the policies and discard others. In 1962 Land Utilization Program grazing policies were formally incorporated into the Forest Service manual, but they applied only to Title III lands. Later, some of the basic philosophy under which the SCS Land Utilization Program land operated started to influence overall Forest Service grazing policies. For example, the following instructions appeared in the general Forest Service manual on range matters:

FSM 2202–1.c.—Contributing to the maintenance of viable rural economies by promoting stability of family ranches and farms in the areas of which the National Forest and National Grasslands are a part.
FSM 2203.1–2.—Through coordinated resource planning, integrate range on all ownerships into logical management units.
FSM 2203.6–2.—Demonstrate effective range management and livestock use, and sound land conservation practices, in association with multiple uses on land management units with mixed ownership.
FSM 2237.03–3.—Policy—Grazing agreements should be used, where practical, in lieu of direct permits on National Forest lands, to place responsibility for a large part of the details of management in local organizations of users to achieve better management and more complete integration of the use of public lands with associated private lands.

Service employees assigned to former Land Utilization projects and later transferred to range positions in many regions were responsible for spreading national grassland management approaches in the Forest Service. Every region except Region 4 (which had extensive rangeland on every forest) and Region 10 (Alaska) has had a regional chief of range management who had previously served in national grassland management. Gerhart H. Nelson, Region 1 range chief, 1979–83; William L. Evans, Region 2 range chief, 1971–73; Willard R. Fallis, Region 3 range chief, 1971–79; John S. Forsman, Region 6 range chief, 1967–76; Robert M. Richmond, Region 6 range chief, 1980–83; Samuel D. Halverson, Region 8 range chief, 1976–83; Deen E. Boe, Region 9, range specialist, 1974–79; and Robert L. Storch, Region 9 range specialist, 1980–81, all previously worked on the national grasslands in Region 1. Glenn E. Hetzel, Region 5 range chief, 1977–81, had charge of the Crooked River unit when he was supervisor of Ochoco National Forest in central Oregon. Several of these men had assignments on the range staff in Washington, D.C. Evans was director of range management in the Washington office from 1975 until his retirement in January, 1983. Forsman was on the Washington office range staff from 1963 to 1967, when he took over in Portland. Hetzel came to the Washington range staff in 1981, and Storch in 1982.[43]

These lands played an important role in developing Coordinated Resource Management Plans with the Bureau of Land Management. In January, 1975, the Forest Service and the BLM issued a memorandum of understanding which provided for "implementing resource management plans on operating units, allotments or other resource areas made up of adjacent BLM and Forest Service administered lands—and private lands." One of the legislative authorities listed in the memorandum was Title III of the Bankhead-Jones Act. Large areas of national forest lands became included with other ownerships in the Coordinated Resource Management Plans developed under this memorandum.

In December, 1979, Deputy Chief of the Forest Service Thomas C. Nelson addressed a workshop on the national grasslands, praising the accomplishments of range management on these lands. He emphasized that Forest Service personnel should understand that the national grasslands played a different role in resource management than the national forests. Title III of the Bankhead-Jones Farm Tenant Act gave the secretary of agriculture the authority to direct and develop a program of land conservation and utilization on these lands. Since the secretary's administrative order of August, 1963, the lands had been devoted to developing grassland agriculture with "the objective of demonstrating sound and practical principles of land use for the areas in which they are a part." He noted that on occasion land acquisition programs had been launched to consolidate or "block-up" government land ownership in national grassland areas "for the sole purpose of easier administration." Nelson declared emphatically, "I want this to stop! Our role is to encourage the integration of federally owned land into logical management units with the associated private lands." He reaffirmed his belief that effective work with grazing associations enhanced

---

[43]John Forsman to Ted Russell, December 1, 1981, and Forest Service Directories, Range Management Office, Forest Service.

the quality and quantity of Forest Service programs because resource conditions were strengthened across larger grassland areas.[44] By the 1980s other resource users threatened grazing interests as coal and gas companies sought energy sources in these lands.

The grassland acquisitions brought the role of the social mission once again into the mainstream of Forest Service range management administration. The service, under the mandate to administer these lands, had to focus on private land owners, their associations, their lands and communities—not just the immediate range resources of the land under direct service management. The Forest Service in its early years had grown out of an intensive conservation movement at the turn of the century aimed not only at conserving resources, but also at promoting the health and economic welfare of the communities dependent upon the resources. The national grasslands helped revive this early spirit of mission.

[44]Remarks by Thomas C. Nelson to National Grasslands Workshop, December, 1979, Range Management Office, Forest Service; Michael Frome, *The Forest Service*, pp. 134–35.

9

The Continuing Challenges

> Early settlers established a predominant and still existing use of the
> land for livestock (cattle, sheep, and horse) grazing. Recently,
> increased emphasis has been placed on public rangelands for their
> mineral value; their value as watersheds, wilderness areas, and
> scenic preserves; and their rich recreational, historical, and cultural
> resources."
>
> —U.S. General Accounting Office,
> *Public Rangeland Improvement*, 1982

BY the 1960s, resource-use issues paled before the problems of domestic
upheavals and a Southeast Asian war. But the spirit of discontent aroused
by these issues also pervaded the long-established institutions of resource
use and protection. For the forest-range users, the 1960s ushered in policy
shifts toward greater multiple-use, the search for the highest economic
use of lands, and the environmental movement, accentuated by heavier
population.

Toward the late 1950s it became clear that stockmen would not get
what they wanted in terms of legislation giving them stronger rights to the
public range. Instead, Congress passed in 1960 the Multiple Use–Sustained
Yield Act, which supported conservationism. It specifically named the
multiple uses of the national forests (except mining) and required their balanced inclusion in the management of the forests. Previously the resources
of outdoor recreation, range, wildlife, and fisheries had not been named in
law. The Multiple Use Act directly stated that the national forests "shall be
administered for outdoor recreation, range, timber, watershed, and wildlife, and fish purposes." The stock industry perceived a threat from the
new multiple-use policies. Because recreation was now clearly recognized
as a major resource use, stockmen feared a challenge to traditional grazing
privileges on the public forest lands. Not even assurances that range re-

sources received equal mention in the act could put to rest fears that the "new" multiple-use scheme posed dangers.

Multiple use was now officially combined with sustained-yield management in the Forest Service. Use-oriented conservationists argued that western forest lands had long been managed under multiple-use principles. The renewable resources of water, forage, timber, and wildlife, and even recreation were manageable and usable resources. Protective use had been at the center of Forest Service policies from the beginning. Some contended the same was true for multiple-use concepts. Chief Forester Ed Cliff in 1961 explained, "A multiple-use program integrates the resource uses into a plan where all are used wisely, but seldom does one use completely exclude any of the others." He believed the principles of multiple-use had been practiced by the Forest Service in its land-use planning ever since 1905. This may have been too sweeping a generalization, but one thing was certain: the Multiple Use Act of 1960 was a far cry from the earlier proposals in the 1950s to open range lands to private ownership.[1]

While the stock industry worried about its future under multiple-use, it was clearly on friendlier terms with the Forest Service than it had been ten years earlier. The reasons grew out of a shift in Forest Service range policies and tactics rather than a change in the objectives of the industry regarding the public ranges in the national forests. Over the past decade the Forest Service range managers pulled back from the aggressive reductions to emphasize cooperation and range improvements. The goal was the same: to bring range capacity into line with range use. Instead of following reduction policies, the range managers sought to improve the ranges in order to handle the large numbers of stock on them. The word *reduction* became a rarity in the Forest Service vocabulary. This is not to say that reductions did not occur when the service deemed them necessary for the protection of forage resources. But cooperation and range improvements became the first options.

At stake were private investments in ranches and stock as well as the

[1] Paul W. Gates and Robert W. Swenson, *The History of Public Land Law Development*, p. 631; Ed Cliff, Address to Third Annual Western Resources Conferences, Fort Collins, Colo., August 8, 1961, Ed Cliff Papers, Special Collections Library, Utah State University, Logan; C. Wayne Cook and L. A. Stoddart, "Grazing and Multiple-Use," *Journal of Forestry* 59 (March, 1961): 216–17; Grant McConnell, "The Multiple-Use Concept in Forest Service Policy," *Sierra Club Bulletin* 44 (October, 1959): 14–28.

continued health of the forage resources of the forests. The message that range managers had tried to deliver to stockmen for nearly fifty years had been that their wealth in stock depended upon a prosperous and protected forage crop: "If range cattle represent wealth, that wealth is chiefly, if not entirely, a derivative of the range vegetation so that the cattleman cannot deem alien to his interest anything pertinent to the welfare of the forage." Armed with this logic, Forest Service range managers attacked the range problem from a public relations standpoint through their cooperative and range-improvement programs.[2] Range improvements could involve proper stocking, the application of a sound grazing plan or system, the removal of harmful or useless vegetation in brush control, reseeding efforts, and coordinating livestock use with other forest uses such as wildlife, watersheds, and timber production.

While emphasizing these positive aspects of forest range management, foresters did point out to stockmen and their political representatives that the removal of stock from some critical lands must continue. This became a burning issue on the overgrazed allotments of Spanish Americans in New Mexico. There, the Forest Service pursued protective cuts against small graziers who could ill afford cooperation with the Forest Service in range improvement programs, including fencing projects. Also the service refused further distribution of grazing privileges to new applicants after 1953. All of these steps saw a gradual removal of many small herdsmen from the forests in the 1950s and 1960s, with a wave of hatred mounting against the service. The hatred found expression in forest arson, threats to Forest Service personnel, and the seizure of a local courthouse in 1968 by a militant group led by Reies Lopez Tijerina.[3]

By 1961 in the intermountain area of the Great Basin, Floyd Iverson, regional forester for Region 4, informed Nevada's Senator Alan Bible that in those areas of the Humboldt National Forest with unstable soils, steep slopes, and depleted vegetative cover, "grazing will undoubtedly need to be curtailed to provide for range-watershed restoration." He said that studies were underway at the Intermountain Forest and Range Experiment Station and the University of Nevada to determine ways of reestablishing a

[2] W. A. Dayton, "Some Outstanding Forage Grasses of Western Cattle Ranges," *The Producer: The National Livestock Monthly* 9 (March, 1928): 3–7.

[3] Patrick C. West, *Natural Resource Bureaucracy and Rural Poverty: A Study in the Political Sociology of Natural Resources*, pp. 92–93.

desirable forage cover. But no quick prospects for rehabilitation had appeared. Iverson suggested that many years of non-use would be upcoming to allow the lands time to recover.

To assure the senator that the Forest Service was working actively in the field of range improvements, Iverson pointed out that his records showed that as of June 30, 1960, the Forest Service had spent nearly $1,191,000 on structural improvement and revegetation on the 298 livestock allotments within Nevada. This was an average of $4,000 per range unit. During 1961, approximately $48,000 was to be spent on range improvements and developments and an additional $85,000 on range revegetation. Iverson estimated that two hundred thousand acres of national forest land in Nevada were "amenable" to artificial treatment either through seeding or by spraying to control undesirable vegetation.

Beyond these immediate improvements, the Forest Service was undertaking a comprehensive range-analysis program for each grazing allotment. The purpose was to determine areas on each allotment suitable for livestock use; the condition and trend of the vegetation; the stability of the soil; how much grazing could be allowed without damage to forage production, watershed values and other resources; which areas would benefit from artificial treatment; and which areas would be more valuable for other forest uses. Many stockmen, of course, feared that grazing would not fare well in this competition for resource use. Still, this new servicewide range analysis served to direct range-management decisions in the Forest Service at the local level throughout the decade.

The permittees were encouraged to participate in the analysis process. The Service attempted to determine if a range were depleted and watershed conditions deteriorating in cooperation with the permittee, who would then be offered a program of stock use to meet the user's and the land's needs. Iverson told Senator Bible that when reduced use was required, the reduction announcement was made one full grazing season prior to its becoming effective. Every possible effort was made to ease the effects on the livestock user. In case of disagreement between the forest supervisor and the permittee, the Forest Service had the authority to go ahead with planned reductions or the removal of certain lands from grazing. If the permittee felt wronged by the supervisor's decisions, that permittee—according to longstanding Forest Service regulations—could make an appeal to the regional forester, then to the chief of the Forest Service, and finally to the secretary of agriculture. The appeals process and arguments with forest-range managers caused stockmen to hire range scientists to do independent studies for presentation of new evidence in appeals proceedings. To some degree these new relationships helped ease a traditional distrust between ranchers and range technicians.

Cooperation with permittees in building and maintaining range improvements had long been a part of Forest Service policy. But the service was always under the obligation to compensate stockmen for their cooperation to avoid private-property claims to the public range. That compensation usually came in the form of determining that reductions were not necessary because improvements increased the range capacity. Still, such improvements required an investment on the part of the stockman on allotments to which he had no permanent guarantee. Certainly this was true under "cost-sharing contracts" for range improvements that became a standard part of Forest Service policy in the 1960s. Some believed that the range-resource agency should "meet the stockman half-way by guaranteeing either a reasonable permanency on the land or a reimbursement for lost investment" should the allotment be denied to him in the future. On the other hand, taxpayers should not be expected to subsidize range improvements for private gains by increasing the capacity of the range. Proposals still surfaced to give permittees a property right over their permits. One argument suggested that perpetual grazing permits be created that could be sold on a free market. Such permits, it was claimed, would offer greater access to grazing lands and equitable distribution of the privilege according to the market forces.[4]

While articles from range experts appeared frequently on how stockmen might better utilize their ranges and how the public agencies could help them, the conservation press complained about ravaged ranges and the threat to western watersheds. Many employees within and supporters outside of the Forest Service asked how the service could reduce the amount of grazing in the face of so much pressure from users to maintain the numbers of permitted stock. By 1963 one forest supervisor declared, "Years ago we were too optimistic about what the land could carry. We didn't foresee the future. Now we are paying the price."[5]

---

[4]L. A. Stoddart, "What Hope for Grazing on the Public Lands," *Journal of Range Management* 18 (May, 1965): 111; Delworth Gardner, "A Program to Stabilize Livestock Grazing on the Public Lands," *National Wool Grower* 52 (November, 1962): 14.

[5]As quoted in Olaus J. Murie, "The Grazing Lands Must Be Restored: What Are We Doing to Our Land?" *American Forests* 69 (February, 1963): 15.

The former head of the Department of the Interior's Grazing Service (the predecessor of the Bureau of Land Management), C. L. Forsling, declared that millions of acres in the arid Southwest should be permanently closed to grazing. Spokesmen in forestry eduction began emphasizing that forage was a major resource, if not the very foundation of the forest resources. The health and maintenance of the plant cover in the forests ultimately determined the vitality of the forest crop. Therefore, a primary purpose of range management was to manage grazing by livestock and wildlife in order to insure sustained yields of forage, not only for the continued security of grazing, but also for the vitality of the forests themselves. Vernon A. Young of the Forestry School at the University of Idaho warned: "Failure by improper range management to maintain a sufficient plant cover on timberlands, burned-over areas, and watershed not only introduces complex soil crosion problems that are vital to the existence of forestry itself, but also to the economic and social welfare of nearby communities."[6]

It was hoped that the new crusade for rangeland restoration would not make the mistakes of the past. In the past livestock had wrongly received most of the blame for range damage without any consideration of other influences both natural and man-made. These errors occurred in the 1936 study *The Western Range*. This study, which had concluded that Forest Service ranges were in better condition than the rest of the public domain rangelands, had failed to take into account that from the outset national forests obtained the best high-elevation rangelands, while the remainder of the public ranges were poorer, low-elevation, and even desert lands. The superior range condition of the national forests was thus not so much a result of better range management, as a difference of climate in these high-elevation lands and the land quality itself. A broad-gauged approach that could account for various influences of human activity and the natural invasion of rangelands by brush and woody species like the juniper, the elevation and annual rainfall was greatly to be desired. In short, all evils should not be traced to grazing.[7]

Many feared that new calls for range restoration and preservation of

[6]C. L. Forsling, "The Grazing Lands Must Be Restored: Revelling Watersheds," *American Forests* 69 (February, 1963): 12–14; Vernon A. Young, "The Role of Range Management in Forestry," *Journal of Forestry* 60 (August, 1962): 15.

[7]Joseph F. Arnold, "Crusade for Rangeland Restoration," *American Forests* 69 (May, 1963): 28.

range resources would not be heard during these years of the Vietnam War and pressing urban problems. For the most part they were correct. In many areas, instead of reinstituting reduction programs the service issued non-use permits and tried range improvements to expand the resource by eliminating unwanted browse and sponsoring reseeding projects. But funding became increasingly difficult to obtain.

As interest in outdoor recreation and wilderness areas grew in the 1960s, a new militant conservation movement arose that ultimately produced the environmental movement. A culmination of the movement was the National Environmental Protection Act of 1969 and the celebration of Earth Day in April of 1970. The environmentalists, unlike the early conservation movement that had helped create the Forest Service, became suspicious of governmental resource protection and management agencies as well as private exploitation.

Environmental groups accused the Forest Service and its range managers of being too closely allied with resource users and stock organizations. Now, in addition to their long-time critics in the stock industry, forest range managers faced the attacks of militant environmentalists, who accused them of coddling stockmen and spending public money to support improvements to maintain stock on overstocked ranges. Criticisms of this type continued into the 1980s. These same environmentalist groups objected to the herbicide and reseeding work in the range-improvement programs. Environmental impact statements were required by the new Environmental Protection Act and public hearings focused on grazing as an environmental question as well as a management process.

In December of 1974 when the Bureau of Land Management brought forth its "programmatic" environmental impact statement on grazing, it believed that it had satisfied the letter of the law. But conservation organizations represented by the National Resources Defense Council, the National Wildlife Federation, and others denounced the statement as "fundamentally inadequate." When they challenged the "programmatic" review in the courts, the courts agreed, directing the BLM to prepare "geographically individualized" impact statements, because "grazing clearly may have a severe impact on local environments." These impact statements proved so costly that ultimately many range-improvement programs were forced to be eliminated.

The environmental movement also sparked interest in wildlife habitat and native-plant values as well as wild horses and burros. The Wild and

Free Roaming Horse and Burro Act of 1971 placed wild horses and burros on public lands under the jurisdiction of the secretaries of agriculture and the interior for protection, management, and control. It prohibited the hunting of these animals by private hunters for sport or commercial reasons. Even the use of pesticides by permittees was required to be written into the permit. If the pesticides were not authorized in the Annual Permit Plan, a separate letter of authorization was required and attached to the plan. The use of herbicides decreased sharply. The demands of the new environmental movement and its new protective laws and assessments increasingly placed similar requirements and standards upon both the BLM and the Forest Service, making them recognize more clearly than ever before their common roles as land managers with similar problems and obligations. By 1972 a Forest Service study, *The Nation's Range Resources*, had declared that much of the western range in both public and private ownership was in a deteriorating condition. Unfortunately, the BLM and the Forest Service were able to spend only about $27 million for range management by the mid-1970s when need was estimated at $182.7 million.[8] Their total fees charged to ranchers was hardly $20 million and represented much less than market value for the rental of the lands for grazing purposes.

All of these problems with the public range prompted Congress to pass in 1976 the Federal Land Policy and Management Act (FLPMA), which provided for funded environmental impact statements on livestock grazing in the eleven western states. It authorized a new grazing-fee study, a range-betterment fund, and more secure tenure for livestock grazing. Most importantly, it acknowledged the intention of the government to retain perpetually the public lands in its ownership. Reported lack of cooperation between land agencies and livestock industry, rumors of higher fees, and the outright declaration by the federal government to its perpetual ownership of the public lands prompted the so-called Sagebrush Rebellion in several western states, with the Nevada State legislature leading the way by 1979. The "rebellion" first called for state ownership of the public lands

[8] Denzel Ferguson and Nancy Ferguson, *Sacred Cows at the Public Trough*; William K. Wyant, *Westward in Eden: The Public Lands and the Conservation Movement*, pp. 325–26; "Use of Pesticides by Livestock Permittees," June 11, 1971, Federal Records Center of the National Archives, Laguna Niguel, Calif.; U.S. General Accounting Office, *Public Rangeland Improvement—A Slow, Costly Process in Need of Alternate Funding*, Report to Congress by the Comptroller General, October 14, 1982, pp. 22–23.

and later touted the idea of privatization of the lands. After the election of President Ronald Reagan in 1980, Secretary of the Interior James Watt defused the issue by declaring a "good neighbor" policy toward the western ranchers on the part of the government land management agencies. But the basic intentions of the 1976 FLPMA legislation and the subsequent Public Rangelands Improvement Act of 1978 (PRIA) remained intact. A provision in the 1978 act launched a "stewardship program" for the combined management of large pilot projects of Forest Service and BLM land. Ranchers would receive greatly reduced grazing fees in return for their cooperation in the projects.[9]

The story of range-management policies in the South is largely a story unto itself. The lack of progress in range management in the South became a major area of concern for the Forest Service in the early 1960s. In his 1964 article "A Review and Analysis of Range Management in Region 8," Chief of Range Management Wayne J. Cloward admitted that the task of establishing control and management of livestock in southern forests remained an unfinished agenda item. Why, after fifty years of national forest administration, was grazing still outside any comprehensive system of control and management in the region? Even the rudiments of control, such as charging for grazing privileges and punishing trespassers were not being enforced in some forests.

Grazing inspectors in the southern region had called for control of the grazing resource by the mid-1930s, but the Washington office refused to demand strict adherence to the recommendations. This refusal was unfortunate because the recommendations came at a time when the region was expanding its land-acquisition and tree-planting program. Cattle, sheep, and hogs ran uncontrolled in the forests, with their number limited only by theft, starvation, Texas tick fever, hog cholera, or screwworm. Cattle from the West and Midwest were being placed on southern ranges to avoid drought, bringing additional pressure on southern forests in competition with timber production. Generally, southern foresters believed that grazing on their lands would not be practiced for long. As soon as the forests grew, available pasturage would be shaded out and cattle and sheep would leave. When the Extension Service advocated a livestock program in the southern

[9] U.S. Forest Service, *The Nation's Range Resources: A Forest-Range Environmental Study*, Forest Resource Report no. 19; Wyant, *Westward in Eden*, pp. 327–32.

Appalachians, forest officials feared that cattle would adversely affect management of forest lands. In Florida there was no regulation of grazing by the Forest Service. In Florida, where cattle grazing existed since 1529, one forest official asserted, "I could discover no possibility for the development of a sound grazing economy or anything of value as a sideline in livestock production."

Unquestionably there was an antigrazing bias in the southern region's forests. This bias arose because large stock interests had not been present in the South as long as they had been in the West. The best thing that Walt Dutton could say about southern grazing policy in 1939 was, "The general grazing policy that has been worked out and applied in Region 8 is the result of individual thinking plus some adherence to the old grazing manual." There had been little interference from the Washington office, but also little help. By 1940, an outline for a southern grazing policy emerged from the Washington office, but it was not finally approved until 1950. Throughout the 1950s range continued to be the southern region's "bastard child." With little financing to do the work, Charles A. Joy, in his 1955 inspection report, said that vacancies in positions of range and wildlife management went unfilled.

Another report in 1959 by Ed Cliff, assistant chief for forest resources, and Russell B. McKennan, general inspector, cited the need to move ahead faster in range management in Region 8. Unauthorized grazing was still occurring there in great numbers. In 1959 approximately 68,000 cattle and horses grazed on the forests without permit in the region, along with 31,000 hogs, and 9,600 sheep and goats. Only 19 percent of the cattle and horses were under permit. The local administration was called upon to prohibit livestock trespass as the first step towards placing all stock under permit. In addition, the forests were asked to consider using a bid system when handing out permits, with accompanying contracts for construction of improvements and maintenance of range lands. Basically Cliff's and McKennan's recommendations insisted that the regional forester should make Forest Service personnel understand the place of range use in the multiple-use management of the national forests in Region 8. By 1960, the region initiated a five-phase program of management. Its short-range goals were "to determine degree of suitability of woodland area for grazing, inventory, and analyze situation and establish business relations with livestock owners." Its long-range goals were "to secure proper use of the woodland grazing resource fully coordinated with other products of the land and need of dependent qualified livestock people." [10]

While grazing control in the South remained an unfinished business in the early 1960s, grazing fees on the public lands once again became a critical question. Agencies within the executive branch began suggesting that the service undertake a revision of its controversial fee policies that had been in effect since the 1930s. The controversy did not arise from the users, who enjoyed remarkably low fees. For almost three decades fees had not been an issue since they had remained unchanged from the 1933 formulas which kept them far below market value for rental of comparable private grazing lands. By the late 1950s, however, it became apparent that the government was preparing to address the issue of raising fees to comparable market value.

By 1960, even Congressman Wayne Aspinall of Colorado saw a need for the revision of the fee structure. In 1961, the newly inaugurated president, John F. Kennedy, delivered a message on natural resources that addressed the question of user fees. He directed the Bureau of the Budget to consult with other departments in a study to formulate general principles for the application of fees and user charges for all kinds of federal natural-resource use, including grazing. The study, entitled *Natural Resources User Charges Study*, appeared in 1964, the same year that the Forest Service had joined in the Interdepartmental Grazing Fees Committee with representatives from the Departments of Agriculture, Defense, and the Interior. The committee sought a uniform basis for establishing livestock-grazing fees on federal lands and made three general conclusions (1) a uniform basis should be used by all federal agencies in establishing fees, (2) fees should be based on the economic value of the use of public lands to the users, and (3) economic value should be set by an appraisal that would provide a fair return to the government and equitable treatment to the users.

As early as 1961 the Forest Service and the Bureau of Land Management undertook a joint study in conjunction with the Economic Research Service and western state universities. The purpose of the study was to develop a system to determine public land grazing values. In 1966 the Statistical Reporting Service of the Department of Agriculture conducted a

---

[10] Wayne J. Cloward, "A Review and Analysis of Range Management in Region 8," August 27, 1964, Range Management Office, U.S. Forest Service, Arlington, Va.

survey of eighteen national forests, nineteen national grasslands, and forty-eight Bureau of Land Management grazing districts. The survey involved interviews with ten thousand individuals and more than fourteen thousand questionnaires. Questions were asked about nonfee costs of using public and private lands, lease rates on private grazing lands, and the market value placed by permittees on grazing permits. The report, published in 1968, arrived at the following conclusions:

1. Forest Service and Bureau of Land Management data can be combined. The survey data do not provide a basis for differential fees between the Forest Service and the Bureau of Land Management.
2. The cost data collected in the 1966 western range survey statistically supported only one base fee in the West. This conclusion was based on a technical analysis of the variation of cost among individual grazing allotments.
3. An adjusted difference between private lease rates and public costs throughout the West, excluding the grazing fee, was $1.23 per animal-unit-month for both cattle and sheep.[11]

It was assumed that raising the grazing fee to $1.23 per animal-unit-month or fair market value would reduce the possibility of permittees claiming a property right in the range and reduce the "permit value" to zero. The stock industry, while not particularly cheerful about the prospects of increased fees, recognized that the resources of the public lands would be used by those who could pay for them. The multiple-use concept introduced the possibility that other uses of higher economic value might be found for the grazing lands of the Forest Service. The secretary of agriculture issued regulations in 1969 calling for grazing fees on the national forests in the western states to be increased gradually to fair market value over a period of ten years. Fees of full market value were to be achieved by 1978.

While the Public Lands Subcommittee of the Senate and House Committee on Interior and Insular Affairs held hearings on the fee issue, the secretaries of agriculture and the interior became defendants in two New Mexico class-action suits: *Pankey* vs. *Freeman*, and *Broadbent* vs. *Hickel*. The suits sought an injunction against the increased 1969 grazing fee and

[11] "Statement of Edward P. Cliff before the Subcommittee on Public Lands of the Committee on Interior and Insular Affairs, House of Representatives," March 4, 1969, U.S. Forest Service Files, Arlington, Va.

charged that the secretaries failed to consider stockmen's capital investments when the new fee rates were developed; in other words, government fee studies had not calculated the value paid for government grazing permits in devising the new fee system.[12] The protests and court cases prevented the scheduled increase in fees for 1970, but the failure of the cases in court allowed the second of the ten incremental adjustments to go forward in 1971 with fair market value to be achieved by 1980. By 1972 some congressmen demanded that a statutory fee system be established to remove fees from the administrative decision-making process. Others still believed that the quickest and simplest route to fair market value was through a competitive bid system for grazing privileges.

In addition to the New Mexico court cases and additional investigations by Congressman Aspinall's committee, adverse economic conditions caused continuous delays in the fair market value rental fee. Prices paid for stock on the hoof remained relatively stable, but the costs of maintaining a livestock operation were ever-increasing. This cost-price squeeze, along with a deemphasis of red-meat protein in the American diet, produced heated arguments against increasing the costs of stock raising through fee hikes for grazing permits on public lands. These arguments flared despite reports that fees represented only a small percentage of livestock production costs.

The Federal Land Policy and Management Act (FLPMA) in 1976 called for renewed fee studies with a report to be made to Congress by October, 1977. Dissatisfaction of the stock industry with the report helped prompt the passage in 1978 of the Public Rangelands Improvement Act (PRIA), which authorized the expenditure of two billion dollars over the next twenty years on range improvements and the implementation of an experimental fee during the period 1979 to 1986. Under this program, market value of forage was rejected in favor of a figure that would be set by the costs of production and the stockmen's ability to pay. Fees in the period were to be based on the 1966 grazing survey of $1.23/AUM fair market value locally adjusted by a forage value index, the current beef cattle price, and the price paid index. When cattle prices moved lower during the recession of the early 1980s, rental fees correspondingly decreased. This reduction also meant less money for range improvements, further demonstrating

---

[12]Ralph R. Hill, "Federal Land Grazing Fees," June 1, 1968, Natural Resource Collection, Denver Public Library.

the power of the stock industry to achieve a fee system far short of the fair market standard that the land-management agencies had sought.[13]

The reemergence of the fee question occurred at a time when the older conservationists worried about graziers obtaining vested rights on public lands and when the commitment to multiple use challenged many of the older uses of the lands, such as grazing. The growth of an urban West oriented toward recreational use of public lands after World War II produced a demand for a share in the lands' use for recreation, wildlife habitat, and the preservation of esthetic values. The Rangeland Renewable Resources Planning Act of 1974 required the Forest Service to offer assessments of renewable resources every five years beginning in 1975. The FLPMA also directed that 50 percent of the fees collected for the grazing of domestic livestock in the national forests be committed to rangeland improvements in the forests, endorsing a widely held industry view that the resource must be expanded.

The new planning mandates placed the Forest Service under heavy burdens in its range responsibilities. It also faced the problem of achieving a single, defensible technique for measuring range condition and trend—a challenge it had struggled with since its range program began. Environmental legislation, dictates from the courts for range improvement, the everpresent multiple use disputes, and the persistent fee question continued to present challenges to Forest Service grazing administration. Moreover, the recent flurry of congressional legislation and demands drew it and the Bureau of Land Management into a clearer realization that many of their tasks would demand concerted actions and policies in the years to come.

[13] "Wyant, *Westward in Eden*, pp. 324–30.

[14] Dennis C. LeMaster, *Decade of Change: The Remaking of Forest Service Statutory Authority during the 1970's*, p. 80.

Forest Service Grazing Chronology

1891   Creation of forest reserves.

1897   Forest Management Act regulates occupancy and use of forest resources (grazing not named).

1901   A. F. Potter comes to Washington, D.C., as grazing expert in USDA and advisor to Gifford Pinchot.

1905   Transfer Act (forest reserves transferred from Department of the Interior to Agriculture; creates the modern Forest Service).

1906   June 11 Act provides that agricultural lands within the forests can be homesteaded; grazing fees first imposed.

1907   Stock experiments such as coyote-proof pastures for sheep and grazing capacity studies initiated on Wallowa National Forest in Oregon.

1910   Office of Grazing Studies established; J. T. Jardine in charge; range reconnaissance conducted on the Jornada and Santa Rita experimental ranges in southern New Mexico and Arizona; employment of quadrat method.

1911   Weeks Act provides for purchase by federal government of forest lands necessary to the protection of the flow of navigable streams. Decision in Light case by U.S. Supreme Court enforces measures against trespass on U.S. forest lands.

1912   Utah Experiment Station in Manti National Forest, Utah (later Great Basin Experiment Station) established by J. T. Jardine and A. W. Sampson to centralize range studies.

1916   Gradually increasing grazing fees; rancher protests; Stockmen's Homestead Bill.

1917   World War I prompts expansion of grazing privileges in the national forests.

1920   Potter retires.

1920   Congress calls for sharp increase in grazing fees; Rachford studies on fees initiated.

1924   Recommended fee increases from Rachford study deferred because of stock industry objections; ten-year permits issued.

1925   Stanfield committee investigates range matters, attacks Forest Service grazing policies; Dan Casement considers fee question and recommends more gradual increase of fees.

1926   McSweeney-McNary Forest Research Act; Casement recommendation of fee reductions in return for allotment improvements accepted by Forest Service.

1930   Secretary of agriculture approves substitution of the name "Region" and "Regional Forester" for "District" and "District Forester"; Soil Erosion Service created.

1932   Cancellation of fees in last half of year to meet Depression emergency; future fees to be tied to market prices.

1934   Taylor Grazing Act for the regulation of the public range.

1935   Soil Conservation Service established.

1936   Ten-year permits again issued; distribution deemphasized; *A Report on the Western Range* published, commenting on the deterioration of a national resource.

1941   Senator McCarran (Nevada) launches investigation of Grazing Service and general western grazing questions.

1942   Forest Service resists overstocking of ranges and repetition of World War I increases.

1946   New efforts by Forest Service to gain control of its range situation; need for reductions.

1947   Congressman Barrett's committee investigates; Bernard DeVoto attacks "land grab" in the West.

1949   Anderson-Mansfield Act for range reseeding.

1950   Granger-Thye Act legislatively recognizes grazing by name as a legitimate use of the national forests; strengthens local Forest Advisory Boards.

1951   Cliff-Sandvig "blow-up" in Region 2.

1952   Parker Three-Step Method for determining range trend and condition.

1954   National grasslands added to U.S. Forest Service.

1960   Multiple-Use Sustained Yield Act recognizes the increasingly varied uses and resources of the national forests.

1964   Wilderness Act (response to public's concern for outdoor recreation); Natural Resources User Charges Study.
1968   Western-wide Fee Study report supports one base fee in the West for grazing.
1969   USDA announces goal of full market value fee for grazing by 1978; fee should be based on economic value of the use of public lands; National Environmental Protection Act passed.
1974   Forest and Rangeland Renewable Resources Planning Act.
1976   Federal Land Policy and Management Act calls for new fee studies.
1978   Forest and Rangeland Renewable Resources Research Act.

Bibliography

Unpublished Material

Manuscript Material

Bible, Allan. Papers. Getchell Library Special Collections, University of Nevada, Reno.

Cliff, Ed. Papers. Special Collections Library, Utah State University, Logan.

Federal Records Centers of the National Archives and Records Service, Denver, Colorado; Seattle, Washington; Laguna Niguel, California; and Washington, D.C.

Forest History Society Archives. Santa Cruz, California.

McCarran, Patrick. Papers. Nevada State Historical Society, Reno.

Medicine Bow National Forest Collection. Western History Research Center, University of Wyoming, Laramie.

Oddie, Tasker L. Papers. Nevada State Historical Society, Reno.

Pinchot, Gifford. Papers. Library of Congress, Washington, D.C.

Pittman, Key. Papers. Library of Congress, Washington, D.C.

Records of the Forest Service. Record Group 95, Sections 3, 63, and 134, National Archives and Records Service, Washington, D.C.

Roosevelt, Theodore. Papers. Library of Congress, Washington, D.C.

Sandvig, Earl D. Papers. Natural Resource Collection, Denver Public Library.

Shoemaker, Leonard C. "History of the Holy Cross National Forest." Manuscript. Colorado Historical Society, Denver.

U.S. Forest Service Range Management Office. Files. Arlington, Virginia.

Work Projects Administration. History of Grazing Papers. Special Collections Library, Utah State University, Logan.

Oral Histories

"Carl B. Arentson, Forty-One Years of Forest Service Career" (1965). Oral History Project. U.S. Forest Service, Region 4, Ogden, Utah.

"Jack Albano's Forest Service Career." Oral History Project. U.S. Forest Service, Region 4, Ogden, Utah.

Kneipp, Leon F. "Land Planning and Acquisition, U.S. Forest Service." Regional Oral History Office, Bancroft Library, University of California, Berkeley.

McArdle, Richard E. "The Western Range." Forest History Society, Santa Cruz, California.

Marvel, Louise. Oral History Project. U.S. Forest Service, Region 4, Ogden, Utah.

Preston, John F. "Early Days in the Forest Service." Oral History Project. U.S. Forest Service, Region 1, Missoula, Montana.

Ringland, Arthur C. "Conserving Human and Natural Resources." Regional Oral History Office, Bancroft Library, University of California, Berkeley.

Theses

Apgar, William Burnet. "The Administration of Grazing on the National Forests." Master's thesis, Cornell University, 1922.

Rakestraw, Lawrence W. "History of Forest Conservation in the Pacific Northwest, 1891–1913." Ph.D. diss., University of Washington, 1955.

Soffar, Allen J. "Differing Views on the Gospel of Efficiency: Conservation Controversies between Agriculture and Interior, 1898–1938." Ph.D. diss., Texas Tech University, 1974.

Interviews

Chapline, W. R. Interview with author. Reno, Nevada, February, 1980.

Cliff, Edward P. Interview with author. Washington, D.C., April, 1980.

Pechanec, Joseph. Interview with author. Bountiful, Utah, March, 1980.

Sandvig, Earl. Interview with author. Portland, Oregon, August, 1980.

Published Material

Government Publications

Aldous, A.E. *Eradicating Tall Larkspur on Cattle Ranges in the National Forests.* Farmers' Bulletin no. 826. Washington, D.C.: Department of Agriculture, 1917.

Barnes, Will C. "Grazing Legislation." *Service Bulletin* [Forest Service] 10, April 26, 1926.

Bennett, H. H., and W. R. Chapline. *Soil Erosion a National Menace.* USDA Circular no. 33, April, 1928.

Carman, Ezra A., H. A. Heath, and John Minto. *Special Report of the History and Present Condition of the Sheep Industry of the United States.* Washington, D.C.: Bureau of Animal Industry, 1892.

Chapline, W. R. *Production of Goats on Far Western Ranges.* USDA Bulletin no. 749, April 30, 1919.

Colorado General Assembly, Senate. *Senate Journal of the 35th General Assembly of the State of Colorado,* November 23, 1945.

Coville, Frederick V. *Forest Growth and Sheep Grazing in the Cascade Mountains of Oregon.* U.S. Department of Agriculture, Division of Forestry Bulletin no. 15. Washington, D.C.: Government Printing Office, 1898.

Congressional Record, 57th Cong., 1st sess., 1902. Vol. 36.

Congressional Record, 53rd Cong., 1st sess., 1893. Vol. 25.

Ensign, Edgar T. *Report on the Forest Conditions of the Rocky Mountains.* U.S. Department of Agriculture, Division of Forestry Bulletin no. 2. Washington, D.C.: Government Printing Office, 1889.

Gates, Paul W., and Robert W. Swenson. *The History of Public Land Law Development.* Washington, D.C.: Public Land Law Review Commission, 1968.

Jardine, James T., and Mark Anderson. *Range Management on the National Forests.* USDA Bulletin no. 790, August 6, 1919.

Powell, John W. *Report on the lands of the Arid Region of the United States.* 45th Cong., 2d sess., 1878. H. Exec. Doc. 73.

Sampson, Arthur W. *Plant Succession in Relation to Range Management.* USDA Bulletin no. 791, August 27, 1919.

Thornber, J. J. *The Grazing Ranges of Arizona.* Arizona Agricultural Experiment Station Bulletin no. 65. 1910.

U.S. Bureau of the Census. *Twelfth Census of the United States, 1900,* vol. 5, *Statistics for Agriculture.*

U.S. Congress, House. *Annual Report of the Commissioner of the General Land Office, 1902.* 57th Cong. 2d sess., 1902–1903. H. Doc. 5.

———. *Annual Report of the Secretary of the Interior, 1897.* 55th Cong., 2d sess., 1897. H. Doc. 5; *1898.* 55th Cong., 3rd sess., 1898–99. H. Doc. 5; *1902.* 57th Cong., 2d sess., 1902–1903. H. Doc. 5; *1903.* 58th Cong., 2d sess., 1903–1904. H. Doc 5.

———. *Letter from the Secretary of the Treasury Transmitting a Report from the Chief of the Bureau of Statistics [Ranch and Range Cattle Traffic*; report prepared by Joseph Nimmo, Jr.]. 48th Cong., 2d sess., 1885. H. Exec. Doc. 267.

U.S. Congress, Senate. *Report of the Committee Appointed by the National Academy of Sciences upon the Inauguration of a Forest Policy for the Forested Lands of the United States.* 55th Cong., 1st sess., 1897. S. Doc. 105. Vol. 5.

———. *A Report on the Western Range: A Great but Neglected Natural Resource.* 74th Cong., 2d sess., 1936. S. Doc. 199. Vol. 7.

———, Committee on Public Lands and Surveys. *Administration and Use of Public Lands: Partial Report of the Committee on Public Lands and Surveys, Pursuant to Senate Resolution 241,* 78th Cong., 1st sess., 1943. S. Rep. 404. Vol. 2.

———, ———. *Hearing Pursuant to S. Res. No. 347.* 69th Cong., 1st sess., 1926, pt. 1. Vol. 246.

———, Subcommittee on Public Lands of the Committee on Interior and Insular Affairs. *Hearings on Grazing on Public Domain Lands.* 86th Cong., 2d sess., Part 1, 1960. Vol. 3.

U.S. Department of Agriculture. "Forest Service to Enlarge Its Research Program." News release, March 28, 1929.

————. *Yearbook of Agriculture (1900, 1901, 1905, 1909, 1911, 1914, 1915, 1917, 1918, 1920, 1933, 1936, 1940)*. Washington, D.C.: Government Printing Office.

————, Economic Research Service. *The Land Utilization Program, 1934 to 1964: Origin, Development and Present Status*. Agricultural Economic Report no. 85. Washington, D.C.: Government Printing Office, 1964.

U.S. Department of the Interior. *Decisions of the Department of the Interior Relating to Public Lands*. Vol. XXX. Washington, D.C.: Government Printing Office, 1905.

————. *Forest Reserve Manual for the Information and Use of Forest Officers*. Washington, D.C.: Government Printing Office, 1902.

U.S. Forest Service. *Annual Report of the Forester (1905, 1906, 1909, 1915, 1916, 1922, 1930, 1933, 1942, 1943, 1944, 1951, 1952, 1953)*. Washington, D.C.: Government Printing Office.

————. *Forest Preservation and National Prosperity*. Circular no. 35. Washington, D.C.: Government Printing Office, 1907.

————. *A National Plan for American Forestry*. Washington, D.C.: Government Printing Office, 1933.

————. *The Nation's Range Resources: A Forest-Range Environmental Study*. Forest Resource Report no. 19. Washington, D.C.: Government Printing Office, 1972.

————. *Use Book—Use of the National Forest Reserves, 1910*. Washington, D.C.: Government Printing Office, 1909.

————, Range Management Staff. *Court Cases Related to Administration of the Range Resources on Lands Administered by the Forest Service*. Washington, D.C.: Government Printing Office, 1964.

U.S. General Accounting Office. *Public Rangeland Improvement: A Slow, Costly Process in Need of Alternate Funding*. Report to the Congress of the United States by the Comptroller General. Washington, D.C.: Government Printing Office, 1982.

U.S. Soil Conservation Service, "Policies and Procedures Governing the Use of Title III Lands" (1945), typescript instruction manual, Range Management Office, U.S. Forest Service, Suitland, Md.

Books

American Forestry Association. *Proceedings of the American Forest Congress*. Washington, D.C., January 2–6, 1905. Washington, D.C.: H. M. Suter, 1905.

Austin, Mary. *The Flock*. Boston: Houghton Mifflin Co., 1906.

Barnes, Will C. *Apaches and Longhorns: The Reminiscences of Will C. Barnes*. Ed. Frank C. Lockwood. Los Angeles: The Ward Ritchie Press [ca. 1941].

————. *Western Grazing Grounds and Forest Ranges*. Chicago: Breeder's Gazette, 1913.

Billington, Ray A. *Westward Expansion: A History of the American Frontier*. New York: Macmillan Company, 1960.

Bryant, Edwin. *What I Saw in California*. Santa Ana, Calif.: Finte Arts Press, 1936.

Calef, Wesley. *Private Grazing and Public Lands: Studies of the Local Management of the Taylor Act*. Chicago: University of Chicago Press, 1960.

Cameron, Jenks. *The Development of Government Forest Control in the United States*. Baltimore: Johns Hopkins University Press, 1928.

Clemen, Rudolf A. *The American Livestock and Meat Industry*. New York: Ronald Press Company, 1923.

Clements, Frederic E. *Dynamics of Vegetation: Selections from Writings of Frederic E. Clements*. Ed. B. W. Allred and Edith S. Clements. New York: H. W. Wilson, 1949.

————. *Plant Succession: An Analysis of the Development of Vegetation*. Washington, D.C.: Carnegie Institute, 1916.

Dale, Edward E. *The Range Cattle Industry: Ranching on the Great Plains from 1865 to 1925*. Norman: University of Oklahoma Press, 1930.

Dana, Samuel T., and Sally K. Fairfax. *Forest and Range Policy: Its Development in the United States*. 2d. ed. New York: McGraw-Hill, 1980.

DeVoto, Bernard. *The Easy Chair*. Boston: Houghton Mifflin, 1955.

Dykstra, Robert R. *The Cattle Towns*. New York: Alfred A. Knopf, 1968.

Elton, Charles. *Animal Ecology*. London: Sedgewick & Jackson, 1927.

Ferguson, Denzel, and Nancy Ferguson. *Sacred Cows at the Public Trough*. Bend, Ore.: Maverick Publications, 1983.

Foss, Phillip O. *Politics and Grass*. Seattle: University of Washington Press, 1960.

Frome, Michael. *The Forest Service*. Boulder, Colo: Westview Press, 1984.

Gau, John M., and Leon O. Wolcott. *Public Administration and the United States Department of Agriculture*. Chicago: Public Administration Service, 1940.

Georgetta, Clel. *Golden Fleece*. Reno, Nev.: Venture Publishing Co., 1972.

Goetzmann, William H. *Exploration and Empire: The Explorer and the Scientist in the Winning of the American West*. New York: Alfred A. Knopf, 1966.

Hampton, H. Duane. *How the U.S. Cavalry Saved Our National Parks*. Bloomington: Indiana University Press, 1971.

Harding, T. Swann. *Two Blades of Grass: A History of Scientific Development in the U.S. Department of Agriculture*. Norman: University of Oklahoma Press, 1947.

Hays, Samuel P. *Conservation and the Gospel of Efficiency: The Progressive Conservation Movement, 1890–1920*. Cambridge, Mass.: Harvard University Press, 1959.

Ickes, Harold L. *The Secret Diary of Harold L. Ickes*. Vol. III. New York: Simon and Schuster, 1953.

Ise, John. *U.S. Forest Policy*. New Haven, Conn.: Yale University Press, 1920.

Johnson, Fred P. "Advantages of Cooperation between the Government and Livestock Associations in the Regulation and Control of Grazing on Forest Reserves." In American Forestry Association, *Proceedings of the American For-*

est Congress, Washington, D. C., January 2–6, 1905. Washington, D.C.: H. M. Suter, 1905.

Kaufman, Herbert. *The Forest Ranger: A Study in Administrative Behavior.* Baltimore: Johns Hopkins University Press, 1960.

Larson, T. A. *History of Wyoming.* Lincoln: University of Nebraska Press, 1965.

LeMaster, Dennis C. *Decade of Change: The Remaking of Forest Service Statutory Authority during the 1970's.* Westport, Conn.: Greenwood Press, 1984.

McCarthy, G. Michael. *Hour of Trial: The Conservation Conflict in Colorado and the West, 1891–1907.* Norman: University of Oklahoma Press, 1977.

McCoy, Joseph G. *Historic Sketches of the Cattle Trade of the West and Southwest.* Kansas City, Mo.: Ramsey Millet and Hudson Printers, 1874.

Malin, James C. *The Grassland of North America: Prolegomena to Its History with Addenda.* Lawrence, Kans.: published by the author, 1956.

Maunder, Elwood R. *Dr. Richard E. McArdle: An Interview with the Former Chief, U.S. Forest Service, 1952–1962.* Santa Cruz, Calif.: Forest History Society, 1975.

Mercer, Asa S. *The Banditti of the Plains, or the Cattlemen's Invasion of Wyoming in 1892.* Cheyenne, Wyo., 1894. Reprint. Norman: University of Oklahoma Press, 1954.

Mollin, F. E. *If and When It Rains: The Stockman's View of the Range Question.* Denver: American National Livestock Association, 1938.

Nash, Roderick. *Wilderness and the American Mind.* Rev. ed. New Haven, Conn.: Yale University Press, 1973.

Osgood, Ernest S. *The Day of the Cattleman.* Minneapolis: University of Minnesota Press, 1929.

Paul, Virginia. *This Was Sheep Ranching: Yesterday and Today.* Seattle: Superior Publishing Company, 1976.

Peffer, Louise E. *The Closing of the Public Domain: Disposal and Reservation Policies, 1900–1950.* Palo Alto, Calif.: Stanford University Press, 1952.

Pinchot, Gifford. *Breaking New Ground.* New York: Harcourt, Brace & Co., 1947. Reprint. Seattle: University of Washington Press, 1972.

Polenberg, Richard. *Reorganizing Roosevelt's Government: The Controversy over Executive Reorganization, 1936–1939.* Cambridge: Harvard University Press, 1966.

Richardson, Elmo. *Dams, Parks and Politics: Resource Development and Preservation in the Truman-Eisenhower Era.* Lexington: University of Kentucky Press, 1973.

Roberts, Paul H. *Hoof Prints on Forest Ranges: The Early Years of National Forest Range Administration.* San Antonio, Texas: The Naylor Company, 1963.

Rollinson, John K. *Wyoming Cattle Trails.* Caldwell, Idaho: Caxton Printers, 1948.

Rowley, William D. *M. L. Wilson and the Campaign for the Domestic Allotment.* Lincoln: University of Nebraska Press, 1970.

Saunderson, Mont H. *Western Land and Water Use.* Norman: University of Oklahoma Press, 1950.

Schlebecker, John T. *Cattle Raising on the Plains, 1900–1961*. Lincoln: University of Nebraska Press, 1963.

Shinn, Charles H. *Mining Camps: A Study in American Frontier Government*. New York: Alfred A. Knopf, 1948.

Shoemaker, Leonard C. *Saga of a Forest Ranger: A Biography of William R. Kreutzer, Forest Ranger No. 1, and a Historical Account of the U.S. Forest Service in Colorado*. Boulder: University of Colorado Press, 1958.

Smith, Darrell H. *The Forest Service: Its History, Activities and Organization*. Brookings Institution Monograph no. 58. Washington, D.C.: The Institution, 1930.

Smith, Frank E. *The Politics of Conservation*. New York: Random House, 1966.

Steen, Harold K. *The U.S. Forest Service: A History*. Seattle: University of Washington Press, 1976.

Stoddart, Laurence A., and Arthur D. Smith. *Range Management*. New York: McGraw-Hill, 1955.

Tobey, Ronald C. *Saving the Prairies: The Life Cycle of the Founding School of American Plant Ecology, 1895–1955*. Berkeley: University of California Press, 1981.

Tueller, Paul T. "Secondary Succession Disclimax and Range Condition Standards in Desert Shrub Vegetation." In *Arid Shrublands: Proceedings of the Third Workshop of the United States/Australia Rangelands Panel*, Tucson, Arizona, March 26–April 5, 1973. Denver: Society of Range Management, 1973.

Voigt, William, Jr. *Public Grazing Lands: Use and Misuse by Industry and Government*. New Brunswick, N.J.: Rutgers University Press, 1976.

Webb, Walter P. *The Great Plains*. New York: Ginn & Company, 1931.

Wentworth, Edward N. *America's Sheep Trails: History, Personalities*. Ames: Iowa State College Press, 1948.

West, Patrick C. *Natural Resource Bureaucracy and Rural Poverty: A Study in the Political Sociology of Natural Resources*. University of Michigan School of Natural Resources, Monograph no. 2. Ann Arbor: The School, 1982.

Wolfe, Linnie Marsh. *Son of the Wilderness: The Life of John Muir*. New York: Alfred A. Knopf, 1945.

Wood, Charles L. *The Kansas Beef Industry*. Lawrence: Regents Press of Kansas, 1980.

Wyant, William K. *Westward in Eden: The Public Lands and the Conservation Movement*. Berkeley: University of California Press, 1982.

Articles

Agrow, Keith A. "Our National Grasslands: Dustland to Grassland." *American Forests* 68 (January, 1962): 10–12, 48, 50.

Arnold, Joseph F. "Crusade for Rangeland Restoration." *American Forests* 69 (May, 1963): 28–32.

Arnold, Oren. "Emergency in Grass." *American Forests*, 50 (June, 1944): 280–83.

Authier, George F. "Both Sides of the Range Controversy." *American Forests and Forest Life* 31 (December, 1925): 715–17.

Baker, John H. "Stockman's Bill in Congress." *Audubon Magazine* 55 (May–June, 1953): 108.

Barnes, Will C. "The Call: An Echo of the War from Distant Forest Depths." *Breeder's Gazette* 74 (December 19, 1918): 1120, 1165, 1196.

———. "The Forest Service and the Stockmen: Cooperation with a big 'C.'" *The Producer: The National Livestock Monthly* 1 (June, 1919): 5–9.

———. Letter to editor. *American Forests and Forest Life* 33 (March, 1927): 186.

———. Letter to editor. *Angora Journal and Milch Goat Bulletin*, 15 (May, 1916): 22–23.

———. "New Grassland in the Southeast." *Breeder's Gazette* 77 (April 15, 1920): 1–7.

———. "A Pioneer Inspector of Grazing." *Breeder's Gazette* 77 (May 6, 1920): 1233.

———. "Sheepmen on the National Forests." *National Wool Grower* 2 (February, 1921): 21–22, 33–35.

Beaman, D. C. "The National Forests and the Forest Service." *Irrigation Age* 23–24 (November, 1908): 10–14.

Beatle, David. "Visit to a National Grasslands." *National Parks Magazine* 38 (October, 1964): 10–13.

Bodley, R. E. "Grazing Reconnaissance on the Coconino National Forest." *Nebraska University Forest Club Annual* 5 (1913): 71–81.

Campbell, R. S. "Milestones in Range Management." *Journal of Range Management* 1 (October, 1948): 4–8.

Carhart, A. H. "Grazing on National Forests." *American Forests* 60 (December, 1954): 3–4.

"The Casement Report." *American Forests and Forest Life* 32 (December, 1926): 743–44.

"The Casement Report." *The Producer: The National Livestock Monthly* 8 (December, 1926): 9–12.

Chapline, W. R. "Erosion on Range Land." *Journal of the American Society of Agronomy* 21 (April, 1929): 423–29.

———. "First Ten Years of the Office of Grazing Studies." *Rangelands* 2 (December, 1980): 223–27.

———. "Range Management History and Philosophy." *Journal of Forestry* 49 (September, 1951): 634–38.

———. "Water Protection on Cattle Ranges." *The Producer: The National Livestock Monthly* 9 (December, 1927): 3–6.

Chapman, H. H. "The Grazing Menace on Our National Forests." *American Forests and Forest Life* 32 (February, 1926): 85–88.

Cook, C. Wayne, and L. A. Stoddart. "Grazing and Multiple-Use." *Journal of Forestry* 59 (March, 1961): 216–17.

Cox, Thomas R. "The Conservationist as Reactionary: John Minto and American Forest Policy." *Pacific Northwest Quarterly* 74 (October, 1983): 146–53.

Darling, J. N. "The Jokers in Western Grazing." *Successful Farming* 34 (April 1, 1936): 9, 22, 47–49.

Dayton, W. A. "Some Outstanding Forage Grasses of Western Cattle Ranges." *The Producer: The National Livestock Monthly* 9 (March, 1928): 3–7.

DeVoto, Bernard. "The Easy Chair." *Harper's* June, 1947, pp. 543–46, and January, 1948, pp. 28–31.

———. "The Easy Chair: An Old Steal Refurbished." *Harper's*, October, 1952, pp. 65–68.

———. "The Easy Chair: Heading for the Last Roundup." *Harper's*, July, 1953, pp. 49–52.

Dillon, Richard. "Comes Now the Plaintiff." *The Producer: The National Livestock Monthly* 5 (April, 1924): 5–9.

Dutton, Walt L. "History of Forest Service Grazing Fees." *Journal of Range Management* 6 (November, 1953): 393–98.

Egler, F. E. "A Commentary on American Plant Ecology." *Ecology* 32 (1951): 673–95.

Fitzgerald, O. A. "Feud on the Ranges." *Country Gentleman* 198 (April, 1938): 15, 203–204.

Forbes, R. H. "The Range Problem." *Forestry and Irrigation* 10 (October, 1904): 476–79.

"The Forest Grazing Fee Case." *National Wool Grower* 21 (October, 1931): 6–7.

"The Forest Service in 1913 and 1914." *American Forestry* 19 (January, 1913): 22–30.

Forsling, C. L. "The Grazing Lands Must be Restored: Revelling Watersheds." *American Forests* 69 (February, 1963): 12–14, 59–63.

Gardner, Delworth. "A Program to Stabilize Livestock Grazing on the Public Lands." *National Wool Grower* 52 (November, 1962): 12–15, 21.

Gill, Tom. "Stanfield Grazing Bill Is Dehorned." *American Forest and Forest Life* 32 (April, 1926): 203–204.

Graves, Henry S. "The New Public Lands Controversy." *American Forests and Forest Life* 32 (January, 1926): 3–8, 63–64.

"The Grazer and the Government." *Outlook* 142 (April 14, 1926): 556–57.

"Grazing." *Outlook* 94 (February 12, 1910): 321–22.

"Grazing for Eleven Million: Livestock Increases on National Forests." *American Forestry* 20 (1914): 436–37.

Greeley, William D. "The Stockmen and the National Forests." *Saturday Evening Post*, November 14, 1925, pp. 10–11, 80, 82, 84.

Hasket, Burt. "The Sheep Industry in Arizona." *Arizona Historical Review* 7 (1936): 3–49.

Hatch, A. B. "Stockmen, Sportsmen to Cooperate." *National Wool Grower* 38 (May, 1938): 9–11.

"Higher Grazing Fees Result of Re-Appraisal." *National Wool Grower* 13 (November, 1923): 13–15.

Hill, Robert R. "Grazing Administration of the National Forests in Arizona." *American Forestry* 19 (September, 1913): 578–85.

"The History of Western Range Research." *Agricultural History* 18 (1944): 127–43.

Hodge, Hugh L. "The Last Straw." *American Cattle Producer* 4 (May, 1934): 15–16.

Jardine, James T. "Efficient Regulation of Grazing in Relation to Timber Production." *Journal of Forestry* 18 (March, 1920): 367–81.

―――. "Improvement and Maintenance of Far Western Ranges." *American Sheep Breeder* 38 (August, 1918): 498–501.

Jones, J. M. "Measuring Range Trends." *National Wool Grower* 41 (September, 1951): 41.

Keck, Wendell M. "Great Basin Experiment Station Completes Sixty Years." *Journal of Range Management* 25 (1972): 163–66.

Koppes, Clayton R. Review of *Public Grazing Lands* by William Voigt, Jr. *Journal of Forest History* 21 (October, 1977): 228–29.

McConnell, Grant. "The Multiple-Use Concept in Forest Service Policy." *Sierra Club Bulletin* 44 (October, 1959): 14–28.

"Mike Frome." *American Forests* 77 (March, 1971): 7, 53–54.

Mortensen, Daniel R. "The Deterioration of Forest Grazing Land: A Wider Context for the Effects of World War I." *Journal of Forest History* 22 (October, 1978): 224–25.

Murie, Olaus J. "The Grazing Lands Must Be Restored: What Are We Doing to Our Land?" *American Forests* 69 (February, 1963): 15.

"National Forest Receipts Increase." *National Wool Grower* 7 (August, 1917): 58.

"National Grasslands Established." *Journal of Forestry* 58 (August, 1960): 679.

Nelson, J. W. "National Forests and the Livestock Industry." *Western Cattle Markets and News*, December 15, 1930, pp. 29–34.

"The Pattern of Grazing Legislation." *American Forests* 60 (June, 1954): 32–33.

Pechanec, Joseph. "Our Range Society." *Journal of Range Management* 1 (October, 1948): 1–2.

Peterson, Charles S. "Small Holding Land Patterns in Utah." *Journal of Forest History* 17 (1973): 9–10.

Pinchot, Gifford. "Grazing in the Forest Reserves." *The Forester* 7 (November, 1901): 276–80.

―――. "How Conservation Began in the United States." *Agricultural History* 11 (October, 1937): 255–65.

"A Plan to Save the Forests." *Century* 27 (February, 1895): 626–34.

Pooler, C. W. "Policies of Forest Service Explained." *American Cattle Producer* 16 (August, 1934): 7.

Potter, A. F. "Cooperation in Range Management." *American National Cattleman's Association Proceedings* 16 (1913): 55.

―――. "Grazing Experiments on Federal Range Reserves." *American Sheep Breeder* 36 (February, 1916): 74–75.

―――. "Improvement in Range Conditions." *American Forestry* 20 (February, 1914): 110–17.

Potter, E. L. "Takes Issue with Colonel Greely." *The Producer: The National Livestock Monthly* 7 (December, 1925): 17–18.

"Progress of Western America." *Irrigation Age* 8 (March, 1895): 69–75.

"Public Lands." *National Wool Grower* 22 (April, 1932): 7–8.

Rakestraw, Lawrence W. "Sheep Grazing in the Cascade Range: John Minto vs. John Muir." *Pacific Historical Review* 27 (November, 1958): 371–82.

"Regulations for Sheep Grazing in the Cascade Reserve." *American Forestry* 4 (July, 1898): 4.

Rutledge, R. H. "Farm Pastures and the Summer Range Problem." *National Wool Grower* 27 (April, 1937): 29–30.

Sampson, Arthur W. "Grazing, Recreation and Game in the Forests." *California Countryman* 12 (March, 1926): 1, 26–28.

———. "The Great Basin Experiment Station." *National Wool Grower* 8 (April, 1918): 19–21.

———. "Natural Revegetation on Rangelands Based on Growth." *Journal of Agricultural Research* 3 (November, 1914): 93–148.

———. "Succession as a Factor in Range Management." *Journal of Forestry* 4 (May, 1917): 593–96.

"The Secretary Stands Firm." *American Forests* 54 (February, 1948): 61, 92–93.

Shinn, Charles H. "Work in a National Forest." *Forestry and Irrigation* 13 (November, 1907): 590–97.

Silcox, F. E. "Forest Grazing Policies for the Future." *National Wool Grower* 25 (February, 1935): 23–24, 46–47.

———. "Grazing Policies for Ten Years." *National Wool Grower* 26 (March, 1936): 6–7.

Stanfield, Robert N. "The Rights of the Shepherds: Definite Status for Public Land Grazing Vital to Prosperity of West." *National Spectator*, April 10, 1926, pp. 3–4.

"Stockmen's Bill Challenged." *American Forests* 59 (June, 1953): 6.

Stoddart, L. A. "What Hope for Grazing on the Public Lands?" *Journal of Range Management* 18 (May, 1965): 109–12.

Tugwell, Rexford G. "Reflections on Farm Relief." *Political Science Quarterly* 43 (December, 1928): 481–97.

Velie, Lester. "They Kicked Us Off Our Land." *Collier's* 120 (July 26 and August 9, 1947): 20–21, 40–42, 72–73, 80.

Young, Vernon A. "The Role of Range Management in Forestry." *Journal of Forestry* 60 (August, 1962): 383–85.

Newspapers

Albuquerque Morning Journal, Oct. 3, 1925.

Arizona Republican (Tucson), June 11, 1925.

Baker Democrat (Baker, Ore.), Dec. 4, 1925.

Baker Herald (Baker, Ore.), Sept. 14, 16, 1925.

Denver News, Jan. 1, 1918.

Denver Post, Feb. 9, 1947; May 29, July 5, Aug. 9, Oct. 26, 1949; Feb. 23, 26, Nov. 30, 1951.

Denver Republican, Jan. 6, 1909.

Elko Free Press (Elko, Nev.), June 27–28, 1941.

Lake County Examiner (Lakeview, Ore.), July 29, 1920.

Miami Evening Bulletin (Miami, Ariz.), June 8, 1925.

Modoc County Times (Alturas, Calif.), Aug. 25, 1949.

Nevada State Journal (Reno, Nev), May 10, 1939.

New York Times, Jan. 6, 1909; Aug. 9, 28, 1925.

Ogden Standard (Ogden, Utah), Feb. 23, 1947.

Portland Oregonian, Sept. 22, 1925.

Record Stockman: The Weekly Livestock Newspaper (Denver, Colo.), Mar. 7, 1946.

Index